# Scottish Mountaineering Trust

# THE
# MUNROS

SCOTTISH MOUNTAINEERING CLUB
HILLWALKERS' GUIDE

Edited by
Donald Bennet and Rab Anderson

First published in Great Britain by the Scottish Mountaineering Trust in 1985

First Edition 1985
Revised and reprinted 1986
Second edition 1991
Third edition 1999
Revised and reprinted 2006
Revised and reprinted 2008
Revised and reprinted 2010
Revised and reprinted 2013
Reprinted 2016
Reprinted 2017

ISBN 978-0-907521-94-5
A catalogue record of this book is available from
the British Library

SMC ® and Munro's Tables ®
are registered trade marks of the Scottish Mountaineering Club

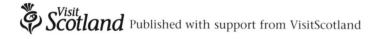 Published with support from VisitScotland

Illustrations
Front Cover:    Clach Leathad and Meall a' Bhuiridh from Rannoch Moor    *Cubby Images*
Title Page:     The summit of Beinn Alligin    *Alan O'Brien*
Facing page:    Ben Lui and the River Cononish    *Derek Sime*
Contents page:  Ben More and Stob Binnein    *Tom Prentice*

In addition to the contributions to the production of this book listed below,
the editors acknowledge the design concepts of Curious Oranj, Glasgow.

Production: Scottish Mountaineering Trust (Publications) Ltd
Typesetting: Aileen Scott
Maps: Lynden Astil, Donald Bennet, Ken Cocket, David Langworth & Tom Prentice
Colour separations: Digital Imaging, Glasgow & Core Image, East Kilbride

Printed & bound in India by Replika Press Pvt Ltd

Distributed by Cordee Ltd
(**t**) 01455 611185 (**w**) www.cordee.co.uk

# Contents

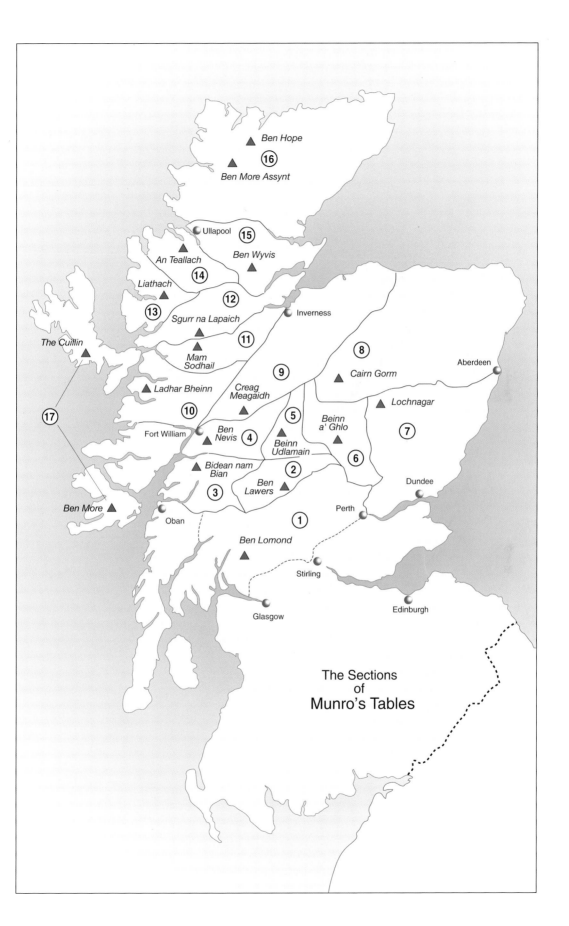

Ben Hope

(16)

Ben More Assynt

Ullapool (15)

Ben Wyvis

An Teallach (14)

Liathach (12)

(13)

Sgurr na Lapaich

Inverness

(11)

(8)

Mam
Sodhail

Cairn Gorm

Aberdeen

(9)

The Cuillin

Ladhar Bheinn

Creag
Meagaidh

Lochnagar

(10)

(5)

Beinn
a' Ghlo

(7)

(17)

Fort William

Ben
Nevis

(4)

Beinn
Udlamain

(6)

Bidean nam
Bian

(2)

Dundee

(3)

Ben
Lawers

Perth

Ben More

Oban

(1)

Glasgow

Ben Lomond

Stirling

Edinburgh

The Sections
of
Munro's Tables

On the Carn Mor Dearg Arete

# Introduction

When Sir Hugh Munro published his first Tables of Scotland's 3000-ft mountains in 1891, he can have had little idea of the influence he would have on later generations of hillwalkers. He could hardly have expected that his name would become synonymous with these mountains, nor could he have foreseen the number of hillwalkers who, just over a century later, would be perusing his work and using his Tables as an inspiration for their hill climbing activities.

Prior to 1891 no one knew exactly how many 3000-ft mountains there were in Scotland. An earlier edition of Baddeley's Guide had listed 31, but the most accurate pre-Munro listing of these hills was in Robert Hall's *The Highland Sportsman and Tourist* (Third Edition, 1884) which gave 236 heights of over 3000 feet. There is no record of Hall having climbed many, if any, of these hills and it is likely that his list was based on the Ordnance Survey maps available at the time. The field survey of Scotland had been completed in 1877 and the One-inch series of maps was all but complete for the Highlands in 1883.

Early in its existence the Scottish Mountaineering Club set out to establish an accurate list, and Sir Hugh Munro, an original member of the Club and an experienced walker in the Scottish hills was the right man for the task. Munro had already climbed many Scottish hills prior to 1891, and he had made some very fine long solo expeditions through the Highlands.

The publication of the first edition of the Tables in 1891 was the outcome of much painstaking research based on his own expeditions and his perusal of the Ordnance Survey maps of the day. These maps, both the Six-inch to the Mile and the One-inch to the Mile versions, would by today's standards be regarded as very inaccurate and incomplete, and no present-day student of Munroism would venture an opinion on the basis of those early maps. When the Tables were published in the 1891 edition of the Scottish Mountaineering Club Journal, quite a stir was caused. Baddeley's guide was shown to be totally inaccurate and Hall's list had to be revised. Munro's Tables were immediately accepted as the most authoritative listing of Scotland's hills over 3000 feet, and soon the name 'Munros' was coined to denote them.

Munro was working on a revision of his Tables when he died in 1919, so he may not have been entirely satisfied with all the classifications in them. Later members of the Club, notably J.Gall Inglis, Jim Donaldson, Wilfred Coats, Hamish Brown and Derek Bearhop, have carried on the process of revision, partly in accordance with accurate aneroid barometer measurements by early climbers and revised measurements of heights by the Ordnance Survey, and partly in an attempt to achieve a consistent distinction between separate mountains (which have by custom become known as the Munros) and Tops.

However, no definitive criterion exists, and such distinction as does exist is based on the drop in height and the distance between adjacent summits, their character and the character of the intervening ground, and the time that might be taken to go from one to the other. This absence of any objective criterion for classifying Munros has given rise to many a controversy, but it is not the intention of this guide to become involved in this debate. We have taken the 1997 edition of Munro's Tables, edited by Derek Bearhop, as the basis for the list of mountains described in this book, which with the 2009 deletion of Sgurr nan Ceannaichean and the 2012 deletion of Beinn a' Chlaidheimh, makes for 282 Munros together with 226 Munro Tops to make a complete list of 508 Tops, as Munro called them.

The publication of the Tables in 1891 must have acted as a stimulus to early climbers to ascend as many of the Munros as possible. The first to be credited with the achievement of climbing all the Munros was the Reverend A.E.Robertson – the first Munroist. In 1901, after what he himself described as a desultory campaign of ten years, he climbed (or should one say claimed) his last Munro, Meall Dearg on the Aonach Eagach ridge above Glen Coe, where he is recorded as having kissed first the cairn and then his wife. Recent historical research by Robin Campbell has, perhaps, cast doubt on Robertson's claim to be the first Munroist. Careful reading of Robertson's notebook reveals that on Ben Wyvis he encountered heavy rain and (to quote his notebook) – "as I did not want to get soaked, I turned." Presumably this was an admission that he did not reach the summit. There is no later record that he returned to Ben Wyvis to rectify this omission. There is also no record that Robertson climbed the Inaccessible Pinnacle prior to 1901, but that might be excused because at the time (for some reason known only to Munro) Sgurr Dearg was listed as a mountain and the Inaccessible Pinnacle as its subsidiary Top in the Tables. It is, however, likely that Robertson climbed the Pinnacle in 1906.

Thereafter about twenty years elapsed before the next climber, Ronald Burn, completed the list, including the Inaccessible Pinnacle and all the Tops. For the next fifty years the number of Munroists increased at an average rate of between two and three per year. Nowadays about a hundred and fifty names are added to the list of Munroists each year, and the number of hillwalkers who are afoot on the Scottish mountains steadily ticking off the Munros is numbered in thousands. It is with them in mind that this book has been written.

The SMC's website <www.smc.org.uk> contains a Munros section with details on how to record your compleation and a list of all those who have recorded their compleation.

The scope and purpose of The Munros is to provide a concise and practical guide to describing natural day expeditions which may be either a single Munro or the traverse of two or three. Most routes are described as starting and finishing at convenient points on public roads as it is recognised that most hillwalkers use cars to reach their chosen hills. However, this should not be interpreted as a discouragement to multi-day bothy or tent based exploration, which brings far greater rewards.

Some of the days described in this book are long, but they have been chosen as providing routes which may be the easiest or the natural choice, or following well-defined natural features or paths, or being of particular scenic interest. Many variations and alternatives may exist, but lack of space precludes a complete description of them. The hillwalker is encouraged to explore and have adventures.

The descriptions apply to summer ascents, but most of them can be applied in winter as well, bearing in mind the hazards of snow and ice, the shorter hours of daylight and the need for additional skills and technical equipment such as ice axes and crampons. A good number of the routes described are intimidating and serious in winter. In these conditions the Aonach Eagach, Liathach or the Cuillin for example, will present difficulties beyond the ability of many hillwalkers with little experience of technical climbing. To keep within one's capabilities is the basic principle of safe winter hillwalking in Scotland.

Distances and heights are rounded up to the nearest 500m and 10m respectively, and times for ascents are calculated on the basis of 4.5km per hour for distance walked, plus 10m per minute for climbing uphill. Times are rounded up to the nearest 10 minutes, but no allowance is made for stops nor the extra time required by rough or difficult ground. These timings are a close metric approximation to Naismith's time-honoured formula. Times quoted are for ascents only, so extra must be added for stops and the descent. Where descriptions relate to the traverse of two or more Munros, times at each summit are cumulative from the day's starting point. Munros are referenced M1 (Ben Nevis) to M282 (Beinn Teallach), depending upon height. For the full list see page 280.

The maps in this book are intended to illustrate the text and serve as aids to route planning. The detail on these maps is not complete, therefore they cannot take the place of a proper map in the field. The recommended maps for hillwalking are the Ordnance Survey 1:50,000 Landranger Series and the OS Sheet number noted beside each hill refers to this series. The OS also produce an Explorer Series of maps at a larger scale of 1:25,000. The heights of hills, passes, cols and bealachs quoted in this book are generally taken from the OS 1:50,000 series, but in some cases are from the 1:25,000 series. Six figure grid references have been used for key locations and are preceded by two OS grid letters to provide a unique reference to within 100m. Details of OS maps can be found at <www.ordnancesurvey.co.uk>. Harvey Maps produce maps for walkers and their 1:25,000 Superwalker Series to many of the popular mountain areas in Scotland is on waterproof paper. Harvey also produce a number of summit map enlargements. Details of Harvey Maps can be found at <www.harveymaps.co.uk>.

The maps in this book use the following symbols to indicate the status of a summit or high point:

▲ Munro (282) summit heights 3,000ft (914.4m) and higher

△ Munro Top (227) less distinct summit heights 3,000ft (914.4m) and higher

● Corbett (220) summit heights 2,500ft (762m) and higher, but below 3,000ft (914.4m) with a drop of at least 500ft (152.4m)

○ Corbett Top (450) summit heights 2,500ft (762m) and higher, but below 3,000ft (914.4m) with a drop of at least 98.4ft (30m)

◆ Graham (220) summit heights 2,000ft (609.6m) and higher, but below 2,500ft (762m) with a drop of at least 492ft (150m)

◇ Graham Top (776) summit heights 2,000ft (609.6m) and higher, but below 2,500ft (762m) with a drop of at least 98.4ft (30m)

⊗ Other summit

*Munros Tables* (SMC) as well as listing the Munros and Tops also lists the Corbetts and the Grahams. Lists of the Corbetts and Corbett Tops as well as the Grahams and Graham Tops can be obtained from TACit Press.

Throughout the text, 'road' means a tarmac surface (usually public), 'track' any unsurfaced way such as used by forestry or estate vehicles (usually private) and 'path', a clear on the ground pedestrian only route (often a stalkers or hillwalkers path). These are clearly differentiated on the maps. A publicly maintained car park is indicated with a **P** on the maps, while a P indicates that there is adequate off road parking for vehicles. Otherwise, parking may not always be easy and convenient. Walkers should avoid blocking gates or hindering local needs and park sympathetically, bearing in mind that other hillgoers will also be vying for space. Just because a walk is shown as starting at a certain point, does not mean parking is possible.

On the maps, continuous red lines indicate the principle routes and dashed lines some alternatives. Hills are sometimes given two route descriptions and it is often possible, without stating it every time, that linking these can give a satisfying and often recommended traverse, though some transport arrangements may be needed. Plenty of time should be allowed for longer expeditions and those into remoter areas. The potential hazards of winter conditions, rivers in spate or challenging navigation from changes in weather should not be forgotten. In the interest of topographical accuracy and therefore safety, the most recent map is best used in the field.

For those dependent on bus, postbus, train, ferry and air services for accessing the Highlands, then up to date timetables are best found via the worldwide web. The SMC publish a CD with detailed GPS way-points and grid references for the primary routes in this book, provided in several popular GPS formats including gpx. See the SMC Book List at the end of this book for other Munros related publications, or visit the SMC website <www.smc.org.uk>, where you can also provide invaluable feedback, updates and corrections to this book.

## Access

The Land Reform (Scotland) Act 2004 gives everyone statutory access rights to most land and inland water including mountains, moorland, woods and forests, grassland, paths and tracks, and rivers and lochs. People only have these rights if they exercise them responsibly by respecting people's privacy, safety and livelihoods, and Scotland's environment. The Scottish Outdoor Access Code provides detailed guidance on these responsibilities. The following is a résumé, full details are available at <www.outdooraccess-scotland.com>.
- Take personal responsibility for your own actions and act safely.
- Respect people's privacy and peace of mind.
- Help land managers and others to work safely and effectively.
- Care for the environment and take your litter home.
- Keep your dog under proper control.
- Take extra care if you're organising an event or running a business.

## Stalking, Shooting & Lambing

The stag stalking season is from 1st July to 20th October, although few estates start at the beginning of the season. Hinds continue to be culled until 15th February. There is no stalking anywhere on Sundays, although requests to avoid disturbing deer on the hills may still be made. There is no stalking on land owned by the National Trust for Scotland. A number of areas are covered by the Hillphones scheme <www.snh.org.uk/hillphones>, run by Scottish Natural Heritage (SNH) and the Mountaineering Council of Scotland (MCofS), which provides daily stalking information, (see page 276).

The grouse shooting season is from 12th August until 10th December, although the end of the season is less used. It is also important to avoid disturbance to sheep, especially from dogs and particularly during the lambing season between March and May.

## Footpath Erosion, Memorials & Cairns

Part of the revenue from the sale of this and other Scottish Mountaineering Club books is granted by the Scottish Mountaineering Trust as financial assistance towards the repair and maintenance of hill paths in Scotland. However, it is our responsibility to minimise our erosive effect for the enjoyment of future hillwalkers. The proliferation of navigation cairns detracts from the feeling of wildness, and may be confusing rather than helpful as regards route-finding. The indiscriminate building of cairns and memorials on the hills should be discouraged.

## Bikes & Car Use

Mountain bikes can cause severe erosion when used 'off road' on footpaths and open hillsides and should only be used on vehicular or forest tracks. Do not drive up private roads without permission, and when parking, avoid blocking access to private roads and land.

## Bothies

The Mountain Bothies Association has about 100 buildings on various estates throughout Scotland which it maintains as bothies. The MBA owns none of these buildings, they belong to estates which generously allow their use as open bothies. Bothies are there for use by small groups (less than six) for a few days. If you wish to stay longer permission should be sought from the owners. The increased number of hill users has put a greater strain on the bothies and their surrounding environment. It is therefore more important than ever that the simple voluntary bothy code be adhered to, this and more information can be found on the MBA website <www.mountainbothies.org.uk>. If you carry it in, then carry it out. Leave the bothy clean and dry, guard against fire and don't cause vandalism or graffiti. Bury human waste carefully out of sight far away from the bothy and the water supply and avoid burying rubbish.

## Mountaineering Scotland

Mountaineering Scotland is the representative body for climbers and hill walkers. One of its primary concerns is the continued free access to the hills and crags. Information about bird restrictions, stalking and general access issues can be obtained from Mountaineering Scotland. Should any climber or hill walker encounter problems regarding access they should contact Mountaineering Scotland, whose current address is: The Old Granary, West Mill Street, Perth PH1 5QP, tel 01738 493 942, email: **info@mountaineering.scot**, website: **www.mountaineering.scot**.

## Participation

"Climbing and mountaineering are activities with a danger of personal injury or death. Participants in these activities should be aware of and accept these risks and be responsible for their own actions and involvement." UIAA participation statement.

## Mountain Rescue

Contact the police, either by phone (999) or in person. Give concise information about the location and injuries of the victim and any assistance available at the accident site. It is often better to stay with the victim, but in a party of two, one may have to leave to summon help. Leave the casualty warm and comfortable in a sheltered, well marked place.

## Equipment and Planning

Good navigation skills, equipment, clothing and forward planning can all help reduce the chance of an accident. While mobile phones and GPS can help in communications and locating your position, consider that the former do not work over all of Scotland and both rely on batteries and electronics which can fail or be easily damaged. Consequently, they can never be a substitute for navigation skills with map and compass, first aid or general mountain skills.

## Avalanches

Hillwalkers venturing onto the hills in winter should be familiar with the principles of snow structure and avalanche prediction. All gullies and most slopes between 22 and 60 degrees should then be suspect. The greater the amount of fresh snow, the higher the risk. Fresh snow can include wind-blown deposits, so that stormy weather can maintain an avalanche risk for prolonged spells. Past and present weather conditions are very important. Hillwalkers preparing for winter journeys should familiarise themselves with basic avalanche theory. In the field, much can be learned by digging a pit and examining the snow profile, looking especially for different layers of snow with different degrees of bonding. Slab avalanches, for example, will be caused when a weakly cohesive layer of snow collapses underfoot. Such a weak layer is usually hidden under a firmer layer, hence its great potential as a killer. The top layer will often break into slabby fragments, the first warning.

If avalanched, try and either jump free, or anchor yourself for as long as possible, depending on circumstances. If swept down protect your access to oxygen by 'swimming' to stay on the surface, by keeping your mouth closed, and by preserving a space in front of your face if buried. Wet snow avalanches harden rapidly on settling, so try and break free if possible at this point. If trapped try to stay calm, which will reduce oxygen demand. If a witness to an avalanche it is vital to start a search immediately, given it is safe to do so. Victims will often be alive at first, but their chances of survival lessen rapidly if buried. Unless severely injured, some 80% may live if found immediately, but only 10% after a three-hour delay. Mark the burial site if known, listen for any sound, look for any visual clue, search until help arrives if possible. Again, a working knowledge of first aid may save a life, as many victims may have stopped breathing.

*A Chance in a Million?* by Bob Barton and Blyth Wright, published by the SMC (see page 282), is the classic work on avalanches. While the ability to make your own assessment of risk is vital to anyone venturing into the area, avalanche predictions for the major mountain areas, produced by the Sportscotland Avalanche Information Service <www.sais.gov.uk> are readily available during the winter. These can be found at police stations, sports shops, tourist information centres and on display boards in mountain areas. A text messaging system may also be trialed in the future.

Sgurr nan Gillean from Sligachan, Isle of Skye

# Scotland. Created for Walking

Whatever type of walking you enjoy, from a short stroll with the kids to a trek through wilderness areas, or climbing the majestic Munros, Scotland's diversity of walking options and spirit-of-place will infuse your spirit and revitalise your senses. And it's not all about the walking! When you're out, look for wonderful Scottish wildlife, remember to look back and admire the amazing scenery, and stop awhile to explore our fascinating historic and cultural heritage.

To help you plan, before you head for the hills, why not check out Visitscotland's dedicated walking website at **visitscotland.com/walking** – Scotland's premier walking website, put together by walkers for walkers. The site is really useful for helping to plan a walking break, whether you decide to visit the hills for a day or longer.

5

The Walking website features:

- **Over 950 walking route suggestions** – for when you want a day away from the Munros or need a bad-weather alternative.
- **Walkers Welcome accommodation** – over 1,200 accommodation businesses in Scotland offer all those essential features such as drying facilities, packed lunches and weather forecasts, that walkers need. Look out for the Walkers Welcome symbol.
- **Walking holiday operators and guides** – details of companies specialising in organising it all for you, or helping you to gain new skills.
- **Useful information about walking in Scotland** – access, stalking and safety information.
- **Events and walking festivals information** – for around 30 different events.
- **Travel information** – how to get here and get around.
- **Online shop** – where we have a selection of useful guides which you can purchase.
- **Munros** – there's even information about the Munros and mountain weather links!

## visitscotland.com/walking

For general information about visiting Scotland, contact the VisitScotland Booking and Information Service on **0845 22 55 121** or **+44 1506 832121** outwith the UK, or log on to

## visitscotland.com

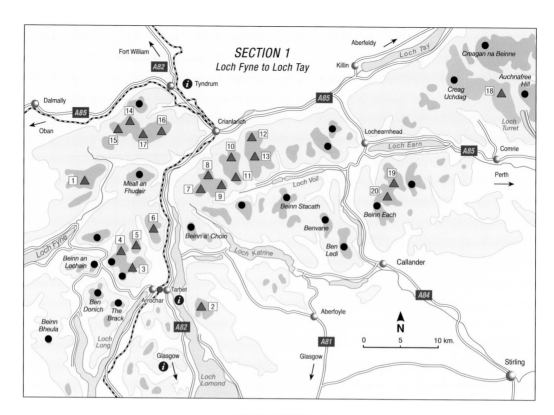

**SECTION 1**
Loch Fyne to Loch Tay

ⓘ VisitScotland Information Centres
**Loch Lomond**; The Old Station Building, Balloch, G83 8LQ, open Apr–Oct
**Tarbet**; Main Street, Tarbet, Loch Lomond, G83 7DE, (01301 702260), open Apr–Oct
**Tyndrum**; Main Street, Tyndrum, FK20 8RY, (01838 400324), open Apr–Oct

*Peter Hodgkiss*

Beinn Bhuidhe from Meall an Fhudair

## Beinn Bhuidhe; 948m; (OS Sheet 50; NN203187); M216; *yellow hill*

Beinn Bhuidhe, situated between the upper reaches of Glen Fyne and Glen Shira, is the highest hill in the extensive tract of high undulating moorland between the north end of Loch Lomond and Loch Awe. It is best seen from the north and east, from where its isolated undulating ridge shows up well. The shortest approach is from Glen Fyne via Inverchorachan, reached by a 7.5km walk or bike ride up the estate road and track in the glen.

Leave the A83 just before the new bridge over the River Fyne, signposted Fyne Brewery and cross the old bridge to a car park on the left (height restriction), opposite the road to Clachan Hydro. Return back over the old bridge and turn left – Private Road, Estate and Brewery Traffic Only – and follow the road through the farm and past the houses at Glenfyne Lodge, to where it swings right and crosses the river. Continue ahead on the track to the upper glen and Inverchorachan.

Beyond the house, go through a deer gate, then left through a wooden gate and follow the path up into a tree-filled gully. Follow this with one short exposed rock-step, then left past a waterfall, to gain the upper corrie at about 550m. Continue north-west by a burn, the path becomes intermittent through a marshy area, then more distinct to gain a shallow gully leading to the lowest point on the ridge between Beinn Bhuidhe and Pt.901m. From the ridge a clear path leads to the summit. (11km; 950m; 3h 50min).

A pleasant return can be made over Pt.901 and down its rocky south-east ridge which turns south into the upper corrie. From here continue down the north side of the burn, or back to the ascent path on its south side.

An alternative, but longer, approach to Beinn Bhuidhe is via the estate road up Glen Shira to the north-west. The lower reaches of Glen Shira are finely wooded, but higher up the lower slopes of Beinn Bhuidhe have been densely afforested. Follow the road to a point just over 1km beyond the bridge across the Brannie Burn, where a break in the forest gives access to the foot of the south-west ridge of the hill. This long and rather featureless ridge leads in 4km over Tom a' Phiobaire and Stac a' Chuirn to the summit. (15km; 950m; 5h).

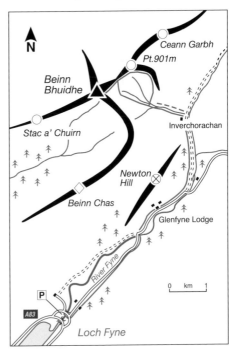

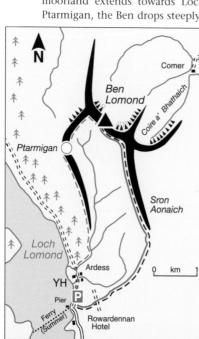

Loch Lomond and Ben Lomond from Duncryne

## Ben Lomond; 974m; (OS Sheet 56; NN367028); M184; *beacon hill*

**BEN LOMOND**

Its isolated position at the southern edge of the Highlands makes Ben Lomond a conspicuous feature from many viewpoints, and from its summit there is an extensive view of both the Highlands and the Lowlands.

Although Ben Lomond appears from many angles to be quite pointed, the summit is the highest point of a short level ridge curving round the head of the north-east corrie. Southwards the mountain has a broad grassy ridge extending down to above Rowardennan, the upper part of which is National Trust for Scotland territory. To the north an extensive tract of featureless moorland extends towards Loch Arklet, and to the west, below the outlying spur called Ptarmigan, the Ben drops steeply in wooded craggy slopes towards Loch Lomond.

The normal route of ascent starts at the car park at the end of the public road just beyond Rowardennan Hotel. From there a much-trodden path leads north-east to gain the grassy lower slopes of the south ridge. The way continues up towards the middle part of the ridge, and on this section of the path much work has been done in recent years to repair the erosion damage caused by many thousands of hillwalkers.

Higher up, a more level section of the south ridge gives easy walking. In due course the steeper cone of the summit is reached, and the path zigzags up the stony hillside to reach the summit ridge. This is a pleasant narrow crest with a steep drop on its north-east side, where a line of cliffs drops into Ben Lomond's high corrie. Continue north-west along this ridge over a few small bumps to reach the top. (5.5km; 940m; 2h 50min).

An alternative descent route goes down a path along the north-west ridge for a short distance, then south-west along the broad knolly crest of Ptarmigan. Beyond the 731m point, the ridge drops steadily southwards and a good path goes along its crest or just to its west, eventually leading more steeply down to Ardess about 1km north of the car park at Rowardennan.

9

*Derek Sime*

Ben Lomond from Beinn Narnain

**Beinn Narnain;** 926m; (OS Sheet 56; NN271066); M259; *hill of the notches*
**Beinn Ime;** 1011m; (OS Sheet 56; NN255084); M118; *hill of butter*

The Arrochar Alps are a fine little group of mountains in the northern part of the Argyll Forest Park north-west of Arrochar, the village at the head of Loch Long. The main cluster of peaks rises opposite the village: The Cobbler, Beinn Narnain and A'Chrois, with Beinn Ime, the highest, hidden behind this trio. These are rocky and rugged peaks with bold outlines.

From the large pay and display car park just round from the head of Loch Long, cross the main road and follow a wide path into the Argyll Forest. Some 40m from the wooden barrier, ignore a vague path off right by the burn and continue for another 30m then take a small stony path on the right which disappears into the undergrowth. Climb directly through the trees, crossing a forest track, and follow the line of an intermittent series of old concrete bases used in the construction of a hydro-scheme. The path is quite steep and eroded in places, and in wet periods becomes a burn.

Emerge from the trees to reach a path which traverses the hillside between dams and continue steeply ahead on a path which climbs onto Beinn Narnain's south-east ridge. Cross a flattening and follow the path up the rocky ridge, a slabby groove can be avoided on the right, to gain the top of Cruach nam Miseag (813m). Beyond a dip, the ridge steepens again and becomes much rockier but the path finds an easy way through to reach the base of the prominent rock prow which crowns the ridge; the Spearhead. Climb a short gully to the right (north) of the Spearhead to gain the flat stony plateau of Beinn Narnain about 200m east of its summit, which is topped by some cairns and a stone trig point (3.5km; 940m; 2h 30min).

**BEINN NARNAIN**

**BEINN IME**

To continue to Beinn Ime, go west-north-west down a short boulder-field followed by a grassy slope to the Bealach a' Mhaim. Cross a fence and climb north-west up a smooth grassy slope to Beinn Ime. Near the top go along a path leftwards to reach the summit ridge which is followed for a short distance to the large cairn surmounting a crag. (6.5km; 1310m; 4h).

Return to the Bealach a' Mhaim and follow a narrow path horizontally south for a few hundred metres to the bealach at the head of the Buttermilk Burn. Go down the path on the north-east side of this burn past the Narnain Boulders to rejoin the uphill route. If an ascent was made via the old concrete blocks path then a descent can be made via the Bealach a' Mhaim and the new forest track, and vice versa, to produce a circular route. This walk is easily extended to include the Cobbler.

Ben Lomond (left) and Beinn Narnain from Beinn Ime

*Donald Bennet*

Jim Renny

Beinn Ime from Ben Vane

Two shorter routes to Beinn Ime are possible from points on the A83 road to Inveraray. One starts 2km south-east of the Rest and Be Thankful pass and follows a stream steeply north-east to the Bealach a' Mhaim where the route described above is joined. The other starts from a parking area at the base of a track in felled woodland about 300m before the bridge in the floor of Glen Kinglas. Follow the track up and left to the aerial. Cross over the fence and follow a path up the south side of the burn past old shielings to the bealach south-west of Beinn Ime, and from there continue up steep and in places rocky ground to the summit. Clear felling on the lower section of the path has littered it with branches, making the going rough and a little tedious.

BEINN NARNAIN

BEINN IME

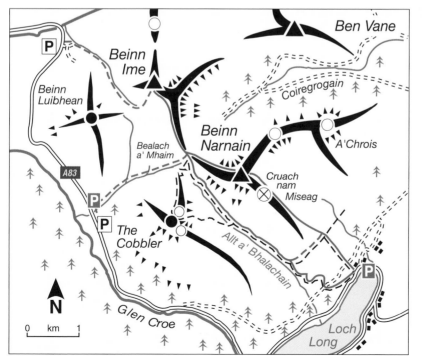

Scott Johnstone

The approach to Ben Vane up Coiregrogain

**Ben Vane;** 916m; (OS Sheet 56; NN277098); M280; *middle hill*

12

BEN VANE

Among the Arrochar Alps, a group of mountains noted for their steepness and rugged character, Ben Vane is one of the steepest. Its rocky south face rising above Coiregrogain has an angle of almost 45 degrees for a height of 600m. On other sides it is less steep, but it is a very fine little mountain, almost the twin of the slightly lower, but otherwise similar A' Chrois on the opposite side of Coiregrogain.

The ascent is most frequently made from Inveruglas on the A82 road up Loch Lomond. From the Inveruglas car park beyond the power station, follow the main road south to the padlocked access road to Coiregrogain. This glen is not particularly attractive as huge electricity pylons march alongside the road, and the Loch Sloy Hydro-Electric scheme, of which these pylons are a part, is visually very obtrusive. Continue up the road for 2km, passing Coiregrogain farm. Turn left over the bridge and follow the track to a small bridge over a burn, just past a small disused quarry. An obvious path follows the right side of the burn, crosses it, then marshy ground left of the fenced enclosure, to gain the south-east ridge. From the crest easy-angled grass slopes gradually steepen until little crags and slabs seem to bar the way. However, it is always possible to find a route, following grassy gullies and ledges between the crags without the need for any scrambling, although for those so inclined there are opportunities for a little mild rock climbing on the many outcrops.

The angle of ascent relents towards the top, which is a small level plateau. The summit rock and its smaller cairn lie to the west above a long steep drop to Coiregrogain. (5km; 880m; 2h 40min).

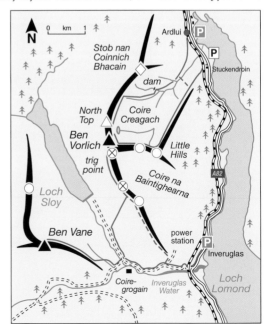

Ben Vorlich is the northernmost of the Arrochar Alps, lying north-west of Inveruglas between Loch Lomond and Loch Sloy. The mountain is a long crescent-shaped ridge running roughly from south to north, with an eastward spur, the Little Hills, jutting out above Loch Lomond. To the north and south of this spur are Coire Creagach and Coire na Baintighearna.

The mountain can be climbed from the vicinity of Ardlui, via Coire Creagach or the Little Hills and from Inveruglas via the south-east ridge, or the west face overlooking Loch Sloy. The latter route, one of the most popular, is also the least attractive.

For Coire Creagach park in the layby opposite the railway underpass to Ardlui Station, walk south along the A82 for 115m and go through the next underpass. Go through the gate or over the stile on the left, cross the burn and traverse the field up and right to a gate. Continue in the same line, the path is boggy and unclear in places, aiming for the wooded river gully at the base of last of the Little Hills, which lies straight ahead. Close to the gully a fence is crossed by a stile. Note that with care and when the river is low, the Little Hills route can be accessed from here by following the fence down to the river, crossing over and following the fence up to join that ridge.

From the stile a clearer path leads up into the corrie and past a small dam, then more directly to gain the upper corrie and the col south-west of Stob nan Coinnich Bhacain. Climb the broad and in places rocky ridge over the North Top (931m) to the summit cairn (943m) overlooking Loch Sloy. The trig point lies on the 941m summit, 200m further south. (5.5km; 890m; 2hr 40min).

Possibly the most aesthetic route up Ben Vorlich is the ridge of the Little Hills, although it requires some route finding, significant ascent and descent and the continuous false summits can become tedious. Park on the roadside south of Ardlui and just north of Stuckendroin farm. From the farm, follow the signs to Ben Vorlich and pass below the railway to open ground. Climb south-west to gain the wooded lower slopes of the ridge to a fence and stile. The ridge leads over several little knolls and two quite distinct tops, the Little Hills, with assorted rocky steps, before dropping to a col and ascending to the trig point and the summit 200m to the north. In some respects the Little Hills are best enjoyed in descent, in conjunction with an ascent via Coire Creagach.

The Inveruglas routes start from the car park by the power station. Follow the main road south to the padlocked access road to Coiregrogain, and follow it past the electricity sub-station and farm and the bridge over the Inveruglas Water. Continue up the road towards the Loch Sloy dam to NN295103, where a cairned path leaves the road. Ascend into the south-west corrie on a relentlessly steep path which is badly eroded in sections, to gain the ridge. The path bypasses the southerly summit (941m) which is topped by the trig point, to reach the summit beyond and to the north. (7.5km; 890m; 3hrs). A bike might prove useful on this route.

A shorter and much pleasanter, although initially pathless, ascent can be had by tackling the front of the south ridge direct. Follow the track which branches off at the electricity sub-station across the front of the ridge, to where the hillside can be accessed to the right of the main burn draining the face, and ascend to the crest. This face is less steep than it appears from below and a path leads from the crest along the delightful south ridge.

Ben Vorlich from Loch Lomond

Donald Bennet

Beinn Chabhair from Glen Falloch

**Beinn Chabhair;** 933m; (OS Sheets 50 and 56; NN367179); M244; *probably hill of the hawk*

This mountain is at the head of the Ben Glas Burn, 4.5km north-east of the north end of Loch Lomond, from which it is not visible. One does, however, get a good view of it from Glen Falloch, from where its principal feature, the long north-west ridge, is well seen rising from the glen over many humps and knolls towards the summit. The upper part of the mountain is quite rugged, there being many rocky outcrops all round the summit, and in misty conditions route-finding may be confusing.

The most direct route to Beinn Chabhair starts from Inverarnan Hotel at the foot of Glen Falloch. Go 300m north along the A82 road, cross the bridge over the River Falloch and follow West Highland Way signposts round Beinglas farm. Then climb steeply behind the farm, following a slanting path up the hillside to reach more level ground above the falls of the Ben Glas Burn. Continue along the north side of the burn following a path which in places becomes lost in the boggy ground, but in due course reaches Lochan Beinn Chabhair.

The upper part of the mountain rises above the lochan in grassy slopes with many rock outcrops. There is no single well-defined route up this face, and possibly the best line of ascent goes north-east from the lochan to reach the north-west ridge of Beinn Chabhair about 1km from the summit. Continue along this ridge, passing a small cairn shortly before reaching the

14

BEINN CHABHAIR

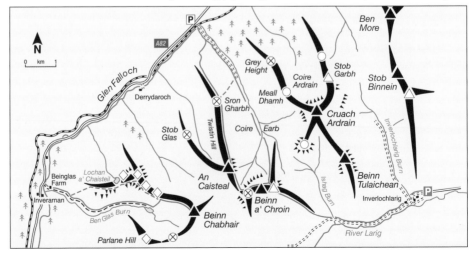

Donald Bennet

Beinn a' Chroin and An Caisteal from the head of Glen Falloch

summit, where a bigger cairn is perched on top of a small crag. (5.5km; 920m; 2h 50min).

The ascent by the north-west ridge past Lochan a' Chaisteil is a fine route, but longer and more strenuous than the one just described. Once fairly level ground is reached above the falls of the Ben Glas Burn, bear north-east over the first knoll, Meall Mor nan Eag, and drop down to the lochan. Go round its south side and save a little effort by traversing below Stob Creag an Fhithich to regain the ridge and traverse one more top, Meall nan Tarmachan, before the route described above is joined.

**An Caisteal;** 995m; (OS Sheets 50 and 56; NN378193); M147; *the castle*
**Beinn a' Chroin;** 942m; (OS Sheets 50 and 56; NN387185); M231; *hill of the sheepfold*

These two mountains stand close together above the headwaters of the River Falloch 6km south of Crianlarich. Typical of the hills in this part of the Southern Highlands, they are grassy on their lower slopes and quite rocky high up near their summits.

An Caisteal has a well-defined summit at the junction of its north-west and north ridges, the latter being known as Twistin Hill. Southwards from the summit, the south ridge drops to a col at 805m below Beinn a' Chroin. This mountain has a 1km-long undulating summit ridge, with the highest point being near its middle.

To traverse the two mountains, leave the A82 road in Glen Falloch at a car park at NN368238 near the obvious bend in the River Falloch. Follow a track under the railway, over the river by a bridge and up its south-west bank. Heading for An Caisteal first, leave this track after about 1km and climb south up the grass slopes of Sron Gharbh, or continue up the track to a gate, then ascend directly. Follow a path along the ridge, Twistin Hill, which is level for some way and then rises over a rocky knoll to reach the summit of An Caisteal. (5km; 860m; 2h 35min).

Descend the south ridge which is grassy at first, then steeper and rocky lower down. Cross the level col and climb the rocky north-west end of Beinn a' Chroin by a zigzag path through the crags. Continue along the undulating crest passing over the knoll of the west top (938m) then a hollow occupied by a tiny lochan to gain the summit just beyond. This is marked by a cairn and stands above a small crag; another tiny lochan lies to the east with another knoll of a similar height just beyond (6.5km; 1020m; 3h 15min).

The east top, which is 2m lower, is 600m further on. From the col (877m) between the two tops go down a grassy ridge which drops to the stream junction in Coire Earb. Continue down the corrie on the west side of the River Falloch to rejoin the track leading back to the glen.

Beinn a' Chroin can equally well be climbed from the east, approaching from Inverlochlarig farm. From there go west for 3km along a track beside the River Larig and across the Ishag Burn. Then climb north-west up grassy slopes, passing a little knoll before reaching broken crags just below the east top.(6km; 800m; 2h 40min).

Cruach Ardrain from Beinn Tulaichean

## Cruach Ardrain; 1046m; (OS Sheets 50, 51 and 56; NN409212); M87; *stack of the high part*

Cruach Ardrain is one of the most familiar of the mountains that encircle the village of Crianlarich. It has a fine pointed outline, enhanced in winter and spring when snow fills the steep Y Gully on the north face above Coire Ardrain. The plan of the mountain itself is rather like the shape of the letter Y, with the summit at the junction of three ridges radiating north-west, north-east and south. The north-east ridge drops steeply from the summit and leads to the rocky Top, Stob Garbh (959m); the south ridge leads to Beinn Tulaichean and the north-west ridge drops towards Crianlarich.

The traditional route of ascent from Crianlarich has deteriorated over the decades due to successive waves of forest planting and felling which have lead to the usual unsightly forest roads, quagmire firebreak paths, hillsides littered with tree stumps and old branches and unpassable deer fences. Accordingly, the most pleasant and aesthetic route nowadays avoids Crianlarich altogether and starts from car parking on a section of old road in Glen Falloch at NN369239. From there pass under the railway and follow the track on the south-west bank of the River Falloch for just over 1km. Go down to the river, cross a bridge and climb east up easy grassy slopes to reach the north-west ridge at the upper edge of the trees.

Turn south-east up the much eroded path to reach Grey Height (686m), and 1km further the next point, Meall Dhamh (814m). From there the path leads on, dropping 50m at first, across a col and then climbing steeply up the shoulder of Cruach Ardrain. The summit of the mountain may be confusing in thick mist as the route just described leads first to a flat top with two cairns about 25m apart. To the north-east, across a slight dip in the ridge, is the true summit with a single large cairn. (5km; 910m; 2h 40min).

Beinn Tulaichean from the south ridge of Cruach Ardrain

The quickest return to Glen Falloch is by the route of ascent. However, a good traverse can be made over Stob Garbh. The start goes steeply down north-east from the summit cairn. The slope is rocky, and in icy conditions needs care. At its foot a wide col is crossed and the ridge to Stob Garbh climbed; this is perfectly straightforward in good visibility, but confusing in mist as there are many knolls and the ridge itself is not well-defined. From Stob Garbh go north down the grassy ridge for about 500m, then descend north-west into Coire Ardrain. Follow the fenced plantation round the corrie to a stile. This leads to a very boggy track leading down to better forest tracks and Crianlarich, but is best ignored. Instead, continue contouring with the fence to skirt below Grey Height. Ascend to a stile on the crest of the north-east ridge to gain the ascent path and descend back to Glen Falloch.

17

### Beinn Tulaichean; 946m; (OS Sheet 56; NN416196); M220; *hill of hillocks*

Beinn Tulaichean is at the southern end of the south ridge of Cruach Ardrain, and is in fact not much more than its south peak, the lowest point of the connecting ridge being about 820m. It is surprising that Beinn Tulaichean is classified as a separate Munro. On its east, south and west sides it falls in long and in places steep slopes, mostly grassy but with some crags here and there.

The ascent of Beinn Tulaichean is invariably made from the south-east. The public road from Balquhidder along the side of Loch Voil ends at a car park 750m east of Inverlochlarig, and the start is from there. Walk along the private road to Inverlochlarig and climb the south-east flank of Beinn Tulaichean directly above the farm. One can chose one's own route up the wide grassy hillside, and towards the summit a band of crags and huge boulders is reached which can be easily passed by keeping to the west. However, there is no difficulty in finding a more direct way through these crags. The south ridge of Beinn Tulaichean is reached a short distance from the top and the climb finishes along a path up this ridge. (4km; 820m; 2h 20min).

The continuation northwards to Cruach Ardrain is straightforward, and gives a good route to this mountain, no longer than the way from Glen Falloch described above. There is a path along the broad grassy connecting ridge, which drops only 120m from Beinn Tulaichean before rising gradually to Cruach Ardrain. The ridge does not lead directly to its top, but rather to its west, and at a point marked by a small cairn one turns right and goes about 70m north-east to the two cairns beyond which is the summit. (5.5km; 1030m; 3h).

On the return to Inverlochlarig from Cruach Ardrain the quickest route is back along the south ridge to the col, and then east down grassy slopes towards the Inverlochlarig Burn to reach a road leading south to the farm.

*Hamish Brown*

Ben More and Stob Binnein from Strath Fillan

BEN MORE

STOB BINNEIN

**Ben More;** 1174m; (OS Sheet 51; NN432244); M16; *big hill*
**Stob Binnein;** 1165m; (OS Sheets 51 and 57; NN434227); M18; *probably conical peak*

These two fine mountains, the highest south of Strath Tay, are among the best known and most popular in the Southern Highlands. From many viewpoints they appear as twin peaks, but Stob Binnein is the more elegant, its ridges being better defined and the tip of its summit being cut away to form a little plateau. Ben More, with a few extra metres of height, appears to be more bulky, particularly when seen from Glen Dochart near Crianlarich from where it shows its full size above Loch Iubhair, and the ascent from that side is a steep haul, but offers tremendous views north to Ben Lui.

The normal route to Ben More starts from the A85 road 150m east of the farm. There is limited verge parking, but the road is fast and busy and a large car park lies just a short distance further east. Cross a stile to reach a track which zigzags uphill for a few hundred metres. Go through a gate and climb south-east up the pathless and ever-steepening grass slopes aiming for the north-west shoulder of the mountain. A stony dyke high up on the shoulder is a useful aiming point and from here an obvious path follows its north side. To its south is a large hanging corrie whose headwall is steep and rocky, a potentially dangerous place in bad visibility or in winter. Higher up the path weaves through a few small crags before the angle of the slope eases below the summit, which is on top of a big crag. (3km; 1010m; 2h 30min).

For anyone making an ascent of Ben More by itself, the return route can be varied by descending the rocky north-east ridge path to the forestry deer fence. From here a straightforward traverse can be made round the pathless north face of Ben More, to arrive back at the gate on the track from Benmore farm.

To continue the traverse to Stob Binnein from the summit of Ben More, descend south for a short distance, then south-west following an indistinct ridge before going down south to the wide flat col called the Bealach-eadar-dha Beinn (the pass between two hills). The ascent of Stob Binnein is up its north ridge, a long uniform slope defined on its east side by the steep edge of the north-east corrie. The cairn is at the south edge of the little summit plateau, which is surrounded by steep slopes and crags on all sides except the north. (5km; 1320m; 3h 20min).

To return to Benmore Farm, retrace your steps down the north ridge to the bealach and from there descend westwards towards the Benmore Burn to reach a track leading down to Glen Dochart.

An alternative but longer route to Ben More's summit is via the north-east ridge, starting

Stob Binnein from Ben More

from the A85 road 4.5km east of Benmore farm at a small car park just west of the bridge over the Allt Coire Chaorach. A path gains a fence behind the car park and leads south-west to a stile and forest track, which is followed left into the forest. Continue on the track as it starts to

ascend, swings round right and divides. Turn left and follow the wide track for 1.5km to NN456260. Just after a large parking area, a cairn indicates a track entering the forest to the right. Follow the track, boggy in places, to exit the forest and cross a bridge before ascending to a gate and stile in the deer fence.

Follow the fence north-west to gain the north-east ridge of Ben More and follow this to the summit. At one point the ridge is quite rocky, but any difficulties can be avoided by traversing to one side or the other. (5.5km; 1010m; 3h).

The usual route to Stob Binnein from the south starts at the end of the public road west from Balquhidder at a car park 750m east of Inverlochlarig. From there climb directly north up steep grass slopes to Stob Invercarnaig, and continue along a pleasant grassy ridge to Stob Coire an Lochain (1068m). Descend slightly and climb Stob Binnein by its broad south ridge, which steepens just below the summit. (4km; 1050m; 2h 50min).

The return can be varied by going east from Stob Coire an Lochain to Meall na Dige (966m) and descending its south ridge to the foot of Glen Carnaig.

BEN MORE

STOB BINNEIN

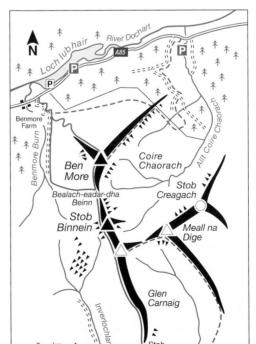

Ben Lui from the road to Cononish

*Des Rubens*

**Ben Lui (Beinn Laoigh);** 1130m; (OS Sheet 50; NN266263); M28; *calf hill*
**Beinn a' Chleibh;** 916m; (OS Sheet 50; NN250256); M279; *hill of the creel or chest*

20

BEN LUI

BEINN A'
CHLEIBH

Ben Lui is one of the finest mountains in the Southern Highlands; it stands high above its neighbours, and its splendid shape is unmistakable. In particular, the great north-east corrie, the Coire Gaothaich, which holds snow most years from midwinter until early summer, gives the mountain an Alpine character. The finest view of it is from Strath Fillan, looking up the Cononish glen directly at the north-east face. Seen from the west, for example from the north-east end of Loch Awe, Ben Lui dominates the upper reaches of Glen Lochy beyond Dalmally and rises high above its neighbour, Beinn a' Chleibh.

The finest way to Ben Lui, scenically at least, is via the Cononish glen, up which it is possible to bike. The approach from the north-west allows it to be combined with Beinn a' Chleibh, while the south ridge enables the link to Ben Oss and a traverse of all four hills.

The Cononish approach to Ben Lui starts either at Tyndrum Lower Station or at Dalrigh just

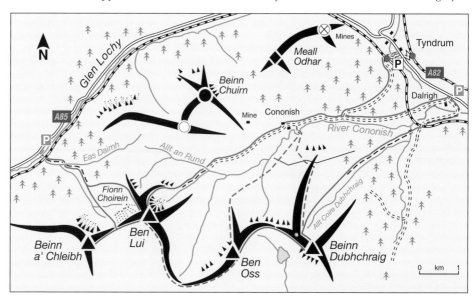

In the Central Gully of Ben Lui, looking towards Ben More and Stob Binnein

off the A82 road at NN343291. The two routes, both following private roads, converge 1.5km before Cononish. The glen just beyond the farm is the scene of a gold mining operation and is not a pretty sight. Continue west up the glen along a track which ends at the Allt an Rund, cross this stream and climb uphill into Coire Gaothach by a path on the north-west side of the stream flowing from the corrie. Once more level ground is reached in the corrie, climb north-west up steeper slopes to reach the north-east ridge of Ben Lui which forms a prominent spur called Stob Garbh. There is a path leading up to the spur and continuing up the crest, which becomes progressively steeper and narrower. There is no difficulty in summer, but in winter this could well be quite a serious climb by hillwalkers' standards. The climb ends suddenly at a cairn a few metres from the North-west Top of Ben Lui (1127m), and there is a short level traverse along the ridge overlooking the steep headwall of Coire Gaothach to reach the summit. (9km; 930m; 3h 40min). Return by the same route.

BEN LUI

BEINN A'
CHLEIBH

The starting place for Beinn a' Chleibh, from a point in Glen Lochy midway between Tyndrum and Dalmally, also gives a shorter approach to Ben Lui, enabling both mountains to be readily climbed together. This is also the start, or finish for a very fine traverse of all four peaks in the range. Start at a car park just off the A85 road at NN239278. There is no bridge over the River Lochy at this point. In dry conditions it is possible to cross the river dryshod by stepping stones near the outflow of the Eas Daimh; otherwise wet feet are likely and wading shoes useful. If the river is in spate it may not be possible to cross at this point; the footbridge 1km downstream leads onto the railway line and should not be used.

Once across the river, follow a path through the forest on the north side of the Eas Daimh for a few hundred metres, then cross this stream and continue along the path which climbs up into Fionn Choirein on the east side of the stream flowing down this corrie. Above the forest cross a stile over the deer fence to reach the open hillside.

From there the direct route to Ben Lui goes east up the grassy hillside to reach the north ridge well above its lower rocky steps, the Ciochan Beinn Laoigh. Continue steeply up this ridge to the North-west Top and the summit. (4km; 950m; 2h 30min).

The route to Beinn a' Chleibh continues from the stile up the grassy Fionn Choirein to the col at its head, the last part of the climb being quite steep. At the col turn right and climb the broad north-east ridge of Beinn a' Chleibh. (3.5km; 740m; 2h). The north-east and north faces of this hill are very steep and craggy, and no attempt should be made to ascend or descend by them.

The traverse between Beinn a' Chleibh and Ben Lui is very straightforward up or down the south-west side of Ben Lui. This slope forms a very broad ridge, defined along its north-west edge by the steep headwall of Fionn Choirein.

Donald Bennet

Ben Oss (left) and Ben Lui from Beinn Dubhchraig

*Ken Andrew*

BEINN
DUBHCHRAIG

BEN OSS

**Beinn Dubhchraig;** 978m; (OS Sheet 50; NN307254); M175; *hill of the black rock*
**Ben Oss;** 1029m; (OS Sheet 50; NN287253); M101; *hill of the loch outlet or elk hill*

These two mountains stand together to the west of Crianlarich between Strath Fillan and Glen Falloch. From Strath Fillan, Ben Oss is almost hidden behind Beinn Dubhchraig which shows its north-facing Coire Dubhchraig. This grassy corrie forms a wide bowl between the north and north-east ridges of the hill, and at its foot is the pine wood of the Coille Coire Chuilc, a remnant of the Old Caledonian Forest.

The traverse of the two hills starts at Dalrigh in Strath Fillan at NN343291 where there is a car park just off the A82. Descend rightwards onto the old road and follow it south-east over the River Fillan. Turn right onto a track which passes over the railway via a bridge. Just beyond the bridge cross marshy ground on the right, towards the pine wood and a footbridge, from where a path leads south-west through the wood to cross two deer fences by old stiles to reach the open hillside. Continue along a path up the north-west side of the Allt Coire Dubhchraig to cross a third fence at the upper limit of the planted forest. From there the route goes more or less directly up the grassy corrie to gain the shoulder by a small lochan, then south-east to the summit of Beinn Dubhchraig. (6.5km, 800m; 2h 50min).

Continuing to Ben Oss, descend north-west, back to the lochan on the shoulder, then more steeply to the col between the two hills. The first rise on the ridge to Ben Oss can be avoided by traversing on its south side and then climbing back to the crest a short distance from the top. (9.5km; 1050m; 3h 50min). Return by the same route.

Another good traverse is to bike to just before Cononish farm where there is a bridge over the River Cononish at NN304283. There is no path to the bridge or after it. Follow the base of the hill south-west for 1.5km to the stream which descends from below the col between Ben Oss and Beinn Dubhchraig. Gain and follow a slight ridge which is right of the next stream and leads diagonally to the north ridge of Ben Oss. This leads to the summit (no scrambling). Reverse the route to Beinn Dubhchraig (above), then back to the lochan on the shoulder and descend the north ridge to a fence. Follow this north-west to pass through a gap where the fence turns left. Continue beside the fence for a short distance to clear the craggy face of Creag Bhocan, then north to the bridge.

Linking these hills to Ben Lui and possibly on to Beinn a' Chleibh makes a very fine day's hillwalking. From Ben Oss descend south, then south-west and finally west down a broad featureless ridge. The col is a grassy expanse and from it the south ridge of Ben Lui leads directly to the summit. (13km; 1460m; 5h 20min). From there one can either return to Dalrigh by the north-east spur (Stob Garbh) and Cononish, or descend the south-west ridge to the col at the head of the Fionn Choirein and Beinn a' Chleibh. From Beinn a' Chleibh a return would need to be made via Ben Lui to Dalrigh, unless a linear route is being followed through to Glen Lochy. Map on page 20.

Looking up Loch Turret to Ben Chonzie

## Ben Chonzie (Ben-y-Hone); 931m; (OS Sheets 51 and 52; NN773308); M250; *mossy hill*

This solitary Munro is the highest point of the extensive tract of flat-topped hills and high moorland between Strath Earn and Loch Tay. At the centre of this area, between glens Lednock, Turret and Almond, Ben Chonzie rises just sufficiently above its neighbouring hills to be the most prominent among them, although it does not itself have any outstanding character. The summit is a long broad ridge, and to its east there is a large corrie ringed by grassy crags.

The normal approaches are from Crieff by Glen Turret, and from Comrie by Glen Lednock. The latter gives the easier climb as it follows a track most of the way. Start from the road up Glen Lednock near Coishavachan and follow the right of way to Ardtalnaig up the Invergeldie Burn. After 1.5km cross the burn and follow a track east up the hillside past shooting butts almost to the ridge. Then strike north-east across heath and blaeberry covered slopes to the broad crest where a fence leads north-west then north-east to the summit. (6.5km; 700m; 2h 40min).

Going by Glen Turret, start from the car park at the dam and walk along the track on the east side of the loch to its head. From there follow a direct line north-west on a rising traverse across the grassy hillside to the summit. Alternatively, continue along the track up Glen Turret, go round Lochan Uaine and climb west between the grassy crags above the lochan to reach the north-east ridge 500m from the summit. (6km; 570m; 2h 20min). Descend either route. An alternative to the Turret Burn descent is the ridge on the west side of the loch.

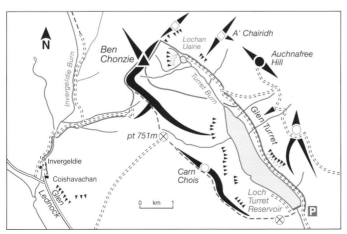

Standing on the southern edge of the Highlands, these two mountains are conspicuous and familiar features of the Highland landscape as seen from the valley of the River Forth. They form two parallel ridges running from south-east to north-west, separated by a col, the Bealach an Dubh Choirein, at a height of about 700m. Ben Vorlich appears from the south-east as a sharp-pointed conical peak, while Stuc a' Chroin has a flatter summit ridge with a steep drop at its east end, the profile of its north-east buttress above the Bealach an Dubh Choirein

Of several possible starting points for the traverse of the two mountains, Ardvorlich on the south side of Loch Earn is probably the most convenient, particularly if one wants to return to the starting point at the end of the day. Glen Ample on the west side of the two hills provides a possible route, but afforestation in the glen makes access awkward. The route from the south up the Keltie Water from Callander is longer than the other two. The Ardvorlich approach follows the right of way from there to Callander for 1.5km up Glen Vorlich along a good track to a junction of paths. The right of way keeps left, but the way to Ben Vorlich goes right along the track for a few hundred metres to the stream in Coire Buidhe. Continue south up the grassy hillside by an obvious path to reach the north ridge. Climb this ridge, which steepens towards the top where the Ordnance Survey trig point is at the north-west end of the level summit ridge and a large cairn stands 100m to its south-east. (4.5km; 890m; 2h 30min).

The continuation of the route to Stuc a' Chroin is easy to follow, there being a line of fence posts down to the Bealach an Dubh Choirein. From there a path leads up to the scree at the foot of the prominent buttress below Stuc a' Chroin's north top, where the path fades at an obvious large boulder with a tall metal fence post before it. From the boulder enter the scree and cross large rocks to locate the scramble up the buttress. The route is steep and loose in places requiring great care, and although well-worn when close up, it is not easily identified from the path.

This scramble can be avoided by descending a short distance north from the Bealach an Dubh Choirein to pick up a path which contours round into the head of Coire Fuadarach, cross-

BEN VORLICH

STUC A'
CHROIN

24

Ben Vorlich and Stuc a' Chroin from the west

Scott Johnstone

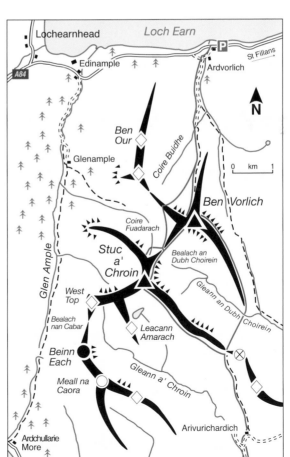

Ben Vorlich from the north-east buttress of Stuc a' Chroin

BEN VORLICH

STUC A'
    CHROIN

es the burn and rises to gain the north-west ridge below Stuc a' Chroin's north top. At the top of the buttress there is a cairn, and the summit of Stuc a' Chroin is about 500m south. (6.5km; 1160m; 3h 30min). To return to Ardvorlich from the Bealach an Dubh Choirein, follow the path horizontally round Ben Vorlich's west face to regain the ascent path.

The approach from Callander starts from a parking place below Drumardoch farm at the end of minor road beyond Bracklinn Falls. Continue along the track past Braeleny farm to the Keltie Water. Ford the river, the bridge was swept away in 2004 and crossing can be difficult in spate, and continue to Arivurichardich. Climb north up the path across the grassy hillside to reach a broad col on the long south-east ridge of Stuc a' Chroin. Descend north-east across Gleann an Dubh Choirein, where the path has largely disappeared in the eroded peat bog of the corrie, and reach the foot of the south-east ridge of Ben Vorlich which is climbed direct to the summit. (From Braeleny: 9km; 900m; 3h 30min). Traverse to Stuc a' Chroin and from its summit descend the long easy-angled south-east ridge to rejoin

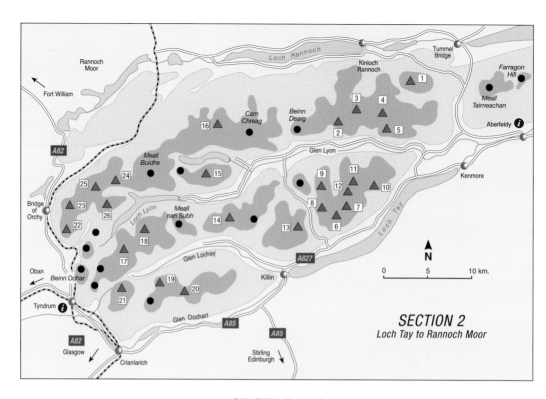

## SECTION 2

### Loch Tay to Rannoch Moor

---

*i* VisitScotland Information Centres

**Aberfeldy**; The Square, Aberfeldy, PH15 2DD, (01887 820276), open Jan–Dec

**Tyndrum**; Main Street, Tyndrum, FK20 8RY, (01838 400324), open Apr–Oct

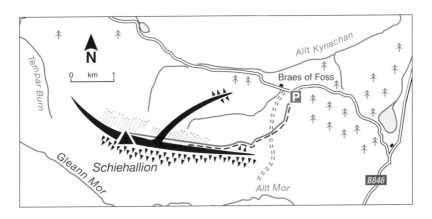

Schiehallion from Dunalastair Reservoir

**Schiehallion;** 1083m; (OS Sheet 51; NN713547); M59; *the fairy hill of the Caledonians*

Schiehallion is one of the best known of Scottish mountains by virtue of its striking appearance and isolated position in the centre of the Highlands. It is a conspicuous feature from many viewpoints; from the east and west it appears as a steep conical peak, but from the north or south its true shape is more apparent: a long whalebacked ridge dropping quite steeply to the west, but much more gradually to the east.

A narrow road leaves the A846 between Coshieville and Tummel Bridge and goes round the north side of Schiehallion to Kinloch Rannoch. Just east of Braes of Foss farm on this road there is a Forestry Commission car park. At it a plaque commemorates the experiment carried out on the slopes of Schiehallion by Maskelyne, once the Astronomer Royal, to determine the earth's mass by observing the deflection of a pendulum caused by the mass of Schiehallion itself.

From the south end of the car park follow a well constructed path south-west across moorland towards the mountain, crossing a faint track from Braes of Foss by an old stone sheep enclosure. The John Muir Trust who own the east side of the mountain, has realigned the former path onto an even older and more sustainable line, restoring the scar created by this former route. There is no waymarking and the good path stops short of the summit where the terrain becomes very stony. The upper part of the mountain is covered with angular quartzite stones and boulders giving rough walking. There are a number of cairns and the actual top is further on than might be expected. The summit panorama is outstanding. (4.5km; 760m; 2h 20min).

Carn Mairg (left) and Meall nan Aighean from Glen Lyon

Donald Bennet

**Carn Gorm;** 1029m; (OS Sheet 51; NN635500); M103; *blue hill*
**Meall Garbh;** 968m; (OS Sheet 51; NN647517); M186; *rough hill*
**Carn Mairg;** 1041m; (OS Sheet 51; NN684513); M91; *probably hill of rust*
**Meall nan Aighean;** 981m; (OS Sheet 51; NN694496); M169; *hill of the heifers or hinds*

**THE CARN MAIRG
GROUP**

This group of hills is on the north side of Glen Lyon, and forms a great arc of broad high ridges above Invervar. The nature of the terrain along the tops is more characteristic of the Grampians or Cairngorms than of the neighbouring Breadalbane mountains such as Ben Lawers. The ridges are wide and level and the corries easy-angled and devoid of crags. Although of no interest for climbing, the corries are of importance for stalking and restrictions may apply during that season.

The south side of the range above Glen Lyon is quite steep, and the southern shoulder of Meall nan Aighean is craggy. The north side is much less impressive and drops gradually across wide tracts of moorland and forest towards Loch Rannoch. Between the four Munros the drops along the ridge are fairly small, although the distances are considerable, so that the traverse of all four is a good high-level expedition from Invervar.

On the south side of the road, opposite the drive to Invervar House and a prominent barn, an access road signposted Invervar Lodge, leads to a small car park hidden from the road. Return to the road, go through the deer fence left of the barn and follow a track through woodland to open hillside. Continue for another 1km alongside the Invervar Burn, passing over the Allt Coire a' Chearcaill and up into the corrie to a springy metal footbridge over the burn. Cross over and follow the burn for a short way before leaving the riverside path and ascending steeply to the edge of the woodland and a better path past an old shieling, where the forest ends.

From that point the ascent of Carn Gorm is very straightforward, bearing west across the rising moorland to the steeper slopes which lead north-west to the level summit ridge. The trig point is about a hundred metres beyond the highest point. (4.5km; 830m; 2h 30min).

Descend quite steeply north and bear round north-east along a broad ridge towards the little pointed Top of An Sgorr (924m); avoided by the main path across its north-west side, although it is easily included. Beyond is a broad col (830m) where there is a cairn. Climb north-east and reach a line of fence posts leading east to the summit of Meall Garbh. The flat summit of this hill has two tops of almost equal height. (6.5km; 1020m; 3h 10min).

Descend east, following the line of fence posts past a small lochan to another wide col, and

Jim Renny

Carn Mairg from the east

reach Meall a' Bharr (1004m) whose summit is a long level ridge. There is only a very slight drop at the east end of this ridge to the next col, and the route lesds onto the north top of Carn Mairg, then bears south-east, still following the line of rusty fence posts. For a short distance the crest of the ridge is quite narrow and bouldery, and beyond it the summit of Carn Mairg, with its large cairn, is reached. (l0km; 1240m; 4h 20min).

In poor visibility, some care is needed on the descent south-east from Carn Mairg as the slope is quite steep and stony, and there is a small crag. Once below this the ground is very easy and a descent south down grassy slopes leads to the col at the watershed between Gleann Muilinn and the Allt Coire a' Chearcaill. From there climb south to the level summit ridge of Meall nan Aighean, heading towards a grassy summit with a small cairn. The highest point is the small rocky tor to the left (east), reached across 500m of flat ground. (12.5km; 1380m; 5h 10min).

Descend due west to get onto the broad grassy ridge on the south side of the Allt Coire a' Chearcaill. Continue very easily down this ridge, gradually bearing south-west to descend towards the Invervar Burn and reach the track on its east side just above the forest.

THE CARN MAIRG
GROUP

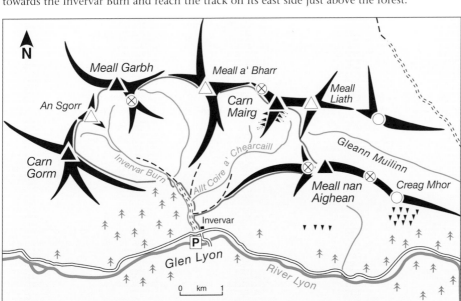

Ruaridh Pringle

The west face of Ben Lawers form Beinn Ghlas

## The Ben Lawers Hills

For much of its length, Loch Tay is dominated on its north-west side by the great sweeping slopes and high summits of the Ben Lawers group. The name applies not only to the highest point, but to the whole range of seven distinct peaks, all of them Munros, linked by a twisting ridge 12km long which at only one point drops below 800m. It is the highest and most extensive mountain massif in the Southern Highlands. The range gives the impression of being very grassy, and this is certainly true of most of the peaks. Only in the north-east corrie of Ben Lawers itself, above Lochan nan Cat, are there crags of any size, and they are vegetatious, of more interest to the botanist than the climber, for the whole area has a reputation for its alpine flora.

Most of the south-eastern side of Ben Lawers, from the summit ridges well down towards Loch Tay, is owned by the National Trust for Scotland, so there are no restrictions on climbing on that side of the mountain at any time of the year. It is worth bearing in mind that the narrow road which crosses the west end of the range from Loch Tay to Glen Lyon is not normally kept open by snow ploughs in winter, and may be blocked when there is much snow on the ground.

It is quite possible for any reasonably fit hillwalker, particularly if a willing car driver is available, to traverse all the peaks of Ben Lawers in a single day. The easiest way to do this is to start near the summit of the Loch Tay to Glen Lyon road, climb Meall a' Choire Leith first and continue over the tops to Meall Greigh, finally descending to Lawers village. Alternatively, if one has to start and finish at the same point, the traverse is best undertaken from the Glen Lyon side, starting at Camusvrachan. This is in effect a circuit of the peaks surrounding the Allt a' Chobhair from Meall a' Choire Leith to Meall Garbh, with a final excursion 3km east to Meall Greigh, followed by a long return to Camusvrachan.

However, attractive as the complete traverse may be for those who are fit, most hillwalkers may find it a bit too strenuous. In the following descriptions the ascent of the seven Ben Lawers Munros will be taken in three separate days, all of them quite short and allowing time for diversions to explore the range and its features of interest. Although these descriptions tend to concentrate on the southern side of the mountain, for it is the most accessible, the northern side overlooking Glen Lyon should not be forgotten. Scenically it is just as attractive, if not more so, and one is much less likely to meet other climbers on that side of the mountain.

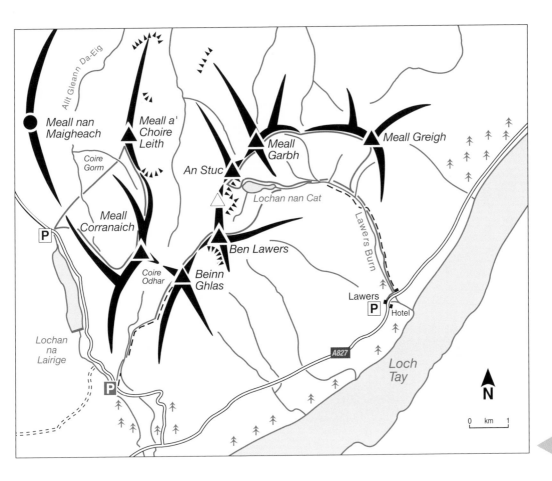

Approaching the col below the south-west ridge of Ben Lawers

Scott Johnstone

**Beinn Ghlas;** 1103m; (OS Sheet 51; NN625404); M47; *greenish-grey hill*
**Ben Lawers;** 1214m; (OS Sheet 51; NN635414); M10; *hill of the Labhair (loud) stream*

These two Munros form the central and highest part of the range. They are most easily climbed from the National Trust for Scotland (NTS) 'contribute and conserve' car park on the road from Loch Tay to Glen Lyon. At a height of 450m, this car park gives a good start for the climb. As noted earlier, this road is not kept open in winter, and in bad snow conditions the car park may not be accessible by vehicle. In that case the climb will have to start some distance lower down the road and further from the mountain.

From the NTS car park take the surfaced path through a walled interpretation area, cross the road and continue into an area fenced off from deer and sheep. Take the main path which climbs north-east up the west side of the Burn of Edramucky. In just over 500m cross the burn and continue north along the path up its east side for a further 500m, then bear north-east up the grassy hillside onto the south ridge of Beinn Ghlas and along this ridge. The summit of Beinn Ghlas is marked by a small pile of stones, hardly a cairn, at the edge of the very steep drop on the north side of the hill. (3.5km; 660m; 2h).

Continue north-east down the broad easy-angled ridge, following an obvious and much eroded path to the wide col at about 995m. The path continues up a broad grassy slope at a uniform angle to reach the summit where little now remains of the huge cairn that was once built to raise Lawers to the select company of Scotland's 4000ft mountains. (5km; 920m; 2h 40min). The best return is probably by the same route.

An attractive alternative route to Ben Lawers, which avoids the usual crowds of the way just described, is to start at Lawers village on the A827 road near the foot of the Lawers Burn. Parking anywhere other than at the walkers car park at the Lawers Hotel is a problem. Walkers not staying at the Ben Lawers Hotel can use the lower of the hotel car parks for a charge on the condition that something is spent in the hotel before, or after the walk. Walk along the road for 500m and on the east side of the bridge take the road to Machuim farm and continue past it by a path along the edge of the fields above the Lawers Burn. The path leads up the east side of the burn to a small dam, from where one continues west beside the stream to Lochan nan Cat. This lochan is at the heart of the range, lying in a beautiful remote corrie above which Ben Lawers and its neighbouring rocky peak of An Stuc rise in steep craggy slopes. Climb south from the lochan to reach the east ridge of Ben Lawers and follow it to the summit. (7.5km; 1000m; 3h 20min). Map on page 31.

Meall Corranaich, Ben Lawers and Beinn Ghlas from Meall nan Tarmachan

*Donald Bennet*

Meall Corranaich from the col between Ben Lawers and Beinn Ghlas

**Meall Corranaich;** 1069m; (OS Sheet 51; NN615410); M68; *probably crooked hill*
**Meall a' Choire Leith;** 926m; (OS Sheet 51; NN612439); M261; *hill of the grey corrie*

MEALL
CORRANAICH

MEALL A' CHOIRE
LEITH

These two hills are at the western end of the Ben Lawers range, Meall Corranaich overlooking Lochan na Lairige on the watershed between Loch Tay and Glen Lyon, and Meall a'Choire Leith lying 3km to the north, halfway along a long ridge extending towards Glen Lyon.

The nearest point of access for both hills is the summit of the road which crosses the western end of the Ben Lawers range. Just north of the north end of Lochan na Lairige there is a prominent cairn above the road, and a short distance to the west there is a rather restricted space where two or three cars can be parked (NN593416).

Going to Meall Corranaich first, cross rough moorland south-eastwards over peat hags to reach the Allt Gleann Da-Eig. Follow this stream uphill and gradually trend east to reach the south-west ridge of Meall Corranaich. Continue up this ridge to the summit. (A shorter and steeper route goes directly up the west face of the hill). The small summit cairn stands close to the edge of the steep north-east face. (3km; 520m; 1h 40min).

The traverse to Meall a' Choire Leith goes north down a broad easy-angled ridge which in 1km divides into two, enclosing Coire Gorm. Go down the north ridge, which is on the east side of this corrie, to the crags at the head of the little Coire Liath and bear north-west round the edge of these crags to reach a col about 780m. To the north of this col the ridge merges into the flat-topped dome of Meall a' Choire Leith. (6km; 670m; 2h 30min).

To return to the day's starting point, descend south-west from Meall a' Choire Leith, cross the stream in Coire Gorm and continue in the same direction to the Allt Gleann Da-Eig. Finally, climb gradually across rough peaty terrain to the col at NN596419 and follow a track down to the road near the prominent cairn.

Map on page 31.

Ben Lawers and An Stuc from Meall Garbh

*Don Green*

34

**Meall Greigh;** 1001m; (OS Sheet 51; NN674438); M136; *hill of horse studs*
**Meall Garbh;** 1123m; (OS Sheet 51; NN644436); M32; *rough hill*
**An Stuc;** 1117m; (OS Sheet 51; NN639431); M36; *the peak*

MEALL GREIGH

MEALL GARBH

AN STUC

These three mountains form the north-eastern end of the Ben Lawers range. Meall Greigh is the furthest point, well seen from the road near the Ben Lawers Hotel; it is a rounded hill, grassy on all sides. Meall Garbh is not well seen from the road, being almost hidden behind the lower rising hillside. An Stuc is the finest of the three, a well-defined peak with a steep and rocky east face overlooking Lochan nan Cat.

The traverse of these three mountains from Lawers village, being almost entirely within National Trust for Scotland territory, can be done at any time of the year, and has the further advantage of giving very fine views of Ben Lawers rising above Lochan nan Cat.

The start is from the A827 road just north-east of the bridge over the Lawers Burn where a private road leads uphill to Machuim farm. Car parking anywhere in Lawers village other than the walkers car park at the Lawers Hotel is a problem. The lower of the Ben Lawers Hotel car parks can be used for a charge on the condition that something is spent in the hotel before, or after the walk. Go along the road for 500m and up the track past the farm beside the edge of the fields above the Lawers Burn. Once beyond the highest wall continue along the path on the east side of the burn for about 2km until the first stream coming down from Meall Greigh is reached. Climb up beside it towards the summit, which is a smooth rounded dome with a lower cairned top 200m north-west of the highest point. (4.5km; 820m; 2h 30min).

The traverse west to Meall Garbh goes along a broad ridge across a col at about 830m. The only difficulty might be in bad visibility when accurate navigation is necessary. (8km; 1110m; 3h 40min). Descend south-west down a steepening ridge to the col below An Stuc. The ascent of its north face (it is hardly a ridge) is steep and involves in summer some mild scrambling. In winter it may be quite a hard climb requiring ice axe and crampons. It is definitely the hardest bit of the Ben Lawers ridge. (9km; 1240m; 4h 10min).

Descend the broad and easy south ridge of An Stuc to the Bealach Dubh and go down the steep grassy gully on its east side to reach Lochan nan Cat. Go round its north side and return along the Lawers Burn to the village.

Map on page 31.

On the ridge from Meall nan Tarmachan to Meall Garbh

**Meall nan Tarmachan;** 1043m; (OS Sheet 51; NN585390); M89; *hill of the ptarmigans*

The Tarmachan Hills, as they are commonly called, are among the best-known peaks of the Southern Highlands, and the outline of their summits seen from the Falls of Dochart is one of the most familiar of our mountain landscapes. They lie about 5km north of Killin and only the highest one, Meall nan Tarmachan, is a Munro, the others being Tops. The southern front of the group has a discontinuous line of crags just below the summit ridge along its entire length.

The nearest approach to Meall nan Tarmachan is from the National Trust for Scotland 'contribute and conserve' car park on the road from Loch Tay to Glen Lyon. Follow the path which climbs uphill above the car park, cross a track and continue on a path up grassy slopes to reach the broad south ridge of Meall nan Tarmachan. Follow this ridge over a small knoll, the South-east Top (923m), and descend a short distance to the col below the craggy south-east face. Continue straight ahead up a steepening slope to reach a rake below the upper rocks, turn right (north) along this rising rake for about 150m and finally climb up steep grass on the left (west) to the summit cairn. (3.5km; 600m; 1h 50min).

The return can be made by the same route, but this hardly does justice to the Tarmachans. It is much better to continue the traverse over the three lower Tops; 'The Ptarmigan Ridge'. A broad grassy ridge, leads south-west from Meall nan Tarmachan to a col with two lochans. From there a path goes up the ridge to the sharp rocky summit of Meall Garbh (1026m), which is the finest peak of the Tarmachans. Continue west along a narrow level ridge for a short distance and then drop steeply to the next col. From there the ascent to Beinn nan Eachan (1000m) might be confusing in mist were it not for the path which twists and turns along the knolly ridge. From that Top go south-west down a grassy slope to the level continuation of the ridge across the next col, and up to Creag na Caillich (914m).

The east face of this top is very steep and rocky, so return north-east towards the col to outflank it before descending south-east into Coire Fionn Lairige. Continue down this grassy corrie to reach a disused quarry and the road which leads in 4km back to the day's starting point.

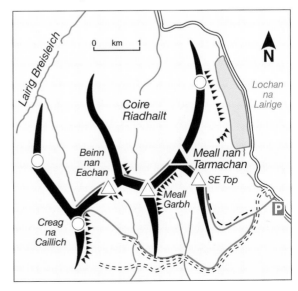

Meall Ghaordaidh from Glen Lyon

**Meall Ghaordaidh;** 1039m; (OS Sheet 51; NN514397); M93; *possibly hill of the shoulder*

MEALL
GHAORDAIDH

Meall Ghaordaidh rises between Glen Lochay and Glen Lyon, about 10km north-west of Killin. It is rather an isolated hill, being far enough away from its neighbours, the Tarmachans to the east and Beinn Heasgarnich to the west, to be climbed by itself, and it gives quite a short day.

On its south side overlooking Glen Lochay, Meall Ghaordaidh has uniform featureless grassy slopes rising from glen to summit in a single sweep. On the north side above Glen Lyon there are two prominent spurs, Creag an Tulabhain and Creag Laoghain, which rise steeply above the glen. Although the Glen Lyon side of the hill is the more interesting, and it is quite possible to climb Meall Ghaordaidh from the bridge over the River Lyon near Stronuich, either up the west side of the obvious spur or up the corrie between the two spurs, the Glen Lochay approach is more usually followed.

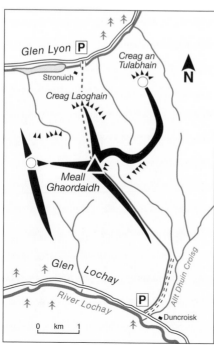

There is an old right of way from Duncroisk in Glen Lochay through the Lairig Breisleich to Glen Lyon, but its line on the east side of the Allt Dhuin Chroisg is rather overgrown. A better route exists on the west side of this stream, starting about 300m west of Duncroisk. Park on a bend at a widening in the road. A rough track leads through fields onto the higher open hillside and in about 1.5km reaches a sheepfank at some old shielings.

From there climb north-west directly towards the summit of Meall Ghaordaidh up a broad shoulder of grass and heather. An iron post marks the way and beyond it for several hundred metres the gradient is easy until some small outcrops of rock are reached, and just above them the summit appears. The Ordnance Survey trig point stands inside a fine circular cairn. (4.5km; 890m; 2h 30min).

*Donald Bennet*

Stuchd an Lochain

**Stuchd an Lochain;** 960m; (OS Sheet 51; NN483448); M197; *peak of the little loch*
**Meall Buidhe;** 932m; (OS Sheet 51; NN498499); M248; *yellow hill*

Far up Glen Lyon, beyond Meggernie Castle, the Allt Conait (a tributary of the River Lyon) flows down from Loch an Daimh. Between this loch and Glen Lyon itself, Stuchd an Lochain occupies a commanding position, its great bulk filling the westward view up the glen. On the north side of Loch an Daimh, Meall Buidhe is an undistinguished hill, the highest point of the vast tract of high undulating moorland between upper Glen Lyon and Loch Rannoch.

Four kilometres west of Bridge of Balgie in Glen Lyon a branch road leads up to the Giorra Dam at the east end of Loch an Daimh, and both hills are accessible from there. The loch is at a height of about 430m, so the amount of climbing on each is not great. In fact, the ascent of both in one day is no more strenuous than many a Munro by itself.

Climbing Stuchd an Lochain first, walk past the south end of the dam for 150m to an obvious path which initially contours the hillside them aims more steeply up into Coire Ban via some eroded and boggy sections to gain the ridge at a cairn and line of fence posts. These are followed west to Creag an Fheadain (887m), then south-west across a dip in the broad ridge to Sron Chona Choirein (927m), and finally west to Stuchd an Lochain. (4.5km; 600m; 2h). The finest feature of this hill is its northern corrie which holds in its depths the dark circular Lochan nan Cat. The return to the Loch an Daimh dam takes a little more than an hour.

Starting again at the dam follow the track north then west above the loch for 600m to NN506469 where a path gains the south ridge of Meall a' Phuill. Follow this path to the col west of Meall a' Phuill, then on to Pt.917m marked with two cairns. Continue north along the broad crest past some small cairns to reach the big cairn which marks the summit of Meall Buidhe at the north end of a level ridge. (4.5km; 520m; 2h).

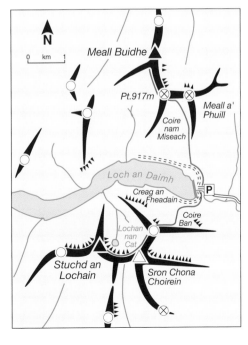

Beinn Heasgarnich from Beinn Achaladair

*Jim Renny*

**Creag Mhor;** 1047m; (OS Sheets 50 and 51; NN391361); M84; *big rock*
**Beinn Heasgarnich;** 1078m; (OS Sheet 51; NN413383); M62; *sheltering hill*

CREAG MHOR

BEINN
HEASGARNICH

These two mountains in the Forest of Mamlorn are on the north side of Glen Lochay near its head, some 17km west of Killin. In common with many of their neighbouring hills in Breadalbane, they are for the most part grassy, with no notable crags or rocky corries. Creag Mhor has two well-defined ridges enclosing Coire-cheathaich at the head of Glen Lochay, and its north face immediately below the summit is fairly steep and rocky. Beinn Heasgarnich is a massive mountain of broad grassy ridges and wide corries, lacking any outstanding features. There is a considerable area of peat moor at a height of about 650m to the east of its summit.

Jim Renny

Summit snowfields of Beinn Heasgarnich

At the time of writing (2012) parking is no longer possible at the end of the public road beyond Kenknock farm and walkers are requested to use the new car park at NN477368, some 1.2km before the road end. A private road climbs north-west out of the glen at the road end and crosses the east side of Beinn Heasgarnich at about 530m before dropping to Glen Lyon near the dam at the east end of Loch Lyon. This road is gated and while there is pedestrian access, vehicle access no longer appears possible, although this may change in the future.

There are two tracks up Glen Lochy from Kenknock. These can both be cycled, but there is no access for vehicles. To traverse these two mountains, climbing Creag Mhor first, walk along this lower estate track for 5km to Batavaime where the track divides, the right-hand branch zigzagging steeply uphill to gain the upper track. Follow the track west to below Sron nan Eun to a wooden gate in the fence. Ascend to an upper gate and an intermittent path into the small boulder strewn corrie forming the frontal face. Keep close to the burn draining the corrie to reach the ridge and follow it to the summit of Creag Mhor. (9km; 830m; 3h 30min).

Avoid the steep rocky descent of the north-east face of Creag Mhor by going north-west for 500m then north for about the same distance down the broad ridge leading to Meall Tionail. Then bear east down a grassy corrie which leads to the wide flat col at Lochan na Baintighearna at about 650m. From there the route to Beinn Heasgarnich climbs steeply at first upgrassy slopes and then continues along a broad undulating ridge to the flat summit.(13km; 1260m; 5h).

Descend east down Coire Ban Mor, following the Allt Tarsuinn until it reaches flat ground north of Lochan Achlarich. From there either continue north-east down the stream to reach the road between Glen Lochay and Glen Lyon and walk down it, or take a more direct line south-east across the level peaty corrie and the west shoulder of Creag nam Bodach to descend the lower grassy hillside above the day's starting point.

CREAG MHOR

BEINN
  HEASGARNICH

MEALL GLAS

SGIATH CHUIL

**Meall Glas;** 959m; (OS Sheet 51; NN431321); M199; *greenish-grey hill*
**Sgiath Chuil;** 921m; (OS Sheet 51; NN462317); M270; *back wing (sheltering spot)*

Between Glen Dochart and Glen Lochay there is a range of low hills. Meall Glas and Sgiath Chuil are the only two Munros in this area, and they can easily be climbed together from Auchessan in Glen Dochart. From this glen both hills rise gradually from the wide strath over rough moorland to their steeper upper slopes. Meall Glas shows a fairly continuous escarpment of steep grass and broken rocks around its southern flank, and Sgiath Chuil is recognised by its prominent summit rocks.

Car parking is possible on the roadside a short distance east of the point where the private

Meall Glas (left) and Ben Challum from Meall Ghaordaidh

road to Auchessan leaves the A85. Walk down the private road across the River Dochart to Auchessan and take the track behind the house on the east side of the stream which flows down from Creag nan Uan. This track ends once high ground is reached, and a course slightly west of north should be taken over rough featureless moorland to aim for the col just east of Meall Glas, where an easy grass slope leads up to the ridge. From there the summit of Meall Glas is a short distance west. (6km; 800m; 2h 40min).

**MEALL GLAS**

**SGIATH CHUIL**

Return east along the broad ridge, passing a prominent cairn at Pt.908m to reach Beinn Cheathaich (937m). The direct descent east from this Top is very steep at first, so go along the ridge north for a short distance and then descend east, thereby avoiding this minor difficulty. Lower down, easy grassy slopes lead to the wide peaty col at the head of the Allt Riobain.

The west face of Meall a' Churain (918m) rises directly above the col in uniformly steep grass slopes 300m high, and the ridge from this Top to Sgiath Chuil is almost level. The cairn on this peak is right at the edge of the crag which looks prominent from below. (10.5km; 1180m; 4h 20min).

Descend south-west towards the Allt Riobain and follow it for about 1km before bearing away south-west below Creag nan Uan to rejoin the uphill route. These hills can also be climbed from Glen Lochay by their north ridges, via Lubchurran, 2km beyond the end of the public road at Kenknock, although the river must be forded.

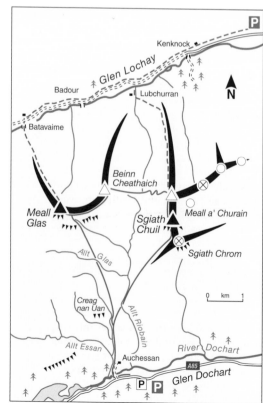

Ben Challum from the north-west, with Ben More and Stob Binnein in the distance

**Ben Challum;** 1025m; (OS Sheet 50; NN386322); M106; *Calum's hill*

The north-east side of Strath Fillan between Crianlarich and Tyndrum is dominated by the slopes of Ben Challum, the largest and highest of the hills on that side of the strath. Seen from the south, the main impression of the mountain is of the wide expanse of grassy hillside above the River Fillan, rising at an easy angle to the dome of the South Top (998m), behind which the true summit is hidden. The remoter side of the mountain above the head of Glen Lochay is steep and craggy, the approach being along either of two estate tracks then up the east ridge.

The most convenient starting point in Strath Fillan is at Kirkton farm. There is a layby on the A82 almost opposite the access road to the farm. Near Kirkton farm are the remains of St Fillan's Priory, and nearby there are two old graveyards. From the priory take the track uphill and cross the railway at an uncontrolled level crossing, or by a footbridge 100m south-east of it. Head north-east to a forestry fence and follow the signposted footpath alongside it, boggy in places, through an area of new broadleaf planting and over assorted stiles in the deer fencing. Rise up to a meeting of three sheep fences before the knoll at Pt. 698m, cross a stile on the right and continue up the south ridge to reach the South Top, whose summit is a large rock with a cairn nearby.

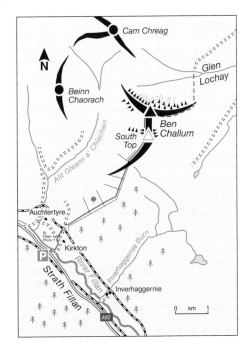

In clear weather the continuation to the summit of Ben Challum is obvious, but in poor visibility the terrain may be confusing as a bearing due north from the South Top would lead one astray. Descend quite steeply west for a few metres from the South Top to cross a little narrow hollow and climb onto the ridge on its far side. Once on this ridge there are no route-finding problems; a gradual descent north followed by a steeper ascent leads to the large summit cairn overlooking the steep north face. (5.5km; 900m; 2h 50min).

**Beinn Dorain;** 1076m; (OS Sheet 50; NN325378); M64; *probably hill of the streamlet*
**Beinn an Dothaidh;** 1004m; (OS Sheet 50; NN331408); M129; *hill of scorching*

These two peaks are the southern half of the semicircular range of mountains which overlook Loch Tulla and the headwaters of the River Orchy. Beinn Dorain in particular, with its great upsweep above the West Highland Railway and its conical shape, is one of the most familiar mountains in Scotland. Beinn an Dothaidh may not be so spectacular in appearance, but it too presents an uninterrupted bastion above Loch Tulla, and has a fine corrie on its north-east face. The two mountains are easily accessible from Bridge of Orchy.

From the station go through the underpass below the railway and emerge onto the rising moorland. Bear north-east for about 100m past a little fenced enclosure along a well-worn path which continues up the south bank of the Allt Coire an Dothaidh. Higher up the corrie, avoid some small crags straight ahead by bearing left beside the stream which flows down from a steep Y-shaped gully on Beinn an Dothaidh. Once a line of rusty fence posts is reached climb east and make a rising traverse rightwards below a line of crags to reach the cairn on the bealach between the two mountains.

Going to Beinn Dorain first, climb south up an easy-angled slabby rib along the edge of a rocky escarpment. In a few hundred metres the rocks end and the ascent continues up a broad grassy slope, bouldery higher up, to a large cairn. This is not the summit, as might be thought on a misty day, and one must continue 200m further south beyond a slight drop in the ridge to reach the highest point of Beinn Dorain. (4.5km 890m; 2h 30min).

After returning to the bealach, climb north-east up the grassy south flank of Beinn an Dothaidh. This leads to the summit ridge of the mountain where there are three tops, the central one being the highest. (7.5km; 1140m; 3h 40min). A few hundred metres away is the West Top (1000m) which is a good viewpoint, and from there a course south leads back to the col and the return to Bridge of Orchy.

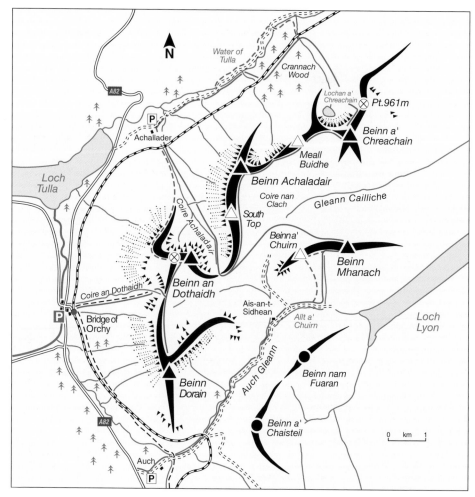

Beinn Dorain

An alternative descent route from the West Top, which gives a good traverse, is to go west then north round the edge of the north-east corrie of Beinn an Dothaidh and follow the ridge towards Achallader farm. After descending quite steep broken slopes for a short distance, continue down easier ground to reach the path on the west side of the Allt Coire Achaladair leading to a bridge over the West Highland Railway just above the farm.

43

Beinn Achaladair (left) and Beinn an Dothaidh from Loch Tulla

**Beinn a' Chreachain;** 1081m; (OS Sheet 50; NN373440); M61; *scallop-shaped hill*
**Beinn Achaladair;** 1038m; (OS Sheet 50; NN344432); M94; *hill of the field by the hard water*

These two fine mountains form the northern perimeter of the Bridge of Orchy range, presenting a great curving rampart above the Water of Tulla and the south-western corner of Rannoch Moor. Beinn Achaladair in particular has a continuously steep hillside above Achallader farm, extending along the flank of Meall Buidhe to Coire an Lochain below Beinn a' Chreachain. The south-east side of these mountains is less impressive, forming a series of shallow grassy corries above Gleann Cailliche. The traverse of these two mountains is best done from Achallader farm, which is 1.5km from the A82 road at the north-east end of Loch Tulla. Cars can be driven along the private road to the farm and parked there.

It is probably better to climb Beinn a' Chreachain first, as the subsequent traverse to Beinn Achaladair has splendid views ahead. From the farm go north-east along a track which is the old right of way to Loch Rannoch. The crossing of the Allt Ur (lower Allt Coire Achaladair) may be a problem if it is in spate. Follow the track to the old bridge over the Water of Tulla. Here a path continues along the south bank to Crannach Wood and ascends through ancient pines to cross the railway by a footbridge at NN349454. Continue north-east alongside the railway to where the Allt Coire an Lochain passes under the railway at NN359467. An alternative avoiding most of Crannach Wood crosses the old bridge and follows the track to a footbridge over the Tulla at NN353468, then ascends east and south round woodland to the Allt Coire an Lochain underpass below the railway. Follow the Allt Coire an Lochain up into Coire an Lochain and Lochan a' Chreachain. Continue east up grassy slopes to reach the north-east ridge of Beinn a' Chreachain just south-west of Pt.961m. Follow the north-east ridge, with one narrow section, to the dome of the summit. (7.5km; 900m; 3h 10min).

BEINN A' CHREACHAIN

BEINN ACHALADAIR

44

Descend stony slopes north-west to the col above Coire an Lochain and climb a short distance west to the north-east end of the level summit ridge of Meall Buidhe (978m). Continue south-west past a cairn and down to the col at 813m. Climb steeply up the rocky east ridge round the edge of the north-east corrie to the top of the north ridge of Beinn Achaladair. From there traverse 200m south-west along the level crest to the summit, which commands a superb view towards the Black Mount and Rannoch Moor. The cairn is right at the edge of a long steep drop to the West Highland Railway, and gives a great sense of exposure. (10.5km; 1070m; 4h 10min).

Continue along the broad high ridge of Beinn Achaladair over the South Top (1002m) and descend the long easy south ridge to the col at the head of Coire Daingean. Go north down this corrie and its lower extension, Coire Achaladair by paths on either side of the Allt Coire Achaladair to reach footbridges over the West Highland Railway just above Achallader farm.

Map on page 42.

Beinn Achaladair from Crannach Wood

*Donald Bennet*

Looking up the Auch Gleann to Beinn Mhanach

**Beinn Mhanach;** 953m; (OS Sheet 50; NN373412); M211; *monks' hill*

The twin rounded summits of Beinn Mhanach and its slightly lower Top, Beinn a' Chuirn (923m), are well seen looking up the Auch Gleann from the A82 road midway between Tyndrum and Bridge of Orchy. They fill the distant head of the glen 8km to the north-east in a remote corner between the Bridge of Orchy mountains and the head of Loch Lyon.

Beinn Mhanach is for the most part a grassy hill, steep on its south side, but craggier on its remote north face. Beinn a' Chuirn is quite steep and craggy at its western end.

The most obvious approach to these hills is up the Auch Gleann, but another route which is slightly shorter is from Achallader farm by Coire Achaladair, and this way enables the ascent of Beinn Mhanach to be combined with Beinn Achaladair and Beinn a' Chreachain.

For the Auch Gleann route there is a small car park on the right, a short distance down the private access road to Auch. Otherwise, there is limited verge-side parking on the A82. Walk down the private road past Auch and along the right of way up the Auch Gleann, keeping left at the West Highland Railway viaduct. Follow the track up the glen crossing and recrossing the Allt Kinglass and keeping right where the track divides. If the stream is in spate, the walker will be forced to stay on the south-east side of the stream as far as the ruined cottage at Ais-an t-Sidhean where the celebrated Gaelic poet Duncan Ban MacIntyre lived for several years.

Continue along the track to its highest point before it bridges the Allt a' Chuirn and follow steep grassy slopes up the west side of the burn to the col and the flat mossy summit of Beinn Mhanach beyond. (9.5km; 760m; 3h 30min).

The descent may be made by the same route, or a traverse can be made to Beinn a' Chuirn along a broad mossy ridge. The descent from this Top in a west or south-west direction is not advised as the slope is steep and craggy, so go south-east with care to avoid these crags and rejoin the uphill route.

The alternative route from Achallader farm goes up Coire Achaladair to the bealach at its head. From there traverse horizontally north-east along a fairly clear path, possibly an old stalkers' path. This crosses the grassy flank of Beinn Achaladair and drops gradually to the 630m col at NN354417. From there follow a fence south-east to reach the flat col 1km west of Beinn Mhanach and continue east along the broad mossy ridge to the summit. (8.5km; 920m; 3h 30min).

This route can be extended to include Beinn Achaladair and even Beinn a' Chreachain. Return to the col at NN354417 and from there climb north-west up grassy slopes into Coire nan Clach and continue more steeply onto the ridge of Beinn Achaladair, where the route described on the preceding page is joined.

Map on page 42.

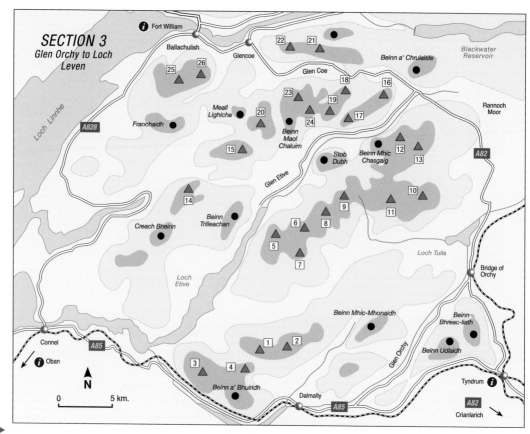

# SECTION 3

## Glen Orchy to Loch Leven

ℹ️ VisitScotland Information Centres
**Oban**; Argyll Square, Oban, PA34 4AN, (01631 563122), open Jan–Dec
**Tyndrum**; Main Street, Tyndrum, FK20 8RY, (01838 400324), open Apr–Oct
**Fort William**; 15 High Street, Fort William, PH33 6DH, (01397 701801),
   open Jan–Dec

Donald Bennet

Beinn a' Chochuill from Beinn Eunaich

**Beinn Eunaich;** 989m; (OS Sheet 50; NN135328); M156; *fowling hill*
**Beinn a' Chochuill;** 980m; (OS Sheet 50; NN110328); M172; *hill of the cowl*

These two hills are the highest points on a 12km-long ridge between Loch Etive and Glen Strae which is separated from Ben Cruachan by Glen Noe. Beinn a' Chochuill has a long, fairly level spine running from east to west, joined to the Ben Cruachan massif to the south by a bealach at 560m. Beinn Eunaich has a more pyramidal shape and is well seen from the A85 road west of Dalmally. With the exception of Beinn Eunaich's west ridge, both hills give easy going on short grass, and both provide magnificent views of Ben Cruachan's majestic peaks and ridges.

Start from the B8077 road in Glen Strae at NN137288 where a private road leads north-west. Follow this road, passing to the west of Castles Farm to reach the hydro road which climbs gradually north-west across the lower slopes of Beinn Eunaich. Follow this for 3km until 300m beyond a bridge the track divides. Take to the hillside of Beinn a' Chochuill and climb steeply north up grassy slopes which gradually steepen to form an ill-defined ridge leading north-west to the main spine of the hill. Follow this ridge west, climbing gradually for 1km to the summit of Beinn a' Chochuill. (5.5km; 930m; 2h 50min).

To continue the traverse to Beinn Eunaich, retrace the route and continue down the ridge east to the bealach at 728m. Above, the west ridge of Beinn Eunaich has a rightward turn at 800m and beyond that point grows rockier and steepens steadily almost to the cairn, set at the north end of a little plateau. (8.5km; 1200m; 4h).

Descend south down the broad grassy ridge leading to Stob Maol and at NN134306 follow a zigzag path steeply down the west flank of the ridge to the hydro road about 1km north-west of Castles Farm. On this descent there are fine views of Loch Awe and the long parallel ridges of the Dalmally Horseshoe.

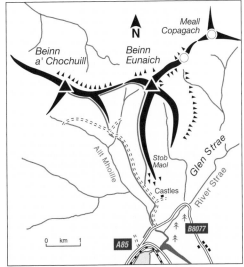

The northern ridges of Ben Cruachan from Beinn a' Chochuill

## Ben Cruachan; 1126m; (OS Sheet 50; NN069304); M31; *heaped hill*

This sharp peak is the culminating point of a huge and complex massif, one of the finest and best known of Scottish mountains. It rises grandly above Loch Awe and the Pass of Brander. The main spine of the mountain runs from east to west, and from it two southern ridges enclose an open corrie holding the Cruachan Reservoir. Ben Cruachan itself is a peak with the classical form of four ridges rising to merge at the pointed summit. Its northern slopes fall very steeply into wild corries. With its high ridge of seven peaks, Ben Cruachan is very distinctive as seen from surrounding hills.

The most direct ascent starts from the A85 road several kilometres west of Dalmally in the Pass of Brander at the Cruachan Power Station. There are one or two roadside parking places nearby, but parking in the power station's Visitor Centre is discouraged.

Opposite the power station scramble under the left-hand arch of the railway bridge over the Falls of Cruachan burn, and climb steeply up the path on the east bank of the burn through open woodland to gain the reservoir access road. Higher up above 300m the best route strikes north-west to the broad and grassy south ridge of Meall Cuanail (918m). An alternative longer route to this point is up the hydro road from Lochawe village to the Cruachan Reservoir.

The south ridge of Meall Cuanail leads easily to that Top. Descend steeply for 70m beyond the summit before starting up the rocky south ridge of Ben Cruachan. This ridge is littered with granite boulders through which a path leads to the sharp summit. (5km; 1200m; 3h 10min).

A fine traverse of the ridge surrounding the reservoir continues with a descent of Cruachan's east ridge, which involves a little very easy scrambling. The next Top, Drochaid Ghlas (1024m), lies a short distance along a northward spur. Further east, at Stob Diamh, the main ridge turns south over Stob Garbh (980m) and drops 250m to a bealach from where easy grassy slopes lead down south-west to the reservoir. This traverse is known as the Cruachan Horseshoe.

## Stob Diamh; 998m; (OS Sheet 50; NN094308); M143; *peak of the stag*

This hill, one of Ben Cruachan's many peaks, lies near the east end of the main spine of the great massif, at the apex of an east-facing arc of peaks and ridges known as the Dalmally Horseshoe. To its north-east and south are two slightly lower Tops, Sron an Isean (966m) and Stob Garbh (980m). The three peaks of the Dalmally Horseshoe are well seen from the east, coming down Strath Orchy along the A85 road. The traverse of them is over smooth terrain set at a generally easy angle.

Start 2.5km west of Dalmally on the B8077 road where a gate at NN133284 marks the

The summit of Ben Cruachan from Stob Dearg

beginning of an old track to a disused lead mine. Follow this track north-west for 2km and continue to a bridge across the Allt Coire Ghlais at NN120295. Go west and climb the grassy ridge which forms the southern arm of the Horseshoe. Above 450m the ridge levels out and there are fine views southwards to the crags of Beinn a' Bhuiridh. At 900m the ridge merges with that dropping south from Stob Garbh, and a path is joined leading north to this Top. Continue north, dropping about 40m and climbing gradually to Stob Diamh along a broad ridge. (5km; 1000m; 2h 50min).

There is a steep descent of 100m north-east from Stob Diamh before climbing again to Sron an Isean. From this last Top a long, easy-angled descent follows its east ridge, eventually bearing south-east and descending steep grass slopes to another bridge at NN127297 below the confluence of the Allt Coire Ghlais and the Allt Coire Chreachainn. From the bridge, regain the track and follow it back to the road.

BEN CRUACHAN

STOB DIAMH

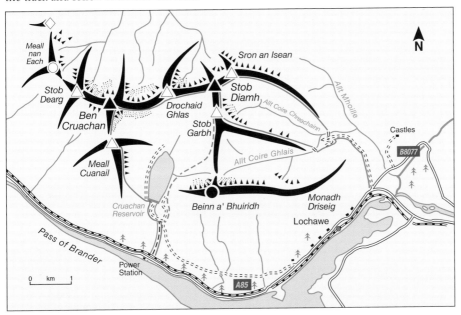

Ben Starav from Glen Etive

**Ben Starav;** 1078m; (OS Sheet 50; NN125427); M63; possibly _hill of rustling_
**Glas Bheinn Mhor;** 997m; (OS Sheet 50; NN153429); M145; _big greenish-grey hill_

These two mountains rise prominently at the foot of Glen Etive. Ben Starav looks its full height and is a grand mountain, having a long north-east ridge rising from near sea-level to its summit. Glas Bheinn Mhor has a classical pyramidal form with a very steep north face.

From the Glen Etive road at NN137468, follow the private road which goes east to cross the River Etive. Continue south-west past Coileitir and along a path to a bridge across the Allt Mheuran. Cross the burn and continue along the path on its west bank for 500m to the foot of the broad lower slopes of Ben Starav's north-east ridge, whose great length and height are very obvious. Although it gives a long and unrelenting climb, it is followed by a good path. Steep slopes fall away on both sides until a parallel ridge merges with it. The final rise to the summit is littered with granite boulders. (5km; 1060m; 3h).

Going south-east along the level summit crest for about 400m, a slight rise is reached. Turn north-east there and traverse a narrow rocky ridge to Stob Coire Dheirg (1028m) where the ridge turns east and drops to a bealach at 767m. Continue east, climbing over a minor grassy top (892m), dropping 70m and finishing up a rockier ridge to the summit of Glas Bheinn Mhor. (8.5km; 1370m; 4h 10min).

Do not descend north from the summit of Glas Bheinn Mhor for the slope in that direction is very steep, possibly dangerously so if the grass is wet or covered with soft snow. Instead, descend the east ridge until after about 500m it is easy to drop down north into the corrie at the head of the Allt Mheuran and follow the path on the right side of this stream back to Glen Etive. Map on page 53.

**Beinn nan Aighenan;** 960m; (OS Sheet 50; NN148405); M196; _hill of the hinds_

This is a truly remote hill, situated 6km south-east of the head of Loch Etive behind Ben Starav at the head of Glen Kinglass. It is a bulky hill with a steep north face and a distinctive undulating ridge running east from the summit over extensive pavements of granite. Beinn nan Aighenan can be climbed with Ben Starav and Glas Bheinn Mhor, adding 4km and 500m of ascent to the route described above, or it may be climbed by itself. In the latter case the start is the same as for Ben Starav for the first 2.5km. Going to Beinn nan Aighenan, continue south up the west bank of the Allt nam Meirleach. There is a good path all the way up this stream to the bealach at 766m on the ridge above.

In poor visibility, careful navigation is needed for the next part of the route, making a descending traverse south-east across featureless slopes and past a few tiny lochans to the next

*Donald Bennet*

Glas Bheinn Mhor from the north ridge of Ben Starav

bealach at 618m, 1.5km north-north-west of Beinn nan Aighenan. From there a rocky ridge leads to the summit of the hill. (8km; 1100m; 3h 40min). Return by the same route, with 150m of re-ascent to the bealach between Ben Starav and Glas Bheinn Mhor.

A much longer route to Beinn nan Aighenan starts from the car park before Victoria Bridge at the west end of Loch Tulla. It can be cycled to above Glen Kinglass. Follow the track and foot-path to the ford below Clashgour. From here a good track leads west past Loch Dochard and over the pass into the head of Glen Kinglass and an old bridge over the river. A new bridge lies out of sight to the south in a small ravine (NN186400). Climb the long east ridge over several knolls and pavements of cream-coloured granite in a superb and solitary setting. (15.5km; 1000m; 5h). Map on page 53.

BEINN NAN
AIGHENAN

Beinn nan Aighenan from the Ben Starav – Glas Bheinn Mhor col

*Donald Bennet*

Meall nan Eun (left) and Stob Coir' an Albannaich from Stob Ghabhar

**Stob Coir'an Albannaich;** 1044m; (OS Sheet 50; NN169443); M90; *peak of the corrie of the Scotsman*
**Meall nan Eun;** 928m; (OS Sheet 50; NN192449); M254; *hill of the birds*

52

STOB COIR' AN
ALBANNAICH

MEALL NAN EUN

These two hills are on the east side of lower Glen Etive. Stob Coir'an Albannaich rises so steeply from the glen that its summit cannot be seen above the lower slopes, while Meall nan Eun can be glimpsed at the head of Glen Ceitlein. However, from the opposite viewpoint near the west end of Loch Tulla, Stob Coir'an Albannaich shows its sharp pointed summit and Meall nan Eun appears as a great dome with a distinctive concave corrie on its south-east flank.

The starting point for the traverse is the same as for Ben Starav, but after crossing the River Etive take the track on the left, then go through a gate in the fence and start climbing south-east directly uphill. At first through scattered birches and then more steeply on one side or the other of the long, straight, tree-filled gully which is an obvious feature of the hillside above Coileitir. It is a long unrelenting ascent of 800m leading directly to Beinn Chaorach, the outlying north-west shoulder of Stob Coir'an Albannaich. Continue south round the edge of Coire Glas and then south-east up an open slope which converges to a narrow ridge where the large summit cairn of Stob Coir'an Albannaich stands above the granite cliffs of the north-east face. (4km; 1040m; 2h 40min).

The continuation to Meall nan Eun requires accurate compass work in bad visibility, although the route is obvious in clear weather. From the summit of Stob Coir' an Albannaich descend east for barely 500m to a level part of the ridge at 880m. At this point there are no cliffs on the north side of the ridge and it is possible to go north-west steeply down mixed rock and grass to a bealach (750m) sprinkled with tiny lochans. From there climb north-east over the top of Meall Tarsuinn (877m), descend to 790m and climb again to the summit plateau of Meall nan Eun, whose cairn lies some distance away to the east. (7km; 1310m; 3h 50min).

To return to Glen Etive, go north-west across the plateau and down a broad ridge to the headwaters of the Allt Ceitlein. Cross to the north bank to reach a path leading down to the foot of Glen Ceitlein and the track back to the day's starting point. An alternative, which avoids the birch wood and brutal ascent up Beinn Chaorach, is to climb Meall nan Eun via Glen Ceitlin (2h 15min), then Stob Coir' an Albannaich (3h 30min) and descend from the col between this and Glas Bheinn Mhor via the Allt Mheuran.

These two mountains can be climbed with considerably more effort from the east, starting from the Victoria Bridge car park near the road end at the west end of Loch Tulla. Follow the right of way to the west end of Loch Dochard. Go north-west across very boggy ground to the

Meall nan Eun from Loch Dochard

foot of Stob Coir'an Albannaich and climb its south-east flank up the right-hand side of the broad ridge overlooking the Allt Coire Chaorach. (11.5km; 870m; 4h). The traverse to Meall nan Eun follows the route described above. (14.5km; 1140m; 5h 10min).

Meall nan Eun, despite its flat-topped, lumpy shape, is very well defended on its north, east and south flanks by steep slabby slopes which make any descent route difficult, if not dangerous, unless great care is exercised. An ill-defined shoulder going east from the summit provides a possible way down to the Allt Dochard. From there it may be preferable to climb 240m to cross the Mam nan Sac and follow the path down to Clashgour rather than negotiate the rough wet ground along the north shore of Loch Dochard.

STOB COIR' AN
ALBANNAICH

MEALL NAN EUN

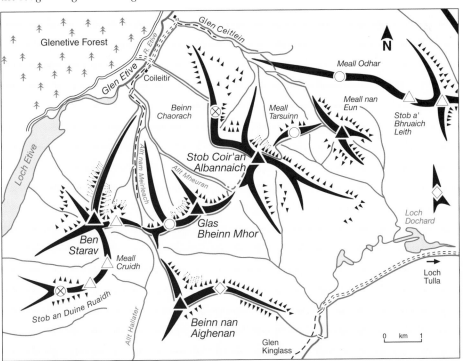

Stob Ghabhar from Loch Tulla

## STOB A' CHOIRE ODHAIR

**54**

## STOB GHABHAR

**Stob a' Choire Odhair;** 945m; (OS Sheet 50; NN257460); M226; *peak of the dun-coloured corrie*
**Stob Ghabhar;** 1090m; (OS Sheet 50; NN230455); M55; *peak of goats*

These two hills lie a few kilometres north-west of the west end of Loch Tulla, from where Stob Ghabhar in particular makes a fine sight through the fringe of mature Scots pine along the lochside. It is a fine peak with an impressive east-facing corrie holding the Upper Couloir, a classic ice climb. Stob a' Choire Odhair, though lower, is more prominent in views from the A82

The summit of Stob Ghabhar

road north of Bridge of Orchy.

The approach to these hills starts from the west end of Loch Tulla at the car park near the road end south of Victoria Bridge. Cross the bridge and follow the track west along the north side of the Abhainn Shira for 1.5km to a small corrugated iron hut. Turn north and continue along a good, but sometimes very wet path on the east side of the Allt Toaig for a further 2km. At NN252446 the path crosses a burn on whose west side a broad ridge rises north towards the summit of Stob a' Choire Odhair with a well-engineered stalkers' path zigzagging for 300m up it. Follow this path to its end high up on bouldery ground, and finish up open slopes to the stony summit of Stob a' Choire Odhair. (6km; 760m; 2h 40min).

Descend west along a broad ridge to the bealach between Stob a' Choire Odhair and Stob Ghabhar at about 680m. Continue west gradually uphill for 500m, then turn south-west and climb more steeply up rough slopes with some scree to reach the crest of a narrow ridge, the Aonach Eagach. Turn west along the crest which at one point is quite narrow and exposed for a few metres across a little gap. Beyond there it merges with the south-east ridge and this is climbed along the edge of the east face of Stob Ghabhar to the top. (9km; 1220m; 4h 10min).

To descend, retrace your steps for 500m to a small cairn at the top of the south-east ridge and follow this down, curving round to cross the burn issuing from the corrie. Drop steeply down an eroded path next to the cascading burn and cross the Allt Toaig to rejoin the upward route.

The traverse of the entire Black Mount range from Inveroran to Kingshouse over Stob Ghabhar, Clach Leathad, Creise and Meall a' Bhuiridh is one of the classic hillwalking expeditions in Scotland, linking two old and famous hostelries. It is quite a long and strenuous day involving about 20km and 1600m of ascent. The shorter traverse of the last three of these mountains is described on the next page.

From the summit of Stob Ghabhar, which is most quickly reached from Stob a' Choire Odhair, by reversing the descent route described above, continue down a broad ridge initially north-west, then north over bouldery ground. After 1km at a flat junction of ridges, go north-north-west along Aonach Mor for 1.5km over three or four knolls. At NN224475 turn north-east and descend along the ridge leading to the Bealach Fuar-chathaidh. From there climb steeply north-east for 300m up grass and broken rocks to easier-angled bouldery ground leading to Clach Leathad (1099m).

Continue north across a slight dip in the broad bouldery ridge to reach the cairn (1068m) which is at the top of the spur dropping east towards Meall a' Bhuiridh. Creise is 500m north along the level ridge. The traverse ends by descending the spur, climbing Meall a' Bhuiridh by its west ridge and continuing down to the car park at the foot of the White Corries chair lift, as described on the next page. (Victoria Bridge to the Glencoe Mountain ski centre car park: 17km; 1600m; 6h 30min).

If returning to Victoria Bridge, descend east from the summit of Meall a' Bhuiridh to the top of the ski tow and go along the level stony ridge for a further 300m. Continue to descend east, at first on the crest of the ridge, then down the shallow corrie of the Allt Creagan nam Meann to reach the ruins of Ba Cottage. From there walk back along the West Highland Way to the day's starting point.

STOB A' CHOIRE ODHAIR

STOB GHABHAR

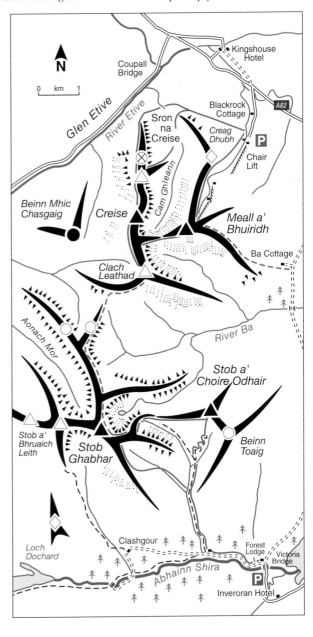

Clach Leathad and Meall a' Bhuiridh from Rannoch Moor

*Douglas Scott*

**Creise;** 1100m; (OS Sheets 41 and 50; NN238507); M50; possibly *from creis, a narrow defile*
**Meall a' Bhuiridh;** 1108m; (OS Sheets 41 and 50; NN251503); M45; *hill of the bellowing (of stags)*

CREISE

MEALL A'
    BHUIRIDH

These two mountains are the highest points at the northern end of the great range on the west edge of Rannoch Moor, the Black Mount. They form a horseshoe ridge to the south of Kingshouse Hotel, from where they are well seen. The finest feature is the steep north-east face of Stob a' Ghlais Choire (996m), the north Top of Creise. Meall a' Bhuiridh is also a prominent mountain, fronting onto Rannoch Moor and having on the long-lasting snowfields of its north-east face the chair lifts and tows of one of Scotland's principal ski mountains. Behind it, Creise is the highest point of the 3km-long ridge which extends from Sron na Creise to Clach Leathad.

The traverse of this group is a fine mountaineering expedition, with possibly some steep scrambling to give it character and interest. However, most difficulties can be avoided, and in bad weather probably should be avoided, by an alternative shorter and easier route.

For the longer traverse, start from the Glencoe Mountain ski centre car park and go along the bottom edge of a small forestry plantation on a vague path which after a slight rise crosses the rough moor below the steep face of Creag Dhubh for almost 2km to reach the Allt Cam Ghlinne. If aiming for the direct route up the north ridge of Sron na Creise, cross this burn and climb south-west to the foot of the rocky ridge. Careful route finding will enable a way to be found up this fine steep ridge, which has some good scrambling high up before the top is reached. Thereafter follow the broad rocky ridge south over Stob a' Ghlais Choire to Creise. (4km; 900m; 2h 30min).

An alternative to the ascent of Sron na Creise is to go up the Cam Ghleann for 1km on the west side of the burn and climb the north-east spur of Stob a' Ghlais Choire. This route is also steep, but easier than the ascent of Sron na Creise.

From Creise continue south along the ridge for 600m (Clach Leathad lies a short way to the south) to an almost imperceptible top (1068m) where a steep spur drops to the east. Descend this rocky spur to a well-defined col, and climb the ridge leading east to Meall a' Bhuiridh. (6km; 1100m; 3h 10min). Continue north down the broad shoulder on the west side of Coire Pollach almost to Creag Dhubh (748m) and go down under the chairlift to the Glencoe Mountain ski centre car park.

The traverse described above involves some steep ground which, particularly in winter, is more mountaineering than hillwalking and calls for mountaineering skills. A much shorter and easier route to Creise is up Meall a' Bhuiridh and along the connecting ridge, reversing the descent route described above. However, even this route, which is quite straightforward in summer, involves steep climbing on snow and possibly the negotiation of a cornice in winter conditions. Map on page 55.

Stob a' Ghlais Choire and Sron na Creise from Kingshouse

Stob a' Choire Odhair from Meall a' Bhuiridh

## Beinn Sgulaird; 937m; (OS Sheet 50; NN053461); M237; *hat-shaped hill*

**58**

**BEINN SGULAIRD**

Beinn Sgulaird stands at the head of Loch Creran, and forms a distinctive undulating ridge running from south-west to north-east. Three kilometres of this ridge lie above 800m, and although the lower western slopes are grassy, much granite is exposed elsewhere, particularly on the summit ridge and in the corrie on its north-west side. There is a fine view of the mountain from the road on the north side of Loch Creran.

Park in a large layby beyond the north (second) entrance to Druimavuic. Walk back to the entrance and follow the rough track on the left through woodland behind the grounds of the house to open hillside. The track swings left then back right, to cross the lower part of the west ridge from where a cairned path on the left leads directly up onto it. Avoid the steep crags on the east side of Point 488m by going north, then south to gain the col. Continue along the ridge to Point 863m, beyond which it becomes increasingly rocky and rough. Pass over Meall Garbh and contour the top of Coire nan Capull to a narrowing ridge of granite slabs and boulders leading to the large summit cairn. (7km; 1110m; 3h 10min). Views to the west down Loch Creran include the island of Lismore and the hills of Mull and Morvern. Return by the same route.

Elleric on the north side also offers a good approach. Park at Elleric and follow the road to Glenure. Behind the house, cross over the River Ure and follow the track up Glen Ure to NN075471, before the track ends at two lochans. Ascend to a small knoll, then skirt the rocky summit of Stob Gaibhre to the south, to reach a tiny lochan. From here continue up the rocky ridge and round Point 909m to the summit cairn. (8km; 980m; 3hr).

Beinn Fhionnlaidh from Glen Etive

**Beinn Fhionnlaidh;** 959m; (OS Sheets 41 and 50; NN095498); M198; *Finlay's hill*

Beinn Fhionnlaidh is a solitary hill rising above the forests on the west side of Glen Etive. It forms an east-west spine about 6km long with steep and craggy slopes to the south and north, and the east end of the spine ends abruptly in a rocky bluff whose precipitous nature is only hinted at on the OS 1:50,000 map. It is mainly composed of quartzite and schistose rock, with bands of limestone providing the fertile basis for some rare alpines on the Glen Creran side. The summit ridge is bare and boulder strewn.

The shortest ascent route is from Glen Etive, starting at Invercharnan, 16km down the glen from the A82 road near Kingshouse Hotel. There is limited parking on the north side of the bridge, before the road swings sharply left to Invercharnan. Cross the bridge and continue straight ahead onto a new forestry track which bypasses Invercharnan, to gain the old track and follow it for 3km south-west then north-west through areas of active felling, to where the track turns sharply right. Go left here onto a cairned track which leads to open hillside after 200m. The alternative route to Sgor na h-Ulaidh continues towards Meall a' Bhuiridh ahead (page 63).

Turn sharp left and follow the forest edge down to two old log bridges across the Allt nan Gaoirean, then ascend the hillside aiming for the burn flowing from the prominent cleft on Meall nan Gobhar. Follow the burn first on its left, then on its right to the small col below the southern flank of the East Top of Beinn Fhionnlaidh. Zigzag up steep stony slopes then bear north-west below the East Top to reach the ridge of Beinn Fhionnlaidh, which is marked by a line of fence posts. Follow these west to a slight dip, at which point the fence-line turns south.

Continue up the narrowing ridge via two short rock steps which are easily avoided by paths on the left, to gain the summit trig point. (7.5km; 960m; 3h). The East Top is best climbed before the final descent, returning to the main ridge to meet the ascent path, rather than straight down the extensive boulder scree of the south face from that summit.

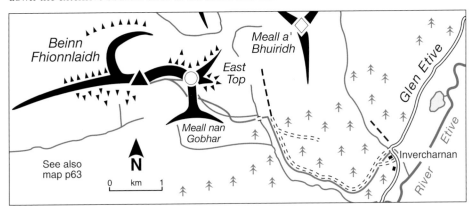

**BUACHAILLE ETIVE MOR;** *big shepherd of Etive*
**Stob Dearg;** 1021m; (OS Sheet 41; NN222542); M110; *red peak*
**Stob na Broige;** 956m; (OS Sheet 41; NN190525); M207; *peak of the shoe*

BUACHAILLE
ETIVE MOR

The Buachaille Etive Mor, and in particular its highest peak Stob Dearg, is one of the grandest and best-known mountains in Scotland, standing as it does in isolation and rising abruptly above the north-west corner of Rannoch Moor. The great walls, gullies and buttresses of Stob Dearg give that peak a decided air of impregnability, at least as far as the hillwalker is concerned. However, the great cliffs which encircle the peak are breached on the north-west by Coire na Tulaich which gives a fairly easy walking route to the summit. Stob na Broige, the second Munro of the Buachaille, is at the other end of its 7km long ridge, overlooking Glen Etive just above Dalness. It also is an impressive rocky peak, surrounded on three sides by crags and giving no easy ascent routes from the glen direct to its summit. Between the two Munros, the summit ridge of the Buachaille rises over two intermediate Tops, Stob na Doire (1011m) and Stob Coire Altruim (941m). These peaks are very steep and craggy on their north-west sides overlooking the Lairig Gartain, but are more accessible on the Glen Etive side by long slopes of grass and scree.

The traverse of the four summits of the Buachaille Etive Mor is best started at Altnafeadh on the A82 road. Follow the track down to the bridge across the River Coupall, go past the climbers' cottage at Lagangarbh and beyond it take the right fork in the path and continue south into Coire na Tulaich, crossing a burn and climbing up the path on its west bank. A few short rocky steps call for a little easy scrambling, and the path continues uphill to the foot of a scree slope at about 700m. Continue up the scree towards a narrowing gully which is probably best avoided by scrambling up rocky ledges on its east bank to emerge onto the broad ridge of the mountain at a flat bealach. Care should be taken in winter since Coire na Tulaich can be prone to avalanche under certain conditions.

Turn east and follow the path over pink rock and boulders, with many cairns, finally trending north-east along the narrowing ridge to the summit. The view is extensive, most notable being the vast expanse of Rannoch Moor with the prominent peak of Schiehallion just visible at its far edge. (3km, 750m; 2h).

The traverse from Stob Dearg to Stob na Broige is a fine ridge walk. Return past the head of Coire na Tulaich and continue along the ridge to Stob na Doire and Stob Coire Altruim following a very obvious path, and finally go along the fairly level ridge to Stob na Broige. (7.5km; 1100m; 3h 30min).

Stob Dubh (left) and Stob na Broige from Glen Etive

The return to Altnafeadh goes back to Stob Coire Altruim and a short distance further down the ridge to NN201529, where there is the start of a path descending north into the Lairig Gartain. Go down it into the glen, cross the River Coupall and finally walk along the path, which is very wet and muddy in places, to reach the A82 road just over 500m from Altnafeadh.

The south-west ridge of Stob na Broige dropping to Glen Etive is steep and encircled by many crags low down, and any descent to the glen by this ridge should only be undertaken with great care. The easiest route to Stob na Broige from Glen Etive starts near NN206513 and goes up grass and scree slopes to Stob Coire Altruim and along the ridge from there to Stob na Broige. This route is the safest descent to Glen Etive from Stob na Broige.

BUACHAILLE
ETIVE MOR

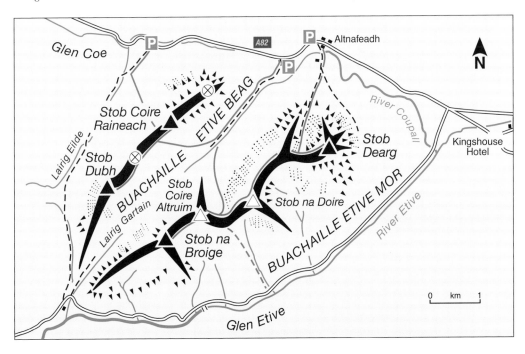

Buachaille Etive Beag from the River Coupall

**BUACHAILLE ETIVE BEAG;** *little shepherd of Etive*
**Stob Coire Raineach;** 925m; (OS Sheet 41; NN191548); M263; *peak of the corrie of bracken*
**Stob Dubh;** 958m; (OS Sheet 41; NN179535); M201; *black peak*

The Buachaille Etive Beag is in size and character the small brother of the Buachaille Etive Mor, and it has many similarities, both when seen from Rannoch Moor and from the lower reaches of Glen Etive. However, it lacks the grandeur of its big brother, and its highest point, Stob Dubh, is at the south-west end of its 4km ridge, the far end as seen from the A82 road. Only when seen from Glen Etive does the Buachaille Etive Beag match its big brother in height and appearance.

From the north one ascent route starts from a car park on the A82 road at NN188563 where a signpost indicates the right of way 'Lairig Eilde to Glen Etive'. Follow the path south-west for 750m and before crossing the burn start climbing south-south-east up the grassy hillside, following an obvious and in places eroded path which leads directly to the 750m col at the centre of the Buachaille Etive Beag ridge. This col can also be reached from its opposite side by taking the right of way from the A82 road at NN213560 through the Lairig Gartain for 2.5km and climbing its south-east side up much drier grass and stony slopes.

From the col a climb of just over 170m up a path on the stony ridge leads to the rocky summit of Stob Coire Raineach and a fine viewpoint for the surrounding peaks of Glen Coe. (3km; 670m; 1h 50min).

Return to the col and continue the traverse south-west, first up steepening slopes to a little top beyond which the ridge is level for 750m to the final short climb to Stob Dubh. (5km; 880m; 2h 40min). There is a fine view down Glen Etive from the cairn just beyond the summit. Return by the route of ascent.

A shorter route to Stob Dubh which might appeal to those staying in Glen Etive is the direct ascent by its south-west ridge from Dalness. This grassy ridge rises at a steady steep angle from the glen, and gives the climber no respite until the summit is reached. (2.5km; 870m; 2h).

Map on page 61.

Sgor na h-Ulaidh and Stob an Fhuarain from the east

## Sgor na h-Ulaidh; 994m; (OS Sheet 41 and 50; NN111518); M149; *peak of the treasure*

Among the Glen Coe mountains, Sgor na h-Ulaidh is very much the unknown one, hidden from the main road by the prominent projecting ridge of Aonach Dubh a' Ghlinne and lacking the bold features of Bidean nam Bian, in whose shadow it lies. Despite its retiring nature, Sgor na h-Ulaidh does have a distinctively mountainous character which is evident as one walks up the Allt na Muidhe into the wild glen which leads to its steep northern face, and it is this glen which provides the approach from Glen Coe.

Start from a small car park on the north side of the A82 shortly before it bends north over the Allt na Muidhe. Go along the track on the west side of the Allt na Muidhe for 1km before crossing to the east side and continuing to the farmhouse of Gleann-leac-na-muidhe, which is skirted by a footpath. The track continues for a further 1km, ending where the glen turns south and Sgor na h-Ulaidh comes into view. Keep to the east bank of the burn and head south up the glen. After 1.5km turn east and climb steeply up grass slopes riven by many little streams to reach the ridge just north of the outlying Top of Stob an Fhuarain (968m). Traverse this peak and descend south-west to the col at 860m. From the col continue south-west by a path up steep rocky ground to the cairn of Sgor na h-Ulaidh, which is on the brink of the steep north face gully. (6.5km; 1040m; 3h 20min).

An easier alternative route to Sgor na h-Ulaidh is from Glen Etive. Start from Invercharnan as for Beinn Fhionnlaidh (page 59) and once through the forest bear north to reach the col between Meall a' Bhuiridh and Sgor na h-Ulaidh. From there climb the south-east ridge direct to the summit. (7km; 950m; 3h 10min).

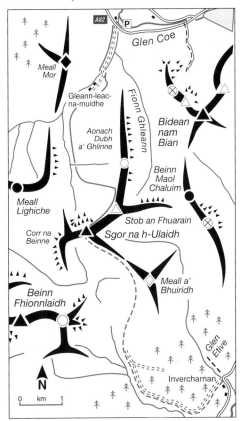

Am Bodach at the east end of the Aonach Eagach

**AONACH EAGACH;** *the notched ridge*
**Meall Dearg;** 953m; (OS Sheet 41; NN161584); M212; *red hill*
**Sgorr nam Fiannaidh;** 967m; (OS Sheet 41; NN140583); M188; *peak of the Fingalians*

64

The north side of Glen Coe is hemmed in by the steep flanks of the Aonach Eagach. From the roadside in the glen it is difficult to appreciate its true character, the narrow crest and sharp pinnacles, and it is not easy to identify the individual summits along the ridge. Meall Dearg is the lower of the two Munros on the ridge, and is near its east end. Sgorr nam Fiannaidh is more easily identified at the west end rising directly above Loch Achtriochtan in a single steep and uninterrupted hillside 900m high.

The traverse of the Aonach Eagach is one of the best ridge traverses on the mainland, continuously narrow and in places exposed, and there is a lot of excellent scrambling. The best way to climb these two Munros is to traverse the ridge, but for those who prefer easier routes, alternatives are suggested. However, it is for the traverse that the Aonach Eagach is renowned.

The best direction for the traverse is from east to west. Start from the A82 road in Glen Coe a few hundred metres west of Allt-na-reigh and take the path which climbs steeply north-east from the roadside. The path soon reaches the crest of the south-east ridge of Am Bodach. Continue up this ridge, which in places is quite steep and rocky, almost a scramble, although there is a path all the way. Higher up the angle eases and the ridge leads directly to Am Bodach (943m), the easternmost peak of the Aonach Eagach.

Descend west along the narrowing crest of the ridge and soon reach a sudden drop of about

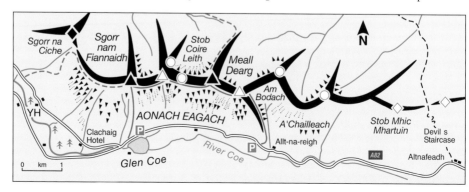

On the ridge between Meall Dearg and Stob Coire Leith

20m. Scramble down ledges on the north side of the ridge and traverse left to the crest where there is a steep descent of a few metres on good holds. It may be prudent to use a rope at this point. The traverse continues along a path on the narrow crest with only one mildly awkward descent, then climb to a little top beyond which a broad rocky slope leads to Meall Dearg. (3km; 870m; 3h).

The next section along the ridge to the col below Stob Coire Leith is the hardest and best part of the traverse. It involves a lot of excellent and in places exposed scrambling, up and down gullies, slabs and chimneys and round and over some little pinnacles. The route is obvious, in summer at least, and the rock is sound. From the col, where all difficulties end, there is a steep pull up to Stob Coire Leith (940m) followed by an easy and fairly level walk to Sgorr nam Fiannaidh. (5.5km; 1000m; 4h 30min).

The most direct descent from this peak to Glen Coe is due south down a continuously steep slope of boulders and stones near the top, and grass lower down. Care is needed not to dislodge stones which might roll a long way down to the hazard of anyone below, but otherwise the route is not difficult. In winter it and the whole traverse of the Aonach Eagach is very different; a serious mountaineering expedition that may be difficult and time-consuming.

For those who seek a less continuously steep descent, the best alternative is to go 750m west from Sgorr nam Fiannaidh, then 1km north-north-west down to the col below the Pap of Glencoe. From there descend south-west by a path to the road between Glencoe village and Clachaig Hotel. Do not descend south from this col as that leads one down across the grazing land above Leacantuim farm, which should be avoided.

There is an obvious path on the west side of Clachaig Gully immediately north of Clachaig Hotel, but it should be avoided as a route of descent or ascent as it is badly eroded with a lot of loose stones and rock which, if dislodged, can be a hazard to climbers in the gully. This route is not recommended.

Easy ascent routes to Sgorr nam Fiannaidh which avoid any scrambling are provided by either of the two recommended descent routes described above. The direct ascent from Loch Achtriochtan is a long continuous slog. (1.5km; 900m; 1h 50min). The route by the Pap of Glencoe col, though longer in distance, is probably more enjoyable. (4km; 950m; 2h 30min).

The only easy route to Meall Dearg is from the north. Start from the A863 road on the south side of Loch Leven just east of Caolasnacon (NN143608) and climb up the north side of the Allt Gleann a' Chaolais on a path to the col at the foot of the north-east ridge of Meall Dearg. A vague path following a line of fenceposts leads easily to the summit. (4.5km; 910m; 2h 40min).

Bidean nam Bian from Stob Coire Sgreamhach

**Bidean nam Bian;** 1150m; (OS Sheet 41; NN143542); M23; *pinnacle of the hills*
**Stob Coire Sgreamhach;** 1072m; (OS Sheet 41; NN154536); M65; *peak of the dreadful corrie*

BIDEAN NAM
BIAN

The highest mountain in Argyll, Bidean nam Bian is a compact and complex massif, the name applying to the highest point as well as to the mountain as a whole. The main ridge is a north-facing arc with the summit of Bidean near its mid-point and a subsidiary Y-shaped ridge projecting northwards from there to enclose three fine corries above Glen Coe. So high and steep are the peaks above the glen, the Three Sisters, that it is difficult to get a view of the summit of Bidean, which is hidden behind them, but from the west end of Loch Achtriochtan there is an impressive glimpse of the two huge buttresses beneath the summit.

Stob Coire Sgreamhach is at the south-east corner of the massif where the main spine of the mountain divides, with a long north-east ridge forming the narrow, undulating crest of Beinn Fhada. Stob Coire Sgreamhach is prominent in views of Bidean from the east, and from Glen Coe it can be seen as the pyramidal peak at the head of Coire Gabhail. The two other high Tops, Stob Coire nan Lochan (1115m) and Stob Coire nam Beith (1107m) are very prominent when seen from the glen, both appearing as great rock peaks and both connected to Bidean by short ridges.

The whole massif is rocky and steep-sided, with great crags and gullies, steep boulder fields and scree slopes on which paths give routes of relative safety, but off the paths there are many dangerous places, so careful route-finding is important. In winter paths become icy and are lost under snow so any route on Bidean needs mountaineering skills and experience.

The following route for the traverse of the two Munros of the Bidean massif is intended to include not only these peaks, but some others as well, and start and finish at the same point in Glen Coe, thereby avoiding the need for any road-walking at the end of the day along the very busy and traffic-ridden A82. The starting and finishing point is the large car park 500m down the glen from Allt-na-reigh.

Go down to the River Coe and cross the bridge at the foot of Coire an Lochan. Follow the path up this narrow corrie on the south-east side of the stream, with high cliffs on both sides, until the path climbs more steeply towards the head of the corrie where its lochans are situated. At that point, below the waterfall, leave the path and climb south to reach the broad grassy ridge between Gearr Aonach and Stob Coire nan Lochan. Climb this ridge south-west then west up steepening rocky slopes to Stob Coire nan Lochan. Descend south-west, dropping

Stob Coire Sgreamhach from Beinn Fhada

100m and then climbing up a steep narrow ridge, past the level shoulder at the top of the Diamond Buttress to reach the summit of Bidean nam Bian. (4.5km; 1150m; 3h).

Descend the south-east ridge for 1km to the bealach at the head of Coire Gabhail and climb 120m to Stob Coire Sgreamhach. (6km; 1270m; 3h 30min). The most direct descent to Glen Coe is to return to the bealach at the head of Coire Gabhail and make an awkward and unpleasant descent down rocks and boulders to reach a path in the screes a short way down. Follow this path down and across the top of the Upper Gorge, then by a descending traverse across the steep slope on the north-west side of the corrie to reach a flat grassy 'meadow' (the Lost Valley) with a huge boulder at its far end. Just before the boulder go up and around the right side of the boulder-field and descend to the stream at the far side. Cross to the left bank and follow the path along the edge of the Lower Gorge to the River Coe.

An alternative descent route from Stob Coire Sgreamhach is to go north-east along the narrow undulating ridge of Beinn Fhada. The first part of this descent involves a short scramble down the east side of a rocky step in the ridge, then traverse Beinn Fhada (952m) and its North-east Top (931m) to a col before the Far North Top. Either descend eastwards into the Lairig Eilde here, or continue a bit further along the ridge before descending into the Lairig Eilde. On no account attempt to descend directly from the end of the ridge. This descent entails a 2km walk back along the road to the day's starting point.

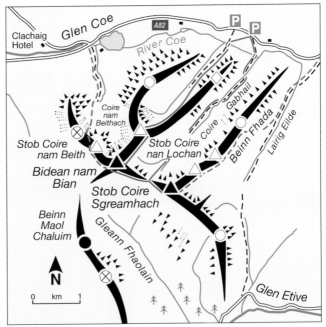

A view of the Glen Coe mountains from the Aonach Eagach

The peaks and corries of Bidean nam Bian

The ridge from Stob Coire nan Lochan to Bidean nam Bian

The view west from Buachaille Etive Mor to the peaks of Glen Coe

Sgorr Dhearg from Sgorr Dhonuill

**BEINN A' BHEITHIR;** *hill of the thunderbolt*
**Sgorr Dhonuill;** 1001m; (OS Sheet 41; NN040555); M137; *Donald's peak*
**Sgorr Dhearg;** 1024m; (OS Sheet 41; NN056558); M107; *red peak*

## BEINN A' BHEITHIR

Beinn a' Bheithir is a fine mountain rising above the narrows at the entrance to Loch Leven at South Ballachulish. Its two peaks lie on a long curving ridge which encloses north-facing corries, and except on their steepest and highest slopes these corries are clothed with vast areas of conifers which cover the lower hillsides and extend high up into the heart of the mountain. Access to the north side of the mountain is therefore restricted to one or two routes following roads through the forest. Above the tree-line the ground is bouldery, that on Sgorr Dhearg being a pink quartzite, and that on Sgorr Dhonuill granite. There is a splendid view of the mountain from the A82 near North Ballachulish and the summits offer superb views of the mountains of Glen Coe and Lochaber, with the seascapes to the west.

Leave the A828 at NN044595 about 1km west of the Ballachulish bridge and follow the minor road south for 500m to the group of houses at the foot of Gleann a' Chaolais where there is a car park. Continue south up the forest track on the west side of the Abhainn Greadhain to the first zigzag, and turn right and very soon left again. Keep straight on south up the glen which in this area has been cleared of trees. After a little over 1km and just before a flat concrete bridge, the apex of the track is reached at NN037567 where it turns back north-east. From here a good path on the west side of the burn leads through the trees up into Coire Dearg to gain the west ridge of Sgorr Dhonuill and follow it to the summit. (5km; 970m; 2h 50min).

Descend east to the bealach at 757m between the two peaks of Beinn a' Bheithir and climb north-east to Sgorr Dhearg. (7km; 1240m; 3h 20min). Return towards the bealach and descend north on a muddy path to the edge of the forest. At about NN050564 leave the old path for a newer one going rightwards over fences into the forest. This leads down and sharp left to meet a track at NN049573. Cross over and descend with a sharp right to meet a second forest track at NN047575. Cross straight over onto a grassy track and follow this down to a track just before the concrete bridge over the Abhainn Greadhain. Turn left over the river to gain the original access track and follow it rightwards back to the car park.

An alternative ascent of Beinn a' Bheithir, which can be combined with the above route to give a fine traverse, starts from the visitor centre in Ballachulish village. Walk up the road, cross the bridge over the river Laroch, then turn off left passing the school. Continue for 1km along a path (the start of the right of way leading to Glen Creran) before climbing south-west towards a steep and well-defined ridge. This becomes narrower and steeper as height is gained, and there

Sgorr Dhonuill from Sgorr Dhearg

is some scrambling up rocky steps, so this should not be regarded as an easy route in winter. The ridge joins the main spine of the mountain a few hundred metres north-east of Sgorr Bhan (947m), the north-east Top of Sgorr Dhearg, and the climb finishes along the beautiful curving arc leading to Sgorr Dhearg (4km; 1040m; 2h 40min). From there the traverse to Sgorr Dhonuill may be continued as described in the route above.

If returning to Ballachulish village, the best route is to descend towards the 757m bealach between Sgorr Dhonuill and Sgorr Dhearg and descend north following the path and tracks through the forest as described above, to the concrete bridge over the Abhainn Greadhain. Do not cross over, but keep right on the track which swings east and make a long descending traverse to reach the A82 at the church less than 1km west of Ballachulish.

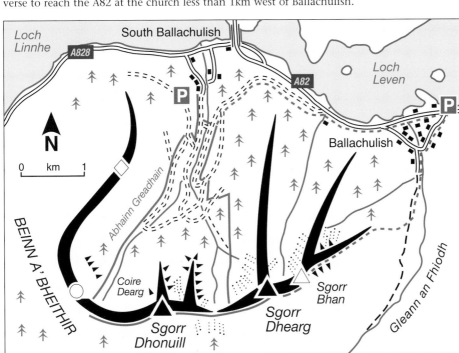

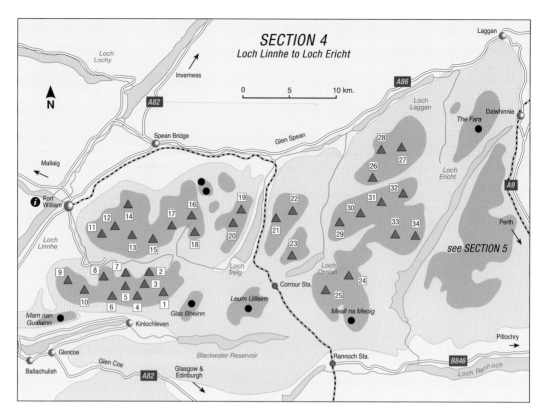

# SECTION 4

## Loch Linnhe to Loch Ericht

---

**ⓘ** VisitScotland Information Centre

**Fort William**; 15 High Street, Fort William, PH33 6DH, (01397 701801),
    open Jan–Dec

# The Mamores

Between Loch Leven and Glen Nevis there stretches for 15km one of the finest mountain ranges in Scotland, the Mamores. Ten Munros are linked by narrow curving ridges, their flanks scalloped by many corries, while through the mountains there is a remarkable network of stalkers' paths, climbing up the corries and along the ridges, some of them taking spectacular lines across steep hillsides thus giving easy routes to many of the peaks.

There are three points of access to the Mamores that are particularly useful. On the south side one can either start at sea-level from Kinlochleven, or possibly drive up a rough road to Mamore Lodge at a height of 200m. In 2013 the Lodge was boarded up and a notice stated the road could be closed at any time. From the lodge a Land Rover track traverses across the hillside, both to the east and west, at a height of about 250m, and gives access to the southern corries.

If starting from Kinlochleven and heading for the eastern peaks, the following directions will be useful: Leave the B863 at the northern end of Kinlochleven, turning east along Wade's Road, to reach a very simple white church in 250m. From the east of the church a path starts north, soon turning east for 200m before descending to a bridge across a burn. Beyond, the path climbs through trees and, at their upper limit, it divides in two. Take the right fork and follow it for 750m through undulating ground to a ford, beyond which is another fork. The left path goes north to the foot of Coire na Ba, the right path goes east towards Loch Eilde Mor, both paths joining the Land Rover track in a further few hundred metres. If heading towards the western peaks from Kinlochleven, follow the West Highland Way from the village school at the north-western end of Kinlochleven and climb diagonally north-west up the wooded hillside, crossing the Mamore Lodge access road and reaching the Land Rover track higher up.

On the north side of the Mamores access is gained along the public road up Glen Nevis. Achriabhach is the starting point for the western peaks. Beyond there the road becomes very narrow and liable to congestion in summer, and it continues for a few kilometres to the car park at its end. From there the walk through the magnificent gorge of the River Nevis leads to the upper glen and the eastern peaks of the range. This approach also serves for the Aonachs and Sgurr Choinnich Mor at the western end of the Grey Corries.

Many different combinations of the Mamore peaks can be climbed in a single day, from one alone to all ten. The latter is a magnificent traverse, but only for the very fit. It is not unduly difficult to do them all in two or three days. However, in the following descriptions a more leisurely approach is taken, none of the expeditions described being at all long or strenuous.

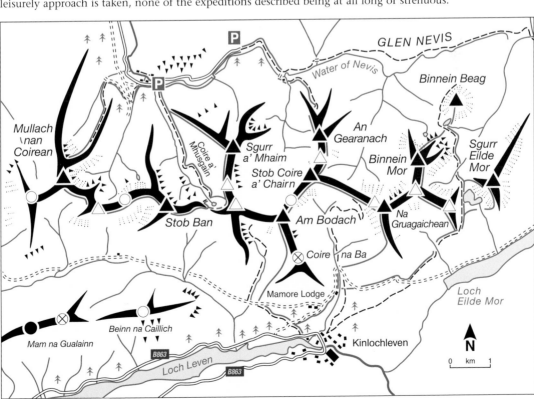

Sgurr Eilde Mor above Coire an Lochain

### Sgurr Eilde Mor; 1010m; (OS Sheet 41; NN230657); M123; *big peak of the hind*

This is the remotest of the Mamores, lying 6km north-east of Kinlochleven and separated from the other peaks at the east end of the range by a col at 740m. In appearance, particularly when seen on the approach from Kinlochleven, it is a steep conical peak of scree and quartzite boulders rising splendidly above Coire an Lochain. North-eastwards from the summit, the spine of the hill goes for 3.5km towards the head of Glen Nevis, its crest paved with schist broken by outcrops of quartz.

Start the ascent from Kinlochleven or Mamore Lodge, see page 73, and follow the Land Rover track east from the lodge to within 1km of Loch Eilde Mor. There take the stalkers' path which climbs north-east, quite gradually at first, then more steeply to reach Coire an Lochain where the loch is set in a fine position amidst spectacular surroundings. Above it Sgurr Eilde Mor rises for 270m in uniformly steep scree slopes of rather uninviting appearance. Two routes are possible. Either cross the level corrie on the south side of the loch and climb the south ridge, or go round the north side and climb the fairly well-defined west ridge. The two routes are very similar, both being on steep and bouldery quartzite with a few small crags. (From Kinlochleven: 7km; 1010m; 3h 20min). Map on page 73.

### Binnein Beag; 943m; (OS Sheet 41; NN221677); M230; *small peak*
### Binnein Mor; 1130m; (OS Sheet 41; NN212663); M27; *big peak*

These two mountains lie north-east of Kinlochleven at the eastern end of the Mamore ridge. Binnein Mor is not only the highest, but also the finest of the range, having the classic mountain form of ridges and corries sweeping upwards to a narrow summit crest. From the north or south it appears as a single sharp peak, while from the east or west its level summit ridge gives it the appearance of a great tent. By comparison, Binnein Beag is small and quite different in shape, being a little conical peak. The two are separated by a bealach at 750m.

The approach from Kinlochleven or Mamore Lodge follows the same route by track and stalkers' path as that described above for Sgurr Eilde Mor as far as Coire an Lochain. From there keep north along the path, dropping slightly, going left at a fork and descending north-west for a further l00m. A rising traverse follows across the east face of Binnein Mor, crossing the headwaters of the Allt Coire a' Bhinnein to reach the wide bealach between the two peaks. Leave the stalkers' path which has been followed to this point, and climb north-east over scree and schistose boulders to the sharp summit of Binnein Beag. (9km; 1080m; 3h 50min). There is a splendid view, very open to the east towards the distant mass of Ben Alder, while the great bulk of Binnein Mor towers above in the south-west.

Return to the bealach and climb to the toe of the north-east ridge of Binnein Mor, which

*Bill Morrison*

Binnein Mor from Binnein Beag

bounds the little north-east corrie on its north side. This ridge is narrow and steep and gives an excellent scramble on sound schist. It emerges on the sharp summit ridge 200m north of the cairn. (11.5km; 1460m; 5h). An easier alternative for the ascent of Binnein Mor is to traverse 750m west from the bealach to reach the north ridge and climb the fine, but perfectly easy crest which curves up to the summit. Continue south along the summit ridge to the South Top (l062m), then turn south-east for 1km to another Top, Sgor Eilde Beag (956m). From there descend the edge a little east of south until at 840m a stalkers' path (not shown on OS maps) is reached which leads in well-engineered zigzags down to join the path of the uphill route, and so back to Kinlochleven. Map on page 73.

BINNEIN BEAG

BINNEIN MOR

*Noel Williams*

Binnein Beag and Binnein Mor

Binnein Mor and cloud-covered Na Gruagaichean from Am Bodach

**Na Gruagaichean;** 1056m; (OS Sheet 41; NN203652); M74; *the maidens*
**Stob Coire a' Chairn;** 981m; (OS Sheet 41; NN185660); M171; *peak of the corrie of the cairn*
**Am Bodach;** 1032m; (OS Sheet 41; NN176651); M99; *the old man*

76

NA GRUAGAICHEAN

STOB COIRE A'
CHAIRN

AM BODACH

These three peaks form an arc of ridges immediately north of Kinlochleven. Na Gruagaichean is particularly prominent when seen from the road on the south side of Loch Leven, from where it has a tent-like appearance. It has two tops separated by a rocky ridge which drops to a narrow gap between them. Am Bodach is another fine mountain with a particularly steep and rocky east face. Between these two, Stob Coire a' Chairn is a more modest peak situated at the point where the An Gearanach ridge goes out to the north. With the exception of the summits of Am Bodach and Na Gruagaichean, this part of the Mamore ridge is fairly grassy and gives easy walking.

An Garbhanach, with Ben Nevis and Carn Mor Dearg beyond

An Gearanach above Glen Nevis

Start from Kinlochleven or Mamore Lodge, see page 73, and reach the bridge across the Allt Coire na Ba on the Land Rover track to Loch Eilde Mor. From there climb north-east up steep grassy slopes to gain the ridge which leads north to the summit of Na Gruagaichean. (4km; 1060m; 2h 40min). Descend very steeply north-west down a rocky slope to a narrow col and climb an equally steep ridge, exposed on its north-east side, to the North-west Top (1041m). Cross the short level summit and continue down the ridge to the bealach at the head of Coire na Ba.

Continue north-west along the path which leads up the broad easy ridge to Stob Coire a' Chairn. (6km; 1300m; 3h 30min). Descend equally easily, crossing a small bump, to the next bealach from where the north-east ridge of Am Bodach rises abruptly. It is steep and rocky enough to give an easy scramble which ends below the summit. (8km; 1550m; 4h 30min).

Descend the south-east ridge of Am Bodach towards Sgorr an Fhuarain. Do not climb this minor top, but keep to its west and go downhill south-westwards to avoid its steep south face. Grassy slopes lead easily down to the Land Rover track 1.5km west of Mamore Lodge at the point where the path forming part of the West Highland Way leads down to Kinlochleven through open woodland. Map on page 73.

### An Gearanach; 982m; (OS Sheet 41; NN188670); M166; *the complainer*

An Gearanach is the northerly and highest point of the short narrow ridge which projects north from Stob Coire a' Chairn on the main spine of the Mamores. The ridge passes over the rocky Top of An Garbhanach (975m) and at that point the crest is very narrow and exposed, falling steeply on both sides. The An Gearanach end is broader and north of this peak the ridge drops steeply towards Glen Nevis.

An Gearanach can be climbed either from Glen Nevis or, with rather more effort, from Kinlochleven. The Glen Nevis route starts at the car park at the road end and goes through the gorge, from where there is a magnificent view of the peak with its pendant waterfall. The path clings to the steep wooded hillside, with crags above and the torrent of the River Nevis rushing below. Shortly after emerging onto the grassy flats of the upper glen, cross the river by a wire bridge and go east past Steall climbers' cottage. Continue for 500m below the Steall Waterfall until the path turns south up a little corrie and becomes better defined. Climb the path in wide zigzags initially on the left of the stream, then on the right, until the last traverse leads out right, the original path shown going out left on OS maps is no longer used, onto the north-west ridge. Follow this to the summit with fine views on either hand. (4.5km; 850m; 2h 30min). The traverse along the narrow ridge to An Garbhanach is a pleasant airy walk, with some scrambling at its far end.

From Kinlochleven the ascent of An Gearanach is an extension of the previous traverse. From Stob Coire a' Chairn descend north-east, then climb the fine, narrow rocky crest over An Garbhanach to reach An Gearanach. Map on page 73.

The Devil's Ridge from Sgurr a' Mhaim to Stob Choire a' Mhail

**Sgurr a' Mhaim;** 1099m; (OS Sheet 41; NN164667); M51; *peak of the large rounded hill*

The dominating mountain in the western half of the Mamore range is Sgurr a' Mhaim, standing at the end of the longest of the arms projecting northward from the main ridge. There is a clear view of the peak from lower Glen Nevis, its great bulk fills the valley and the quartzite capping of its summit is very evident in certain lights. On its north and north-east sides there are two finely sculptured corries, below which the lower slopes of the mountain end abruptly in cliffs dropping into the Nevis gorge.

Southwards from the summit of Sgurr a' Mhaim the ridge leading to the main spine of the Mamores is one of the finest sections of the range; it forms a sharp arete, the Devil's Ridge, which near its mid-point rises to Stob Choire a' Mhail (990m) and continues to Sgor an Iubhair (1001m), a flat-topped summit on the main ridge. The traverse of the Devil's Ridge is one of the highlights of hillwalking in the Mamores. It is an exhilarating scramble, but some may consider it to be a bit too exposed for their liking.

Start in Glen Nevis 300m east of Achriabhach and take the path up the east bank of the Allt Coire a' Mhusgain. After 500m leave the path and climb south-east up the steep shoulder between the north and west faces of Sgurr a' Mhaim. Half way up, the zigzags of a stalkers' path on the west side of the shoulder give some respite from the steady steep climb, then at 800m the angle eases and the grassy slopes of the lower hillside give way to quartzite boulders and scree. Higher up the route follows the rim of the north corrie to the cairn of Sgurr a' Mhaim. (3km; 1050m; 2h 30min). To return direct to Glen Nevis, reverse the route of ascent. However, this leaves undone the traverse of The Devil's Ridge, which should not be missed.

To continue the traverse, descend south down open slopes which soon converge to the narrow arete of the Devil's Ridge. Near the lowest point there are two short, exposed and awkward sections (Grade I) where some might welcome the security of a rope, particularly in winter. Continuing up the ridge, there is an airy climb up the very narrow crest to Stob Choire a' Mhail. From there the route is much easier, descending to a broad col, then south-west on a path to Lochan Coire nam Miseach. An alternative is to take in the Top of Sgor an Iubhair before descending the west ridge to the col before Stob Ban and descending north to Lochan Coire nam Miseach.

To return to Glen Nevis, follow a stalkers' path down Coire a' Mhusgain to join the approach and finish at Achriabhach. The path is often rough and muddy and takes more time and effort

The summit ridge of Stob Choire a' Mhail

than expected. The full traverse of the peaks from Sgurr a' Mhaim to An Gearanach which includes the Devil's Ridge can be made in either a clockwise or counter clockwise direction with a return along paths in Glen Nevis. Known as the Ring of Steall, it gives a magnificent outing. Map on page 73.

Stob Ban from the east

Mullach nan Coirean from Stob Ban

**Mullach nan Coirean;** 939m; (OS Sheet 41; NN122662); M236; *summit of the corries*
**Stob Ban;** 999m; (OS Sheet 41; NN147654); M140; *white peak*

MULLACH NAN
COIREAN

STOB BAN

These two peaks rise at the western end of the Mamore ridge, and are most easily accessible from Glen Nevis. Mullach nan Coirean is a sprawling mass of grassy ridges enclosing several corries, as befits its name. Stob Ban makes a contrast with its shapely summit cone and fine line of buttresses and gullies on the north-east side of the peak. It is an impressive sight from the road near Glen Nevis youth hostel with its cap of quartzite looking curiously like snow in some lights. Though Mullach nan Coirean is itself rather shapeless, it does present an attractive profile when seen from the path through the Nevis gorge, and its summit is an unexpectedly rewarding viewpoint.

Start the traverse at Achriabhach in Glen Nevis, NN145683, from where access to the north-east ridge of Mullach nan Coirean can be gained through the forest. Go back along the road and opposite the cottages, take the path signposted 'forest walk' which leads uphill through the forest to meet a road at a hairpin bend. Go north-west along the upper road for about 700m to the start of a stepped path on the left. Climb up this waymarked path through the forest to cross a stile onto the open hillside and follow a fence south-east up a rough path to reach the north-east ridge of Mullach nan Coirean. A better path leads up this ridge at an easy angle for 2.5km to the summit. (4km; 890m; 2h 30min). There are good views from this ridge of the great hump of Ben Nevis, and from the summit there is an equally expansive view down Loch Linnhe.

To continue to Stob Ban, descend south-east down easy slopes along the rim of one of the northerly corries and follow an undulating ridge that goes south-east over a minor bump to the Mullach's South-east Top (917m). Beyond, the ridge becomes better defined and rockier, bearing north-east over a minor top, then dropping east to the col (846m) between the two mountains. At this point the red granite rocks of Mullach nan Coirean suddenly change to the pale grey quartzite that gives Stob Ban its name. Finally, climb east then south-east more steeply up angular quartzite boulders along the rim of the north-east cliffs to the summit of Stob Ban. (7.5km; 1130m; 3h 40min).

In descent, follow the narrow shattered east ridge steeply down to grassier slopes, reaching a stalkers' path near the col at the head of Coire a' Mhusgain. Follow the branch of this path that goes north down the corrie on the east side of the stream, leading directly back to the car park at Achriabhach. Map on page 73.

Ben Nevis and Carn Mor Dearg from An Garbhanach

**Ben Nevis**; 1345m; (OS Sheet 41; NN166712); M1; *possibly venomous hill or cloudy hill*
**Carn Mor Dearg**; 1220m; (OS Sheet 41; NN177722); M9; *big red hill*

For the average hillgoer, Ben Nevis is not just the highest mountain in the British Isles, its traverse combined with that of Carn Mor Dearg provides a taste of mountaineering amongst scenery of a magnificence not to be found elsewhere on the mainland of Britain. The two peaks form a vast horseshoe facing north-west, with the simple shape of Carn Mor Dearg's slender ridge contrasting starkly with the huge and complex mass of Ben Nevis, whose north-east face presents the grandest array of cliffs of any Scottish mountain. Another contrast appears between the pink granite of Carn Mor Dearg and the grey andesite of the Ben, a contrast made more obvious by the great exposure of rock, boulders and scree on both mountains.

BEN NEVIS

CARN MOR DEARG

However, the hillwalker on the 'tourist route' up Ben Nevis gets little impression of its great mountain architecture, and one has to go round to the north-east side of the mountain, into the glen of the Allt a' Mhuillin, to appreciate its scale and grandeur. For this reason the traverse from Carn Mor Dearg to Ben Nevis is recommended as the finest way for a fit and competent hillwalker to reach the summit of Scotland's highest mountain. The best roadside view of these mountains is from the A82 road just beyond Spean Bridge, and even from a distance of several kilometres their great scale can be appreciated.

The route to Ben Nevis starts in Glen Nevis, either at the visitor centre car park on the west side of the river or at Achintee on the opposite side, and follows the excellent path from there which climbs across the flanks of Meall an t-Suidhe. The same path can be reached from the Glen Nevis youth hostel. After 2.5km and 500m of ascent the path emerges onto the broad bealach holding Lochan Meall an t-Suidhe, and starts a series of uphill zigzags. Above, the path crosses a deep gully, the Red Burn, then zigzags up increasingly bouldery ground to the extensive summit plateau. At the top there are the remains of the observatory, a small shelter, several cairns and a trig point, and a few metres to the north the cliffs drop vertically. In spring and early summer the cornices at the cliff-edge are likely to be dangerously unstable, so beware of approaching the edge too closely. There are likely to be climbers on the cliffs below so take great care not to dislodge any loose material onto them. (8km; 1340m; 3h 20min).

To make the traverse over Carn Mor Dearg, follow the Ben Nevis path as far as Lochan Meall an t-Suidhe. Continue north along a level path past an old fence where the path turns south-east below the cliffs of Carn Dearg, and a few hundred metres further leave the path to descend east and cross the Allt a' Mhuilinn. Then climb rough bouldery slopes for 600m towards Carn Beag Dearg (1010m), and traverse the high ridge which stretches for 2km over Carn Dearg

The north face of Ben Nevis from Carn Dearg Meadhonach

Meadhonach (1179m) to Carn Mor Dearg. (8km; 1450m; 4h 10min). The crest of this ridge provides easy walking with splendid views of the great cliffs of Ben Nevis's northern cirque.

To continue the traverse to Ben Nevis, follow the well-defined ridge south. After 200m of descent it sharpens to a narrow arête composed of huge granite blocks. Keeping to the crest makes for a fine scramble, but a faint path just below the crest on its south-east side avoids the tricky sections and much of the exposure. Throughout its length the Carn Mor Dearg Arête gives a superb view of the Ben's great ridges and corries, with the outline of the North-East Buttress growing more and more impressive. About 300m beyond the lowest point of the arete, at a level place below the final steep climb towards Ben Nevis, a post on the right-hand edge of

**BEN NEVIS**

**CARN MOR DEARG**

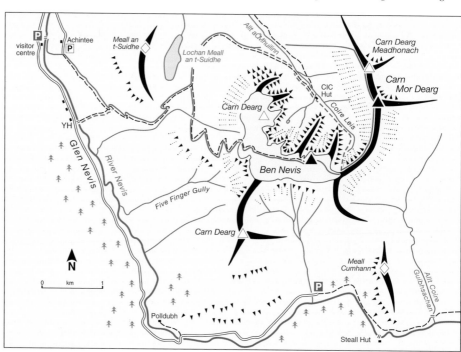

Ben Nevis from the Carn Mor Dearg Arete

the ridge marks the start of a moderately easy descent into Coire Leis which might be used as an escape route in bad weather or failing light. However, if there is snow on the headwall of Coire Leis this descent is not advised unless the party has ice-axes and crampons. Above that point the arête merges into the bulk of Ben Nevis and it is worthwhile hunting for the faint path that climbs for 250m through the litter of giant boulders to the top. (10km; 1750m; 5h 10min). Descend by the 'tourist route'. The traverse, or both hills individually, can also be made from the north via the Allt a' Mhuillinn, accessed from the North Face car park at NN146764 near Torlundy.

83

BEN NEVIS

CARN MOR DEARG

Carn Mor Dearg from Aonach Beag

Aonach Beag (left), the summit of Ben Nevis and cloud-covered Aonach Mor from the east

*Donald Bennet*

**Aonach Beag;** 1234m; (OS Sheet 41; NN196715); M7; *little ridge*
**Aonach Mor;** 1221m; (OS Sheet 41; NN193729); M8; *big ridge*

**AONACH BEAG**

**AONACH MOR**

The Aonachs, as these two mountains are often called, form a great high ridge, several kilometres long from south to north, lying to the east of Ben Nevis and Carn Mor Dearg, and connected to the latter by a high bealach at 830m. Although the crest of the ridge, particularly on Aonach Mor, is fairly flat and broad, the slopes to east and west are very steep, forming wild and remote corries.

Aonach Mor is a long flat-topped mountain whose finest feature is its steep and scalloped east face which holds snow well into summer. Aonach Beag has a more rounded summit guarded by crags and corries on all sides. The best impression of this pair is gained from the Grey Corries, from where their east-facing corries are well seen, with Ben Nevis appearing over the connecting ridge.

The end of the public road in Glen Nevis is probably the best place from which to traverse these two mountains. Follow the path through the Nevis gorge and along the north side of the Water of Nevis to the bridge across the Allt Coire Giubhsachan at the ruined Steall cottage. Above, to the north-east, Aonach Beag forms a wide corrie, enclosed by its south-west ridge on one side and the pointed Top of Sgurr a' Bhuic (963m) on the other. The most direct route goes north towards the corrie for 1.5km to reach the south-west ridge, which leads easily to the top. (6.5km; 1100m; 3h 20min).

A longer and more scenic route bears north-east from the Steall ruin to reach the south-west ridge of Sgurr a' Bhuic. Traverse this Top and continue along the ridge, north-east at first, then north-west to Stob Coire Bhealaich (1101m) and finally up stony ground to the summit of Aonach Beag. (8km; 1200m; 3h 50min).

Descend north-west down rocky slopes that fall away to the right in steep crags, and reach the bealach at 1080m. Beyond, an easy rise up a broad grassy ridge leads in just over 1km to the cairn of Aonach Mor, which in poor visibility may not be easy to find on the featureless expanse of the summit plateau. (9.5km; 1330m; 4h 20min).

To return to Glen Nevis, retrace the route south, keeping near the western cliffs of Aonach Mor for about 750m to NN192722. At this point turn west down a steep, ill-defined spur (cairn) to the bealach at 830m under Carn Mor Dearg. In bad visibility careful navigation is required to find the correct point of descent, as the ground on both sides is very steep. Finally, go south down Coire Giubhsachan to reach the path in Glen Nevis.

The northern approach to Aonach Mor has been made easier by the ski developments on the mountain and the completion of the traverse described above is much shorter and easier if one goes from the top of Aonach Mor to the gondola and gets a lift in it. Purists can follow the mountain bike trail to the base.

Sgurr Choinnich Mor from the west

## Sgurr Choinnich Mor; 1094m; (OS Sheet 41; NN227714); M52; *big mossy peak*

This sharp and shapely peak lies directly north of the watershed at the head of Glen Nevis, and with its smaller companion Sgurr Choinnich Beag (963m) it marks the south-western end of the Grey Corries ridge. Sgurr Choinnich Mor has a narrow rocky summit ridge, dropping steeply on both sides, and it is the finest of the Grey Corries, comparable with Binnein Mor on the opposite side of Glen Nevis.

Although Sgurr Choinnich Mor can be climbed from the north in combination with other peaks of the Grey Corries, that approach is quite long. A shorter route is from the car park at the road end in Glen Nevis. Follow the path through the Nevis gorge, and stay on the path along the north side of the Water of Nevis to the bridge over the Allt Coire Giubhsachan and the ruined cottage at Steall. Continue along the path for a further 2km until it leaves the main river to cross a side stream. From that point climb north-east up grassy slopes beside this stream to reach the bealach at the foot of the south-west ridge of Sgurr Choinnich Beag. Climb this ridge, which steepens and becomes quite narrow as it nears the distinctive Top. Descend east for 70m to a high col and continue north-east up increasingly rocky ground to the summit of Sgurr Choinnich Mor. (8.5km; 1030m; 3h 40min).

The return follows the same route, and a small saving of time and effort can be made by descending directly from the col between the two peaks to Glen Nevis.

The north-east ridge of Sgurr Choinnich Mor, which connects it to the rest of the Grey Corries, has a rocky section at about its mid-point where the path goes on the east side of the crest. Below that point the ridge drops to a broad col from which rises the rocky south-west ridge of Stob Coire Easain.

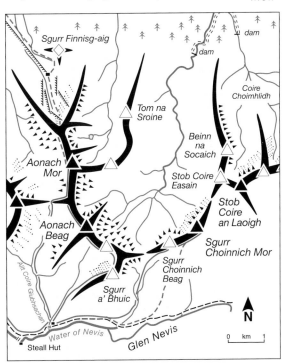

Stob Coire na Ceannain

**Stob Choire Claurigh;** 1177m; (OS Sheet 41; NN262738); M15; *claurigh is probably from Gaelic clambras, brawling or clamouring*
**Stob Coire an Laoigh;** 1116m; (OS Sheet 41; NN240725); M38; *peak of the corrie of the calf*

**STOB CHOIRE
CLAURIGH**

**STOB COIRE AN
LAOIGH**

These two peaks lie 3km apart at the ends of a high ridge to the south of Spean Bridge and the extensive Leanachan Forest. They are part of the long chain of mountains extending eastwards from Ben Nevis over Aonach Beag and Sgurr Choinnich Mor. The pale grey quartzite screes which cover their higher slopes earn them the name The Grey Corries. The roll-call of two Munros and six or seven Tops gives an excellent high-level ridge walk, which flatters to deceive, for the crest of the ridge undulates gently, its lowest point being 980m.

The best approach is from the north by the narrow public road which goes eastwards from Spean Bridge up the south side of the River Spean. There is very limited space for parking cars at the end of this road near Corriechoille. It may also be possible to park 1.5km up the track, at the start of a forestry track, or 500m further on, opposite the old tramway clearing. This is the start of the right of way through the Lairig Leacach to Corrour and Rannoch.

Go up this rough road to reach the old tramway used at the time of the construction of the Fort William aluminium works. Continue south-east through the forest up the road which leads to the Lairig Leacach. In 1.5km leave it and turn south-west up steep grassy slopes which continue for 600m to the first Top, Stob Coire na Gaibhre (958m). Beyond, the route is defined by the steep slopes on the left dropping into Coire na Ceannain, above which the shapely Top of Stob Coire na Ceannain is worth ascending. Higher up, the ridge forms a narrow rocky crest for a few hundred metres before the summit of Stob Choire Claurigh is reached, (6km; 1020m; 3h 10min).

Turning south-west, the crest undulates gently and a faint path eases the rough going over angular quartzite scree. From east to west the traverse includes Stob a' Choire Leith (1105m), Stob Coire Cath na Sine (1079m), and Caisteal (1106m) before reaching the second Munro, Stob Coire an Laoigh, notable for its dark northern cliff. (9km; 1220m; 4h 10min).

The crest continues west to Stob Coire Easain (1080m) at which point a broad ridge running north to Beinn na Socaich (1007m) provides the line of descent. Continue along it for 1.5km past this Top, then turn north-east down into Coire Choimhlidh by grassy slopes. Cross the Allt Coire Choimhlidh above the forest and descend past a small dam to reach the end of a road. The dam cannot be crossed and if a river crossing is to be avoided, stay on the shoulder and follow a narrow break through the forest to gain the forestry track and follow this back. The apparent short-cut along the line of the old tramway requires more effort than the track.

A useful and shorter alternative can be made by parking in the forest at a fork in the track (rough), just before the Coire Choimhlidh Dam.

Douglas Scott

Stob Ban from the north

## Stob Ban; 977m; (OS Sheet 41; NN266724); M178; *white peak*

Stob Ban is a remote peak, far distant from any main road and hidden behind its higher neighbours. It lies at the east end of the Grey Corries ridge, separated from it by a bealach of 800m, and it is from viewpoints near the head of Glen Nevis or in the Lairig Leacach that one gets the best views of this solitary conical peak.

The shortest approach is from Corriechoille in Glen Spean, as described opposite for Stob Choire Claurigh, by the track to the Lairig Leacach. Cross this pass and descend on its south side for 1.5km to the MBA Lairig Leacach bothy from where there is a good view of Stob Ban. It is possible to bike to the bothy.

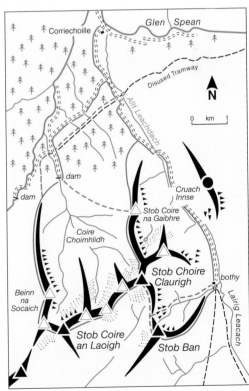

Cross the Allt a' Chuil Choirean by a bridge just up from the ford to pick up a path which leads all the way up the north-east ridge to the summit of Stob Ban (9km; 790m; 3h 20min). The easiest return is the same way.

An alternative ascent can be made by following the north side of the Allt a' Chuil Choirean to reach quartzite slabs at the head of the corrie which give pleasant easy scrambling leading to an 800m bealach with a small lochan. A path up the scree slope then leads south-east up the summit cone to the top and a descent back down the north-east ridge to the bothy.

Stob Ban can be combined with other peaks of the Grey Corries. From the 800m bealach, a broad ridge leads north then north-west to Stob Choire Claurigh. If descending north from there back to Glen Spean, it is worth making a short diversion to Stob Coire na Ceannain (1123m). This is a fine-looking peak, rather detached from the rest of the Grey Corries. The short connecting ridge is narrow and rocky, and gives a pleasant easy scramble.

Stob a' Choire Mheadhoin from Stob Coire Easain

## STOB A' CHOIRE MHEADHOIN

**88**

## STOB COIRE EASAIN

**Stob a' Choire Mheadhoin;** 1105m; (OS Sheet 41; NN316736); M46; *peak of the middle corrie*
**Stob Coire Easain;** 1115m; (OS Sheet 41; NN308730); M39; *peak of the corrie of the little waterfall*

These two mountains form a high ridge 10km long to the east of the Grey Corries. The two summits are near the middle of this ridge, and are separated by a col at 960m. To the east and west there are steep slopes, those to the east being particularly so and giving Loch Treig a fiord-like character. The two mountains are prominent in views from the south, appearing like twins, while from the north in Glen Spean there is a fine view of Stob a' Choire Mheadhoin, with Stob Coire Easain just appearing behind it. It is from Glen Spean that the two are most usually climbed. Leave the A86 road in Glen Spean 7.5km east of Roy Bridge and drive along the narrow public road to Fersit almost to the outflow of An Dubh Lochan at NN349790. Start the ascent from there and go south-west across level ground for a short distance, cross the line of the old tramway and continue south-south-west along the broad heathery ridge, passing a concrete pillar. A drier route gains this point by going to the dam, taking the upper track, then a path leading to the pillar. In 3km there is a steep climb to Meall Cian Dearg by a fairly obvious scrambly path up the nose of the ridge. Continue with level sections and short rises along the broad ridge to the summit of Stob a' Choire Mheadhoin. (7km; 870m; 3h). Descend stony slopes south-west to the col and climb quite steeply to the summit of Stob Coire Easain. (8km; 1030m; 3h 30min).

The descent may be made by retracing the ascent. Alternatively, from the col between the two peaks descend north-west into a fine corrie and continue downhill, gradually bearing north then north-east down Coire Laire. In due course a path is joined on the south-east side of the Allt Laire, and further down the line of the old tramway leads back to the starting point.

Chno Dearg from Stob Coire Sgriodain

**Stob Coire Sgriodain;** 979m; (OS Sheet 41; NN356743); M174; *peak of the corrie of the scree*
**Chno Dearg;** 1046m; (OS Sheet 41; NN377741); M86; *red hill*

These two hills make an easy hillwalking circuit from Fersit, the small group of cottages at the north end of Loch Treig reached by a minor road leaving the A86 7.5km east of Roy Bridge. Stob Coire Sgriodain is a rugged hill which rises steeply above the east side of Loch Treig. Above 500m it forms a north-south ridge that is rough and craggy and has three distinct tops. This ridge bends round to the south-east and merges with Chno Dearg, a rounded and featureless hill with open and easy-angled northern slopes. Both hills are clearly seen from the main road in Glen Spean.

Starting at Fersit, follow the road east for almost 500m and then turn south across rough and boggy ground. Beyond a minor craggy top at 450m, the slopes steepen to form a ridge with small crags which can easily be turned on one side or the other and the next top, Sron na Garbh-bheinne, is reached. A short level shoulder is passed, and the ridge narrows and rises to the summit of Stob Coire Sgriodain from where there is a splendid view of the fiord-like Loch Treig far below. (4.5km; 730m; 2h 20min).

The traverse of the next two tops may be confusing in bad visibility. Descend south to a pronounced col and turn south-east up the South Top of Stob Coire Sgriodain (958m). Continue south-east over knolly ground and reach another distinct double-headed top (924m) in 500m. A short descent south-east leads to an open col with some tiny lochans. Continue in the same direction, climbing easily to the ridge of Meall Garbh, and turn south to reach the cairn on its south top (976m). Return north then north-east across another col above which easy slopes covered by dwarf vegetation lead to the flat, boulder-strewn summit of Chno Dearg. (8.5km; 1020m; 3h 40min). Descend the wide grassy corrie in a direct line back to Fersit.

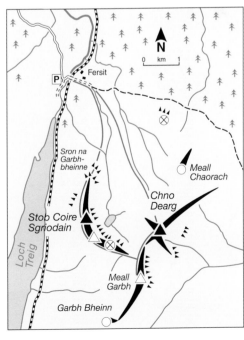

Beinn na Lap from Loch Ossian

**Beinn na Lap;** 935m; (OS Sheet 41; NN376695); M241; *dappled hill*

Beinn na Lap may be classed as one of the easiest ascents among the Munros, although it does require a train journey to reach its foot; <www.scotrail.co.uk> provides the relevant train information). It lies 4km north-east of Corrour Halt, altitude 400m, on the West Highland Railway and looms quite steeply above the northern shore of Loch Ossian. There is a clear view of the hill from Corrour, but from elsewhere its featureless whaleback shape is not readily identified.

BEINN NA LAP

From Corrour Halt, follow the estate road east towards Loch Ossian. After 1.25km take the left fork in the road round to the north-west side of the loch, and soon leave it to climb north on easy-angled slopes of dwarf vegetation. At 700m a broad ridge is reached and followed north-east to the summit of Beinn na Lap, which provides a remarkable contrast in views, with the wide expanse of Rannoch Moor to the south-west and a complicated tangle of peaks around the northern and western arc. (5km; 540m; 2h).

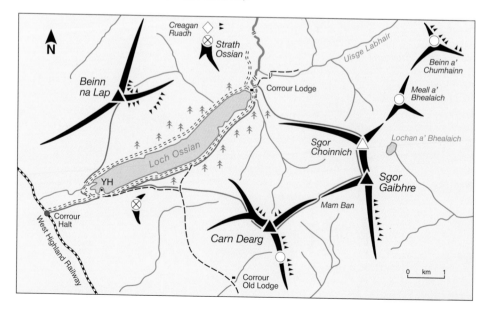

Sgor Gaibhre from the north-west ridge of Carn Dearg

**Sgor Gaibhre**; 955m; (OS Sheets 41 and 42; NN444674); M208; *peak of the goat*
**Carn Dearg**; 941m; (OS Sheets 41 and 42; NN418662); M232; *red hill*

These hills, together with the Top, Sgor Choinnich (929m), make a fine round from Corrour Halt on the West Highland Railway (see opposite). It is quite a long circuit, and one may have to move fast to complete it within the train timetable. Sgor Gaibhre and Carn Dearg lie between Loch Ossian and Loch Ericht and enclose in their open corries the gathering grounds for some of the largest herds of red deer in Scotland.

In general they are rounded hills without distinctive features, and from Corrour there is not a clear view of them, but the two Sgors rise steeply above Lochan a' Bhealaich and present a bold profile when seen from the east. The total distance of 22km for this round is lightened by easy going along the estate road for the first 7km and the smooth terrain of the hills themselves.

Follow the road north-east from Corrour Halt along the south shore of Loch Ossian to reach the cottages at the north-east end of the loch. Cross the bridge over the outflow, then immediately turn north-east along a path to recross the river by a wooden footbridge and continue along the path north then east round a copse at NN415698. (This avoids having to find a way through the forest at the east end of the loch). Bear south-east and climb at an easy angle, passing through a gate in a deer fence after 400m, to reach Meall Nathrach Mor, and beyond a short drop continue at an even easier angle to Sgor Choinnich. Descend south for 120m to a well-defined bealach and climb a broad steepening ridge to the summit of Sgor Gaibhre which provides a splendid view of Ben Alder and Loch Ericht. (12km; 720m; 4h).

Turn south-west and descend easy slopes of moss and heath to the broad bealach, the Mam Ban, riven by peat-hags. Continue in the same direction up Carn Dearg, climbing 220m to the cairn which overlooks the whole expanse of Rannoch Moor, while to the north the glacial trench of Strath Ossian is very prominent. (15km; 940m; 5h).

For the return to Corrour Halt, descend the north-west ridge to reach the head of an open corrie at NN412668. Go down this corrie and in 2km reach the path, known as The Road to the Isles, which can be followed west to the station.

Beinn a' Chlachair from the north

*Jim Renny*

**Beinn a' Chlachair;** 1087m; (OS Sheet 42; NN471781); M56; *stonemason's hill*
**Geal Charn;** 1049m; (OS Sheets 42; NN504812); M81; *white hill*
**Creag Pitridh;** 924m; (OS Sheet 42; NN487814); M264; *possibly Petrie's rock*

92

BEINN A'
CHLACHAIR

GEAL CHARN

CREAG PITRIDH

This group of mountains lies south of Loch Laggan and is most readily approached from the A86 road. Beinn a' Chlachair is prominent in the roadside view from Moy, looking like a great whaleback with a prominent corrie scooped out of its north flank just below the summit. To its north-east Creag Pitridh is a much smaller peak with a pointed summit and broken crags on its west face overlooking Lochan na h' Earba. Between these two Geal Charn (also known as Mullach Coire an Iubhair) appears as rather a featureless flat-topped hill. The group is penetrated by an extensive system of estate roads and stalkers' paths which makes access to the tops fairly easy, even though they are some distance from the road.

Leave the A86 road at the concrete bridge over the River Spean 1km south-west of the outflow of Loch Laggan near Moy and follow estate roads going south at first, then east round the foot of Binnein Shuas to Lochan na h-Earba. Leave the track (which continues along the loch) and follow a stalkers' path south-east up the Allt Coire Pitridh for about 1.5km, then bear south up the north-east flank of Beinn a' Chlachair. Above 900m the ground levels out at a shoulder and the route bears round the rim of Coire Mor a' Chlachair over a waste of boulders, many of them of surprisingly regular shape. The large summit cairn is set a short distance back from the edge of the corrie. (9km; 840m; 3h 30min).

Go north-east down a broad ridge and over the East Top for almost 2.5km, at which point the shoulder ends abruptly above a large crag. Descend north to avoid this crag and reach a stalkers' path which forks a short distance lower. Take the right-hand path and go north, climbing slightly to its highest point on the west flank of Geal Charn. Turn east and climb easy slopes of heath and boulders to the flat summit. (14km; 1150m; 5h 10min).

Retrace the route to the col west of Geal Charn and make the short easy ascent of Creag Pitridh, keeping to the left of craggy ground. (16km; 1300m; 5h 50min). Descend south-west to regain the stalkers' path along the Allt Coire Pitridh, and return by the outward route.

Beinn a' Chlachair and Geal Charn can also be climbed from the east, although Creag Pitridh is not so accessible from that direction. It is necessary to reach Loch Pattack first, possibly by bike from Dalwhinnie along the estate road beside Loch Ericht or up the River Pattack from Kinloch Laggan. From Loch Pattack follow the track west to the ford across the Allt Cam and continue up the path towards Loch a' Bhealaich Leamhain. From a point 1km beyond the ford it is straightforward either to bear west to reach the outer end of Beinn a' Chlachair's north-east ridge, or bear north-west up open slopes to Geal Charn.

These two remote mountains lie in the hinterland between Loch Laggan and Loch Ericht, part of the range which forms the northern wall of the long glen cutting through the hills in a straight line from Loch Ossian to Loch Pattack over the Bealach Dubh. The only view of these hills from any public road is from the north, on the A86 near the west end of Loch Laggan, from where they can be seen rising beyond the forests of Glen Spean.

Aonach Beag is a fine peak, with three well-defined ridges converging at its top. Beinn Eibhinn is a more extensive mountain, with a level summit ridge curving round Coire a' Charra Mhoir and its south-west side forming a series of rounded ridges and open corries well seen from Loch Ossian.

The ascent of these two mountains can be made from Corrour Halt on the West Highland Railway. Given good conditions, it should be possible to fit the round trip in with the railway timetable <www.scotrail.co.uk>. Fortunately half the distance to and from the peaks is along the estate road beside Loch Ossian which makes for quick progress.

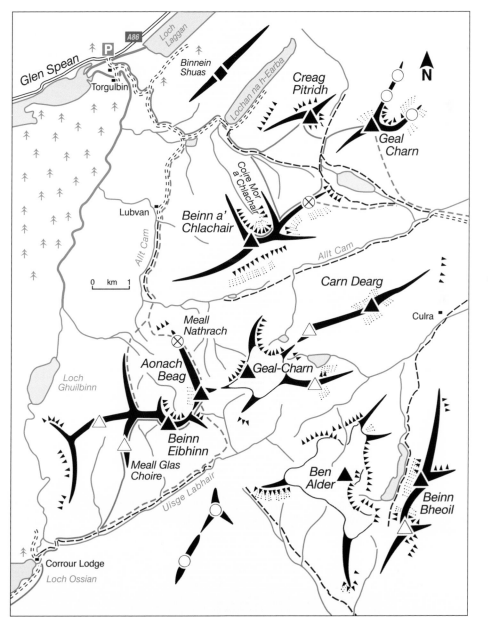

93

BEINN EIBHINN

AONACH BEAG

Beinn Eibhinn from Loch Ossian

From Corrour Halt follow the route described for Sgor Gaibhre to the outflow of Loch Ossian. Take the path north-east across the River Ossian, round the west side of the copse and continue along this path to the footbridge across the Uisge Labhair. A fair path continues up the north side of this stream past a fine rocky linn. After crossing the Allt Feith a' Mheallain head north up the grassy slopes of Creagan na Craoibhe. Higher up the going becomes very easy on short heath and grass, past a huge rounded boulder on the crest to the Top of Meall Glas Choire (924m). Beyond a short drop into a square-cut col, easy slopes lead onto the stony summit ridge of Beinn Eibhinn, whose north-east face drops steeply to Lochan a' Charra Mhoir. The summit cairn is at the east end of this ridge. (13.5km; 730m; 4h 20min).

**BEINN EIBHINN**

**AONACH BEAG**

**GEAL-CHARN**

**CARN DEARG**

The narrow ridge continues north-east, dropping 120m in a graceful curve before climbing again to Aonach Beag, whose summit is a small flat plateau. (15km; 860m; 4h 50min).

The return to Corrour Halt may be by the outward route over Beinn Eibhinn. Alternatively, from the col between Aonach Beag and Beinn Eibhinn descend south-east into Coire a' Charra Bhig and reach the Uisge Labhair. Then follow the path down this stream to Loch Ossian.

A totally different approach to these two mountains may be made from the A86 road in Glen Spean at the bridge across the River Spean just south-west of Loch Laggan. From there go along the private road towards Lochan na h-Earba for 3.5km, then turn right and go for another 2km to the ruins of Lubvan. It should be possible to bike as far as there. Continue along the path up the Allt Cam for 2.5km, ford the river and make a circuit of Aonach Beag (2h 30min from Lubvan) and Beinn Eibhinn (3h 15min from Lubvan) by their northern ridges which enclose Coire a' Charra Mhoir. The rocky termination of Aonach Beag's northern ridge can be avoided by gaining Meall Nathrach from its west side. Map on page 93.

**Geal-Charn;** 1132m; (OS Sheet 42; NN470746); M26; *white hill*
**Carn Dearg;** 1034m; (OS Sheet 42; NN504764); M98; *red hill*

These hills lie in a great tract of mountainous country between Loch Laggan and Loch Ericht which is penetrated by no public roads. Geal-Charn is the highest point on the high ridge stretching from Strath Ossian to Loch Pattack, the north-easterly extension of Beinn Eibhinn and Aonach Beag just described, and Carn Dearg continues the range to its end above Loch Pattack. Geal-Charn has a large summit plateau surrounded by corries and steep hillsides, and its two easterly spurs enclose Loch an Sgoir. The southern one forms a well-defined Top, Sgor Iutharn (1028m), whose terminal ridge is the steep and narrow Lancet Edge. The ascent of this ridge and descent of the more northerly spur is a fine traverse which can be continued over Carn Dearg.

The shortest approach from Dalwhinnie station, 40km for the round trip, may entail a night out, possibly at Culra Bothy which is well situated at the base of these hills. A bike can be used

GEAL-CHARN

CARN DEARG

*Bill Morrison*

Geal-Charn from the ridge to Carn Dearg

along the estate road from Dalwhinnie, either to Loch Pattack or beyond to Culra; 16km. If walking though, 500m east of Loch Pattack, take the path for 3.5km south-west across the moor and along the south-east bank of the Allt a' Chaoil-reidhe to cross the river by a footbridge near Culra bothy.

Continue past the bothy for 3km, on a track then a path, to cross the stream from Loch an Sgoir. Break off up steep rough ground leading to the Lancet Edge, a ridge sharp enough to require careful scrambling, and providing magnificent views, right to the waterfalls feeding Loch an Sgoir and left to the mass of Ben Alder. The ridge ends at Sgor Iutharn, beyond which the ground broadens to form a wide col. Continue west across this col then north-west up the steep slope to the rim of the plateau which has to be crossed for 1km westwards to reach Geal-Charn's summit. (From Culra: 6.5km; 800m; 2h 30min).

To continue the traverse, cross the plateau north-east for 1km to reach the spur dropping steeply between the north and east corries of Geal-Charn. In poor visibility an exact compass bearing is needed to find the correct route. Descend to a narrow level ridge and climb a short way to an intervening Top, Diollaid a' Chairn (925m). Finally, a long, broad and stony ridge leads to Carn Dearg. (15km; 1000m; 3h 50min).

For the return descend due east to Culra bothy, or alternatively go down the long easy-angled north-east ridge to the track at the south-west corner of Loch Pattack, and retrace the outward route. Map on page 97.

Ben Alder (left) and Sgor Iutharn from Culra bothy

**Ben Alder;** 1148m; (OS Sheet 42; NN496718); M25; *hill of rock and water*
**Beinn Bheoil;** 1019m; (OS Sheet 42; NN517717); M112; *hill of the mouth*

BEN ALDER

BEINN BHEOIL

Ben Alder is one of the great remote mountains of Scotland, a vast high plateau surrounded by corries in the heart of the Central Highlands between Lochaber and the Cairngorms. For such a remote hill, however, there is a remarkable roadside view of it from Dalwhinnie, the eye being drawn 20km along the length of Loch Ericht to its great north-eastern corries, which hold snow into early summer. Other views from the west tell more of the plateau-like form of Ben Alder, but only a traverse can reveal its enormous bulk and fascinating complexity of ridge and corrie. By contrast, Beinn Bheoil has a simple north-south ridge, dropping steeply on both sides, but its position between Ben Alder and Loch Ericht gives it a very mountainous setting.

There is the feeling of a mountain expedition in the traverse of these two peaks, and their remoteness may make necessary an overnight stop in the hills, possibly at Ben Alder Cottage or Culra bothy. Alternatively, the use of a bike along the estate road from Dalwhinnie brings them within easier reach on a long summer day. Ben Alder can also be climbed from Corrour Halt on the West Highland Railway, but one would have to move fast to fit this in with the train timetable <www.scotrail.co.uk>. For anyone staying at Loch Ossian youth hostel this constraint would not matter.

The Dalwhinnie approach starts just south of the station. Cross the railway and follow the estate road along the north-west shore of Loch Ericht. There are locked gates, but a bike can be used beyond Loch Pattack as far as the bridge at NN525765, close to Culra bothy; 15.5km from Dalwhinnie. If on foot, 500m before reaching Loch Pattack, take the path which cuts south-west across wet level moorland to the bridge. A well constructed path now leads alongside the river, past Culra on the opposite side, before heading uphill to reach the burn flowing from Loch a' Bhealaich Bheithe. Ahead are two prominent ridges. For the Long Leachas cross the burn and traverse north-west to it. For the Short Leachas continue to the loch, cross the outflow and gain the ridge. The Short Leachas is the most convenient and involves some easy scrambling, while the Long Leachas is easier but longer. Both emerge onto the summit plateau near a minor top, beyond which 1km of very gradual ascent leads south to the summit cairn. (From Culra: 7km; 750m; 2h 30min).

To continue the traverse, follow the rim of the Garbh Choire for 1.5km, first south then south-east over Sron Bealach Beithe to descend abruptly (still south-east) down steep bouldery ground to reach the Bealach Breabag. From there climb north-east to Sron Coire na h-Iolaire (955m) which is a splendid viewpoint above Loch Ericht. Ahead, the spine of the hill stretches north for 3.5km above 800m, dropping to 860m before rising to Beinn Bheoil. (11.5km; 1030m; 4h). Follow the ridge north for a further 2km, then descend north-west to

Loch Ericht and Beinn Udlamain from Sron Coire na h-Iolaire

reach the path returning to Culra, Loch Pattack and Dalwhinnie. Altogether a very long expedition of 48km, two-thirds of which can be done by bike.

The ascent of Ben Alder from Corrour Halt follows the same route as for Beinn Eibhinn, first along the private road beside Loch Ossian to Corrour Lodge. Continue along the path up the Uisge Labhair for 5.5km and cross to the foot of Ben Alder's broad west ridge, which is followed for 3km to the top. (16km; 750m; 4h 50min).

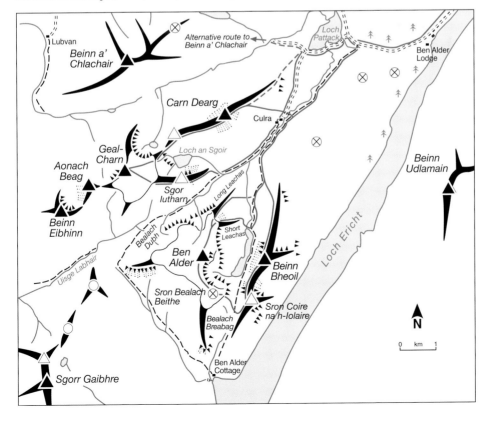

**BEN ALDER**

**BEINN BHEOIL**

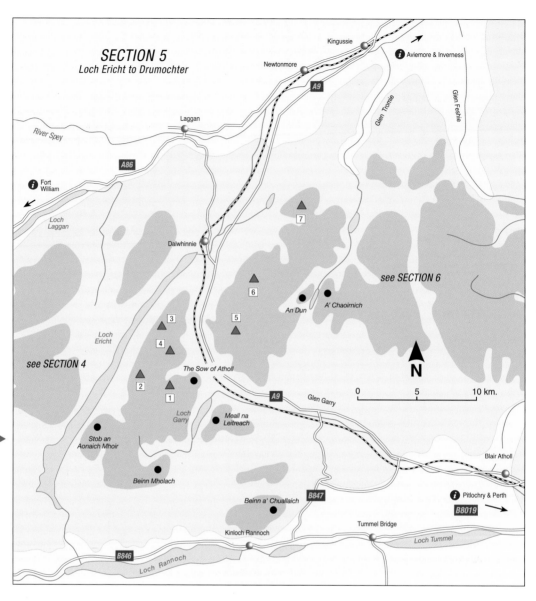

# SECTION 5

## Loch Ericht to Drumochter

**VisitScotland Information Centres**
**Pitlochry**; 22 Atholl Road, Pitlochry, PH16 5BX, (01796 472215), open Jan–Dec
**Aviemore**; Grampian Road, Aviemore, PH22 1RH, (01479 810930), open Jan–Dec
**Fort William**; 15 High Street, Fort William, PH33 6DH, (01397 701801),
     open Jan–Dec

Looking north-east from Geal-charn to Meall Chuaich (left) and Carn na Caim

# The Drumochter Hills

These hills, although themselves not of great character, stand astride one of the great dividing lines of the Highlands, the Pass of Drumochter. Once an important route for drovers and soldiers, it still carries the most important lines of communication in the Highlands. It also marks an obvious divide in the topography of the Highland mountains. Looking to the west from Beinn Udlamain across the deep trench of Loch Ericht, there is Ben Alder, the eastern outlier of the great peaks of Badenoch and Lochaber which culminate thirty miles away at Ben Nevis, and to the south-west far down Loch Ericht the hills of Breadalbane and the Black Mount are visible on the horizon. Turning round and looking in the opposite direction, there is the undulating plateau of the Mounth, dissected by many deep glens, stretching eastwards towards the distant mountains of the Cairngorms and Lochnagar.

The Boar of Badenoch, Sgairneach Mhor and A' Mharconaich from the east side of Drumochter Pass

Beinn Udlamain from Sgairneach Mhor

**Sgairneach Mhor;** 991m; (OS Sheet 42; NN599731); M155; *big scree*
**Beinn Udlamain;** 1011m; (OS Sheet 42; NN579740); M119; *jointed hill, or unsteady hill*

SGAIRNEACH
MHOR

BEINN
UDLAMAIN

These two hills lie between the Pass of Drumochter and Loch Ericht. Sgairneach Mhor is prominently seen from the A9 dual carriageway east of Dalnaspidal as a high rounded mass. It is also well seen from further north near the summit of the pass from where its most obvious feature is the steep north-facing Coire Creagach, which often holds snow until early summer. Beinn Udlamain, on the other hand, although the highest of this group of hills, is screened by its satellites and is only visible from the A9 directly opposite the foot of Coire Dhomhain. The two hills lie on either side of the head of this corrie, and can be conveniently climbed together in a single expedition.

From Layby 79 on the A9 opposite the entrance to Coire Dhomhain, first head south down the old road for a few hundred metres to pass beneath the railway on a track, then come back up the other side and follow the Allt Coire Dhomhain into the corrie by the track on its north side. After 1.5km cross the stream and climb south up grass and deep heather to a col on the east ridge of Sgairneach Mhor. From this col the ridge is broad and easy-angled at first, but becomes steeper and narrower before reaching the summit along the edge of Coire Creagach. (5km; 550m; 2h 10min).

If the Allt Coire Dhomhain is in spate and difficult to cross, it may be necessary to walk 3km up the corrie almost to the end of the track before crossing the stream and climbing the ridge on the west side of Coire Creagach.

From the summit of Sgairneach Mhor walk south-west for almost 500m before turning west to the 810m col at the head of Coire Dhomhain. The terrain of the descent is featureless, and in misty weather care should be taken not to be diverted south by the slope of the ground. From the col continue west up a short steeper slope to reach the south ridge of Beinn Udlamain, and follow the remains of a fence north up this ridge to the summit. (8.5km; 750m; 3h 10min). Descend north-east along the broad ridge, following the fence for 2km until the 860m col is reached. From there descend south-east down easy slopes to reach the track in Coire Dhomhain.

A'Mharconaich can easily be included in this traverse by continuing north-east from the 860m col, still following the fence until it goes off leftwards. The summit of A'Mharconaich is at the north-east end of the level summit ridge. From there descend steeply south-east towards the Boar of Badenoch col and regain the track near the foot of Coire Dhomhain.

Sgairneach Mhor and A' Mharconaich from Drumochter Lodge

**Geal-charn;** 917m; (OS Sheet 42; NN597783); M278; *white hill*
**A' Mharconaich;** 975m; (OS Sheet 42; NN604763); M179; *the place of horses*

These hills, which lie north-west of the Pass of Drumochter, are the continuation northwards of Sgairneach Mhor and Beinn Udlamain. Geal-charn is a rounded hill formed by a broad ridge running from south-west to north-east. A' Mharconaich is a fine looking hill seen from the road, with a very steep east face forming a high corrie just under the summit. They are both very easily accessible from the road which is 425m above sea level, so their traverse is a pleasant and undemanding day.

GEAL-CHARN

A' MHARCONAICH

Leave the A9 road at Balsporran Cottages, 3km north of Drumochter Pass, and cross the railway. Follow the path west, crossing the Allt Beul an Sporain, and then climb directly up the broad north-east ridge of Geal-charn by an obvious path through the heather. Above about 650m the path leads up the south-east side of the ridge to the flat shoulder of the hill at 850m. Finally, a broad stony slope leads to the summit of Geal-charn. (3.5km; 500m; 1h 40min).

Descend the stony ridge south-west then south for 1.5km to the col at the head of Coire Fhar at 740m. From there ascend south-east up grassy slopes to reach the flat plateau of A' Mharconaich, where the summit is at the north-east end. (6.5km; 730m; 2h 40min).

Descend north, steeply at first down rocky ground, then easily along the north-east ridge which leads directly back to Balsporran Cottages, with rough ground of peat bog and heather near its foot. This rough ground can be avoided by leaving the ridge to cross the Allt Coire Fhar to the path on its north side. However, if this stream is in spate the crossing should be made high up as there is no bridge across it.

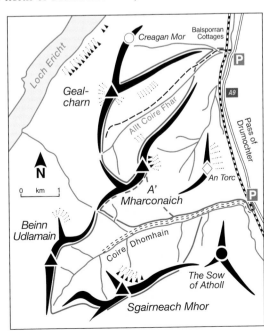

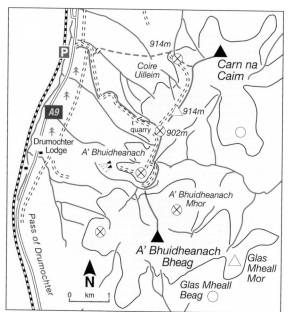

Carn na Caim from the Allt Coire Chuaich bothy

**A' Bhuidheanach Bheag**; 936m; (OS Sheet 42; NN661776); M240; *the little yellow place*
**Carn na Caim**; 941m; (OS Sheet 42; NN677821); M233; *hill of the curve*

A' BHUIDHEANACH
BHEAG

CARN NA CAIM

These two hills are the highest points of the plateau which extends north-east from the Pass of Drumochter to Loch an t-Seilich in the Gaick Forest. Both are flat-topped and their most distinctive features when seen from the A9 to the west are the many gullies and corries descending from the plateau in shallow curves. A' Bhuidheanach Bheag lies well back from the edge of the plateau and its summit is not visible from the road. Carn na Caim, on the other hand, is on the western edge of the plateau and, viewed from Dalwhinnie, it is the obvious rounded summit whose north and west sides are scalloped by shallow corries.

The two hills may conveniently be climbed together. Start from Layby 87 on the west side of the A9, 500m south of the road junction to Dalwhinnie. Cross over to a new gated track (no parking) and ascend past a junction to the old track which climbs south-east to old quarry workings, where the track divides; left to Carn na Caim and right to A' Bhuidheanach Bheag.

Climbing A' Bhuidheanach Bheag first, follow the track south to where it rises from the second col towards a prominent quartz cairn with an upright marker stone. This is about 1.1km from the track division and before the top of A' Bhuidheanach. Turn hard left off the main track onto another track which descends east then south-west to the col below A' Bhuidheanach Bheag. Cross the burn and ascend due south to an old fence-line which leads to the summit trig point. (7km; 620m; 2h 30min).

For Carn na Caim retrace your steps past the track division to meet the fence-line beyond the first 914m knoll. As the track ascends north-west round the head of Coire Uilleim towards the furthest 914m knoll, leave the track for the fence-line, which heads north-east towards Carn na Caim. The summit cairn lies about 185m north-east of the point where the fence turns sharply south. (13.5km; 780m; 4h). A return can be made via the quarry track or via the 914m knoll west of Carn na Caim. For the latter, return to the track and continue over the knoll to where the track fades. Descend steeply into the lower corrie and cross the Allt Coire Uilleim, from where open heather slopes lead to a footbridge at NN644822 and the ascent track.

Beinn Dearg from the head of the Allt Sheicheachan

## The West Mounth

The Mounth is the high ground south of The Cairngorms, stretching from Beinn Dearg to Lochnagar, conveniently split into two by the natural route through Glen Shee taken by the A93 Perth to Braemar road.

### Beinn Dearg; 1008m; (OS Sheet 43; NN853778); M124; *red hill*

Pointed Beinn Dearg rises above a multitude of flat and rounded hills and peaty plateaux, in the middle of the Atholl deer forest north-east of Bruar Lodge and 12km north of Blair Atholl. It is a lone granite peak, surrounded by a vast area of schist hills. The approaches from the south start from Blair Atholl, Bruar or Calvine, and are long. The route from Calvine up Glen Bruar follows a long-established right of way, the Minigaig Pass, but it is not the most attractive way to this hill.

The Glen Banvie route starts from Old Blair, 1km north of Blair Atholl. Follow the estate road on the north-east side of the Banvie Burn, and continue up the east side of the Allt an t-Seapail to the bothy beside the Allt Sheicheachan. The path continues along the north-west side of this burn to a height of 800m on Meall Dubh nan Dearcag. From there an easy broad ridge leads north to the summit of Beinn Dearg up dwarf heath and the reddish-coloured screes which give the hill its name. (14km; 890m; 4h 40min).

An alternative route of similar length and character also starts at Old Blair, but follows the high road on the west side of Glen Tilt through Blairuachdar Wood and up the Allt Slanaidh by a track passing a wooden shed. Continue up the burn, bearing north across the west side of Beinn a' Chait, then descend slightly to the col at the head of the Allt Sheicheachan and join the route described above on the final ascent up the south ridge of Beinn Dearg. (13km; 890m; 4h 30min).

On both of these routes it is possible to use a bike to quite high on the hill, considerably shortening the times involved and making a circular route possible.

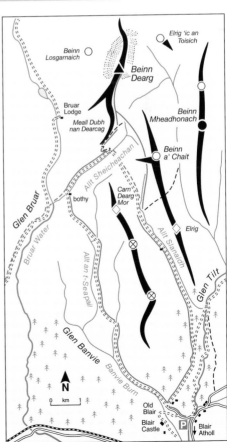

Braigh Coire Chruinn-bhalgain (left) and Carn Liath from the west

**BEINN A' GHLO;** *hill of the veil or mist*
**Carn Liath;** 975m; (OS Sheet 43; NN936698); M181; *grey hill*
**Braigh Coire Chruinn-bhalgain;** 1070m; (OS Sheet 43; NN946724); M66; *height of the corrie of round blisters*
**Carn nan Gabhar;** 1121m; (OS Sheet 43; NN971733); M33; *hill of the goats*

BEINN A' GHLO

A beautiful, stony mountain of many remote peaks and corries, Beinn a' Ghlo is the finest mountain in the Mounth between Drumochter and Aberdeen, with the sole exception of Lochnagar. It rises to the north-east of Blair Atholl, a complex range of summits, ridges and corries which looks particularly fine seen from the Cairngorms. The general orientation of the range is from south-west to north-east, rising above the farms on the north side of the River Garry between Killiecrankie and Blair Atholl. On its north-west side the range is bounded by the long straight trench of Glen Tilt, and on its south-east by the shallower valley of Glen Girnaig. Far to the north-east the mountain ends in 600m of remarkably steep slopes above the deep and narrow defile of Glen Loch, holding the curiously named Loch Loch. This end of the mountain is very wild and impressive compared with the comparatively pastoral appearance of the south-western slopes rising above Glen Fender.

The highest summit, Carn nan Gabhar (erroneously marked 1129m on older OS maps), is the remotest, 12km from Blair Atholl as the crow flies, and the finest way to it is the traverse of the other two Munros *en route*, starting with Carn Liath. From Killiecrankie the pointed hill of Carn Liath, with its grey screes, looks more prominent than the higher tops beyond it. It is best approached from Blair Atholl by the narrow public road on the south side of Glen Fender which ends near Loch Moraig, where cars can be parked. From there walk along the track north-east towards Glen Girnaig for 2km, to a little hut, and then climb Carn Liath by a path which is easily identified by the big scar higher up the slopes. (4.5km; 640m; 2h 10min).

Follow the twisting ridge north-west then north-east down to the col at 760m, and continue up the broad ridge of heath and stones to Braigh Coire Chruinn-bhalgain. (7.5km; 950m; 3h 20min). There is a fine view down into Glen Tilt from this summit.

Continue north-east along the ridge for 1km before turning east to descend a grassy slope to the next col, the Bealach an Fhiodha (847m), at the centre of the Beinn a' Ghlo range. Climb east to the col between Carn nan Gabhar and Airgiod Bheinn (1061m; *silver hill*), and finally go north-east along the broad easy-angled ridge to the top where there are two large cairns. The highest point is at the north-east end of this nearly level summit ridge, at a cairn about 200m beyond the trig point. (11km; 1230m; 4h 30min).

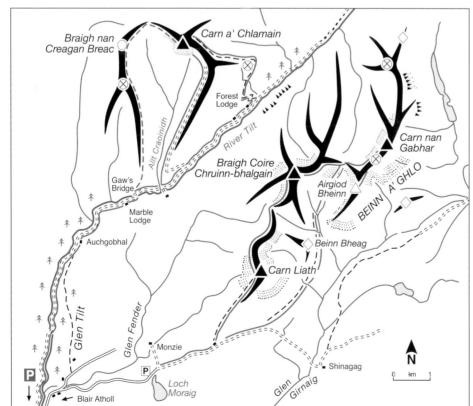

Carn nan Gabhar from Airgiod Bheinn

From here the Munro Top Airgiod Bheinn is a short diversion offering fine views to the south-west. Return to the col between Carn nan Gabhar and Airgiod Bheinn and descend south into the corrie. A well trodden path (not shown on OS maps) traverses around the base of Beinn Bheag to join the track to Loch Moraig. There may be access restrictions during the stalking season.

BEINN A' GHLO

The approach to Carn a' Chlamain along the south ridge

**Carn a' Chlamain;** 963m; (OS Sheet 43; NN916758); M192; *hill of the kite*

CARN A'
CHLAMAIN

CARN AN
FHIDHLEIR

AN SGARSOCH

This hill is the highest point of the undulating plateau, intersected by two or three deep glens, on the north-west side of Glen Tilt. Carn a' Chlamain has a pointed summit rising slightly above the level of the plateau, and the prominent patch of grey screes on its south-west side makes it recognisable from as far away as the A9 road near Blair Atholl.

From the signposted car park a short distance beyond Old Bridge of Tilt on the road to Old Blair, follow the estate road on the west side of the River Tilt, crossing to the east side after 2km. Continue past the farm at Auchgobhal and Marble Lodge and cross Gaw's Bridge. Some 750m beyond, a bridge crosses the Allt Craoinidh at the foot of the long south ridge of Carn a' Chlamain. It is possible to bike to this point, a significant saving in time and effort.

Follow the path up the broad crest of the ridge to gain a new track and occasional sections of old path, before leaving the track north then north-west to the summit of Carn a' Chlamain. (12km from Old Bridge of Tilt; 820m; 4h 10min).

Alternatively, on foot or by bike, go 3km further up Glen Tilt to Forest Lodge and climb the path which starts 400m beyond the lodge and zigzags up the steep hillside on the north-west side of the glen, offering an easy way up with spectacular views from the top. This path, continuing at an easier angle beyond the edge of the plateau, joins the previous route just southeast of the summit of Carn a' Chlamain. (From Forest Lodge, 4km; 660m; 2h). Both of these routes can be linked with Braigh nan Creagan Breac to give a pleasant round, with a final rough descent of Sron a' Chro to near Gaw's Bridge. Map on page 107.

**Carn an Fhidhleir;** 994m; (OS Sheet 43; NN905842); M148; *hill of the fiddler*
**An Sgarsoch;** 1006m; (OS Sheet 43; NN933837); M125; *the place of the sharp rocks*

These two very remote hills stand in one of the wildest and most inaccessible parts of the Highlands, more or less at the centre of the headwaters of the rivers Feshie, Geldie and Tarf. They are both smooth, gently sloping hills, with rough heather and peaty ground on their lower slopes, but excellent walking on mossy turf on their upper parts. Carn an Fhidhleir is also known as Carn Ealar.

They are a long way from any starting point, and a bike is a great help in reaching them along rough roads which, although private and not accessible to cars, nevertheless follow long-established rights of way. The three possible access points to which cars can be driven are Linn of Dee, Old Bridge of Tilt and Achlean farm in Glen Feshie. If approaching by

The view north-west from Beinn a' Ghlo towards the hills beyond Tarf Water

bike from Glen Feshie the onward track is on the west side of the glen. The Linn of Dee approach follows a track for most of the way which makes for fast walking, and although it is rough and stony in places, it is negotiable by bike for much of its length.

From Linn of Dee the route follows the track on the north bank of the River Dee to White Bridge, and then along the Geldie Burn to the ruined Geldie Lodge. From there a bulldozed track climbs west-south-west and is followed to its highest point. Continue south-west across peaty ground and climb the north-east slopes of Carn an Fhidhleir, up grass and heather, to reach the north ridge near the summit. (18.5km; 630m; 5h 10min).

CARN AN
FHIDHLEIR

AN SGARSOCH

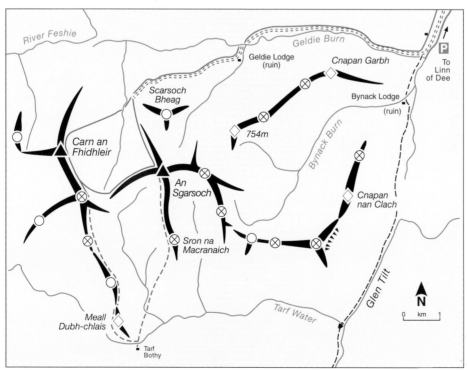

Descend south along the broad ridge for 1km and then drop down its east side to reach the 710m col between the two hills. From there climb north-east up a broad ridge to the large cairn on the flat summit of An Sgarsoch. (22km; 930m; 6h 30min). The easiest way back is due north, avoiding the steep north-east corries which may hold snowdrifts well into summer. Keep west of Scarsoch Bheag across peaty ground and reach the bulldozed track leading down to Geldie Lodge.

The route up Glen Tilt goes first to Forest Lodge, then up the zigzag path to Carn a' Chlamain. Once fairly level ground is reached at about 750m, bear north across rough terrain of peat and heather over the col between Carn a' Chlamain and Conlach Mhor and descend to the MBA's fine Tarf 'Hotel' bothy (Feith Uaine) at NN927789.

## CARN AN FHIDHLEIR

## AN SGARSOCH

From the bothy cross the Tarf Water and head north. To find the best ground for walking it is preferable to go up the very broad south ridge of An Sgarsoch rather than follow the shallow glen of the Allt a' Chaorainn. (From Forest Lodge: 11.5km; 930m; 4h 10min). Traverse to Carn an Fhidhleir across the 710m col by reversing the route described above, and descend the long south ridge of this hill over two or three knolls down to the Tarf Water. A short stop at the bothy will be needed before making the last climb over the hills to return to Forest Lodge in Glen Tilt.

## GLAS TULAICHEAN

## CARN AN RIGH

**Glas Tulaichean;** 1051m; (OS Sheet 43; NO051760); M80; *grey-green hillocks*
**Carn an Righ;** 1029m; (OS Sheet 43; NO028773); M102; *hill of the king*

These two hills stand rather remotely between Glen Shee and Glen Tilt, and can be most easily reached up Glen Lochsie, an offshoot of Glen Shee. There is an estate road from Spittal of Glenshee for 2km to Dalmunzie Castle Hotel, where cars may be parked for a payment (£2 in 2011). Alternatively, walk up the estate road to the hotel from Spittal of Glenshee.

Glas Tulaichean is a typical green Mounth hill, with crisp mossy turf and heath giving excellent walking on its upper slopes, and with grassy corries to the east. Carn an Righ is much more remote, the western outlier of the group of hills which extends from the Cairnwell Pass to the head of Glen Tilt, and includes Glas Tulaichean and Beinn Iutharn Mhor. It is a rounded hill, with much scree on its slopes.

From the hotel follow the track towards Glenlochsie farm. Avoid the farm by the path diversion to regain the track and continue to a ford. Do not cross over, but ascend the short slope immediately right of the track to gain the line of the old railway (hidden from below) which used to link Dalmunzie with Glenlochsie Lodge, a former deer-stalking lodge now in ruins.

Glas Tulaichean from Creag Bhreac

Nick Picozzi

Carn an Righ from the hills to the west above Tarf Water

Beyond the lodge, follow the track all the way up the Breac-reidh ridge to just south of the summit of Glas Tulaichean, which lies close to the edge of Glas Choire Mhor, which can be corniced in winter. (8.5km; 710m; 3h 20min).

To continue to Carn an Righ, go down the north ridge of Glas Tulaichean for 1km and then descend north-west to reach the path on the south side of Mam nan Carn. Follow this path west for 1km to the col east of Carn an Righ and climb to the summit through areas of quartz scree. (12.5km; 1000m; 5h).

On the return journey retrace the outward route and follow the upper of two paths beneath Mam nan Carn to reach Loch nan Eun then descend beside the Allt Easgaidh into Gleann Taitneach. Further on, a track leads down this steep-sided glen to a footbridge over the burn at NO089724. From here a path leads to the track just north of the hotel.

If returning to Spittal of Glenshee, do not cross the footbridge, but stay on the track on the east side of the river.

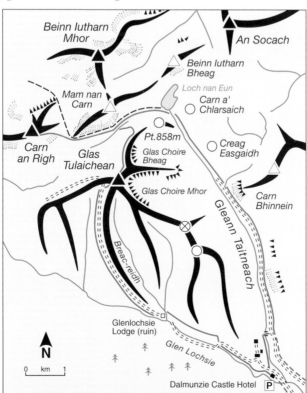

Beinn Iutharn Mhor from Carn an Righ

**Beinn Iutharn Mhor;** 1045m; (OS Sheet 43; NO045792); M88; *probably big sharp-ridged hill*
**Carn Bhac;** 946m; (OS Sheet 43; NO051832); M221; *hill of peatbanks*

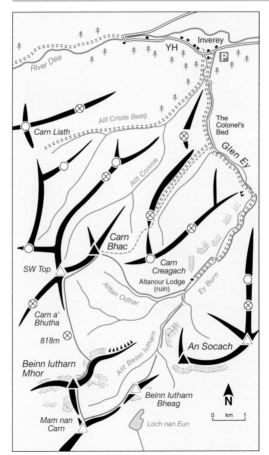

Beinn Iutharn Mhor is a rounded hill, the second highest in the Mounth between Beinn a' Ghlo and Glas Maol. It rises boldly in the view from upper Glen Ey, thrusting its long north-east ridge out into the glen, which gives a very pleasant approach.

From Inverey bike or walk up the road which starts on the east side of the Ey Burn. This road climbs through decaying birch woods past The Colonel's Bed, and higher up through beautiful grassy haughs to the ruined Altanour Lodge, 8km from Inverey. From there walk up the Allt Beinn Iutharn for a further 2.5km, and then climb south up the shoulder of Beinn Iutharn Bheag (953m); the western edge of the steep north-east corrie is the easiest route.

From Beinn Iutharn Bheag there is a short drop to a col above Loch nan Eun, and then a gentle rise to the flat top of Mam nan Carn (986m). Again there is a short drop north-west to a col below the mainly mossy and grassy slopes leading to the stony summit of Beinn Iutharn Mhor. (15km; 900m; 4h 50min).

From there the route to Carn Bhac goes north-east along a fairly level ridge

Looking south from Carn Bhac to the hills at the head of Glen Ey

for 1km, then north-west down steep stony slopes, possibly hazardous in winter if there is hard snow or ice, to reach the lowest point of the connecting ridge. Continue for 2km along a broad undulating ridge of eroded peat bogs to the 920m south-west top of Carn Bhac. Finally, an easy walk for 1.5km north-east leads to the true summit, 5km from Beinn Iutharn Mhor. (20km; 1080m; 6h 20min). The best descent route for those who have biked in is south-east down to the headwaters of the Alltan Odhar to reach the ruins of Altanour Lodge. An alternative, if a descent does not have to be made to Altanour, is to follow the north ridge of Carn Creagach to a track which leads down into Glen Ey.

Looking up Glen Ey to An Socach and Beinn Iutharn Bheag

An Socach from the foot of the Baddoch Burn

**An Socach;** 944m; (OS Sheet 43; NO080800); M227; *the snout*

AN SOCACH

THE CAIRNWELL

CARN A'
GHEOIDH

CARN AOSDA

An Socach is a broad ridge rising between upper Glen Ey and the Baddoch Burn, several kilometres west of the A93 road from Perth to Braemar. The ridge is about 2km long between the east and west summits, with the East Top at 938m being slightly lower than the main west summit.

The shortest approach to An Socach is from the summit of the A93 road at the Glenshee Ski Centre. Follow the bulldozed track north-west into Butchart's Corrie past several ski tows and bear west up to the col between The Cairnwell and Carn Aosda. Descend west from the col, traversing the heathery slopes and peat bogs north of Loch Vrotachan to reach the Baddoch Burn. Once on the north-west side of the burn make a rising traverse to reach the col at the middle of An Socach's summit ridge. Finally, go 1km west along this level stony ridge to the summit. (6.5km; 560m; 2h 30min).

The 938m East Top is 2km away, with very little drop along the ridge, and it can easily be included in the return.

A much more attractive approach to An Socach, avoiding the ski slopes, is up the Baddoch Burn from Glen Clunie, starting 6km north along the A93 road from the Cairnwell Pass. An estate road leads to Baddoch farm and a track from there onwards goes far up the glen to the point where the previous route is joined. It is equally possible to leave the track lower down the glen and climb the long ridge to the East Top, and then traverse the summit ridge to the highest point. (8km; 580m; 2h 50min).

**The Cairnwell;** 933m; (OS Sheet 43; NO135774); M245; *hill of bags, baggy peatbanks*
**Carn a' Gheoidh;** 975m; (OS Sheet 43; NO107767); M180; *hill of the goose*
**Carn Aosda;** 915m; (OS Sheet 43; NO134792); M281; *ancient hill*

These three hills lie on the west side of the A93 road from Perth to Braemar, and are most easily accessible from the summit of the road where the Glenshee Ski Centre has its many tows, lifts and pistes.

The Cairnwell stands out boldly in the view from Spittal of Glenshee to the south. Carn Aosda rises to the north of The Cairnwell, a heathery hill with pale grey screes on its bald top. The flanks of both these hills have snow fences and ski lifts going up right to their summits. Carn a' Gheoidh, on the other hand, lies well to the west of its two neighbours, hidden from the road.

The Cairnwell from Gleann Beag

The Cairnwell and Carn Aosda are the two most accessible Munros in Scotland, particularly The Cairnwell for there is a chairlift which operates in summer as well as winter and goes up to 910m, a short distance from the summit.

Going to The Cairnwell first, and starting just south of the Ski Centre, steepish slopes of short dry heather and, higher up, windclipped heath and patches of grey screes lead to the big cairn where there is also a small hut. (0.6km; 270m; 40min). It is a very good viewpoint, offering fine panoramas of the Cairngorms and south towards Central Scotland.

Descend north past the top of the chairlift and along the broad ridge with snow fences. After 1km, and 500m before reaching the Cairnwell-Carn Aosda col, diverge west and drop down to another col at 810m which is the lowest point between The Cairnwell and Carn a' Gheoidh.

Continuing south-west, the walking is easy up a gentle slope of crisp mossy heath along the edge of the Coire Direach rocks, past Carn nan Sac (920m) and west to Carn a' Gheoidh across a little plateau. (4.5km; 440m; 1h 50min).

Return along the same route to The Cairnwell-Carn Aosda col and climb north-east then east along the broad ridge of windclipped heath, passing the top of the ski tow in Butchart's Corrie to reach the flat stony summit of Carn Aosda. (9km; 570m; 3h). Descend south by vehicle tracks to the road at the foot of Butchart's Corrie.

If one wants to avoid the pistes and ski tows of Butchart's Corrie, there are alternative ways to The Cairnwell and Carn a' Gheoidh. The starting point for these routes is a layby about 2.5km south of the summit of the A93 road. From there The Cairnwell can be climbed directly up its broad south ridge, and a possible route to Carn a' Gheoidh is north-west up the ridge of Carn nan Sac on the west side of Coire Direach.

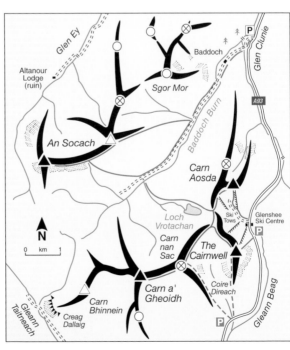

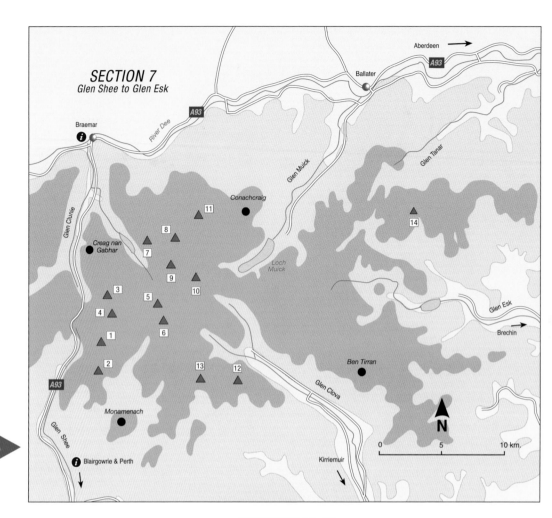

# SECTION 7

## Glen Shee to Glen Esk: The East Mounth

ℹ️ VisitScotland Information Centres
**Blairgowrie**; 26 Wellmeadow, Blairgowrie, PH10 6AS, (01250 872960), open Jan–Dec
**Braemar**; The Mews, Mar Road, Braemar, AB35 5YL, (01339 741600), open Jan–Dec

On the ridge from Glas Maol to Creag Leacach

## The East Mounth

Lying to the east of the A93 road over the Cairnwell Pass, the Mounth plateau extends from Creag Leacach in the south-west for 20km to Lochnagar in the north-east, never falling below 800m. Its outline is defined by the surrounding glens and corries: Callater to the west, Muick, Clova and Isla to the east. North of the Tolmount drove road, which crosses the Mounth between Glen Callater and Glen Doll, the underlying granite yields a poorer soil and sparser vegetation than the grassier tundras further south which are based on varied metamorphic rocks.

Thirteen Munros and sixteen Tops are scattered across the Mounth plateau, with no great drops between them. This is an area of easy but expansive high-level walking. The following routes involve a variety of approaches by different glens, but do not include any long days.

GLAS MAOL

CREAG
LEACACH

**Glas Maol;** 1068m; (OS Sheet 43; NO167765); M69; *grey-green hill*
**Creag Leacach;** 987m; (OS Sheet 43; NO154745); M159; *slabby rock*

These two hills are at the south-west corner of the Mounth plateau. The dome of Glas Maol rises 3km south-east of the Cairnwell Pass just south of the point where the plateau narrows between the Garbh-choire and the Caenlochan Glen. A long ridge ridge extends south-west from Glas Maol to Creag Leacach and beyond it for a further 5km over a series of lesser tops towards Glen Shee.

Start the traverse from the car park on the east side of the A93, 2km south of the summit of the Cairnwell Pass and go east on a path downhill for 100m to cross the Allt a' Ghlinne Bhige. Follow the path or a rough track up onto the grassy ridge of Leacann Dubh and continue for 2km, passing a small hut and now on a good track. Swing east and climb a stony slope to the side of the ski-tows and cross Meall Odhar to reach a flat col. From there a path zigzags steeply up the dome of Glas Maol and crosses the grassy plateau for 500m to reach the summit cairn. (4.5km; 570m; 2h).

To the south-west of the summit, screes and grass slopes lead down towards the Creag Leacach ridge. A dry stone dyke is a useful guide, and it can be followed downhill to the col and from there south-west to Creag Leacach. The ridge is quite narrow for this part of the Mounth, and even rocky in places, although broken into large scree and boulders. The summit of Creag Leacach is 500m beyond the col. (7.5km; 660m; 2h 50min).

Continue down the widening stony ridge to the South-west Top (943m) and then leave the crest to descend steeply north-west to the saddle between Creag Leacach and the outlying knoll of Meall Gorm. From there go north down grassy slopes to cross the burns in the floor of the corrie just before they join. Make a short climb up the other side to gain a path which then traverses the hillside then descends to the burn below the car park. Map on page 119.

*Tim Rennv*

Carn an Tuirc

**Carn an Tuirc;** 1019m; (OS Sheet 43; NO174804); M113; *hill of the wild boar*
**Cairn of Claise;** 1064m; (OS Sheet 43; NO185789); M71; *hill of the hollow or ditch*
**Tolmount;** 958m; (OS Sheets 43 and 44; NO210800); M202; *from doll, a valley, and monadh, a hill*
**Tom Buidhe;** 957m; (OS Sheets 43 and 44; NO214787); M204; *yellow hill*

CARN AN TUIRC

CAIRN OF CLAISE

TOLMOUNT

TOM BUIDHE

Of these four hills, Carn an Tuirc and Cairn of Claise overlook the head of Glen Clunie a few kilometres north-east of the Cairnwell Pass, showing shallow grassy corries and rounded shoulders to the A93 road. Tolmount, a few kilometres east, stands at the head of Glen Callater with a steep craggy face above this glen, and Tom Buidhe to its south is a rounded swelling on the Mounth plateau. The four can be climbed in a round tour from the head of Glen Clunie.

There is a small car park at NO148800 on the east side of the A93, 2km north of the Cairnwell Pass and a larger one 700m beyond, on the west side. From the former, descend to the Cairnwell Burn and cross the old bridge, a remnant of the 18th-century military road. The military road goes left and down to the bridge by the lower car park.

Follow the Allt a' Gharbh-choire east for 1km by a path and cross the tributary coming down from the north-east. Continue up the intermittent path beside the tributary, which leads round below the north side of Carn an Tuirc avoiding the unpleasant boulder slopes of the north-west face, and reach the flat stony summit. (3km; 510m; 1h 40min).

Continue east across the summit boulder field and, where the slope steepens towards Coire Kander, turn south-east down a wide grassy ridge to the saddle from where Cairn of Claise lies 1.5km south. Climb the easy slope by a track which leads close to the summit. (5.5km; 620m; 2h 20min). A pleasant walk east-north-east down grassy slopes leads to a shallow peaty col from which a wide shoulder leads to Tolmount. (8.5km; 700m; 3h 10min). The summit stands near the steep headwall of Glen Callater.

To the south the rounded top of Tom Buidhe rises from the plateau. It is best approached by going round the upper part of the shallow green corrie, one of the sources of the River South Esk, which separates Tolmount from Tom Buidhe. A short ascent south-east up a grassy slope studded with a few boulders leads to the rounded summit of the latter. (10km; 790m; 3h 40min).

Return due west along the highest ground over Ca Whims. After about 2km bear south-west, contouring at about 970m between the upper slopes of Cairn of Claise on the right and steepening ground dropping towards the Caenlochan Glen on the left. This traverse across tussocky grass and blaeberry leads in about 2km to the more level ground of the watershed where the Mounth plateau is reduced to a broad ridge between the Caenlochan Glen and the Garbh-choire. Go south-west, then west along this ridge, following a vehicle track, to reach the path of the Monega road, the highest drove route in the Highlands, which comes up from Glen

The Mounth Plateau between Cairn of Claise and Glas Maol

Isla over Little Glas Maol. The path crosses the ridge and leads north-west down the spur of Sron na Gaoithe towards Glen Clunie. Follow it, and leave the crest of the spur to descend its north flank just before reaching the rocky knob at its termination. Below this the path disappears, but an easy grass slope leads down to the Cairnwell Burn which is crossed by a footbridge, to regain the car park.

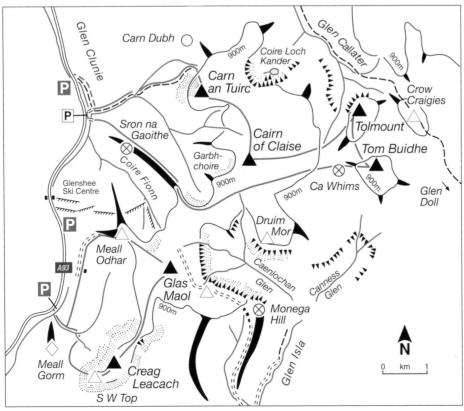

CARN AN TUIRC

CAIRN OF CLAISE

TOLMOUNT

TOM BUIDHE

Cairn Bannoch and Carn an t-Sagairt Mor from Broad Cairn

**Carn an t-Sagairt Mor;** 1047m; (OS Sheets 43 and 44; NO208843); M83; *big hill of the priest*
**Carn a' Choire Bhoidheach;** 1110m; (OS Sheet 44; NO226845); M42; *hill of the beautiful corrie*

Between the north-facing corries of The Stuic and Lochnagar and the deep glen of Loch Muick and the Dubh Loch further south is the corner of the high Mounth plateau known as The White Mounth. To its east the summit of Lochnagar, Cac Carn Beag, is the highest point, while in the middle Carn a' Choire Bhoidheach rises only marginally higher than the top of The Stuic buttress just to its north. Westwards the plateau rises and falls in individual hills of which Carn an t-Sagairt Mor is the highest. It is possible to climb these hills in a single long day from Glen Muick and include Lochnagar, Cairn Bannoch and Broad Cairn. However, this involves a walk of nearly 30km, and it is more usual to enjoy them in shorter sections by the routes described here and in the following pages.

For these two hills, start at Auchallater Farm on the A93 road in Glen Clunie, voluntary pay and display car park, and follow the estate road up Glen Callater for 5km to Lochcallater Lodge and the MBA maintained Callater Stable bothy. This is the first part of the old drove road over the Tolmount which leads to Glen Clova; a bike can be used to here. Just outside the lodge enclosure a path strikes uphill, then turns south-east to traverse the hillside above Loch Callater, gradually gaining height. It goes north-east below the small rocky bluff of Creag an Loch to gain a col below the west slope of Carn an t-Sagairt Mor. Follow the path up this slope until it starts to contour south-eastwards across the hillside, and then climb directly to the summit by the line of a fence. (9km; 680m; 3h 10min).

Continue north-east, descending about 80m and reascending the same height to pass over Carn an t-Sagairt Beag (1044m) and reach the rim of the plateau 750m beyond. The top of The Stuic buttress rises a little higher, 500m east along the edge of the cliffs, and is well worth

CARN AN T-
SAGAIRT MOR

CARN A' CHOIRE
BHOIDHEACH

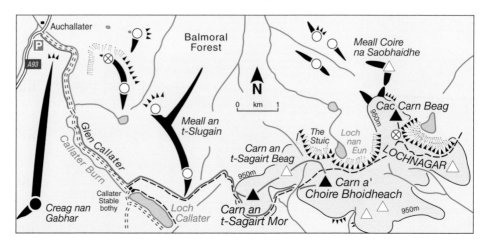

visiting for the view over its rocky corries to the Dee valley far below. From there an easy walk south for 500m over the sparse stony tundra of the high plateau brings one to Carn a' Choire Bhoidheach. In thick weather, with snow on the ground, careful navigation is needed to find the summit of this flat-topped mountain. (11.5km; 880m; 4h 10min).

Return by descending west to intersect the path which leads south-west across the headwaters of the Allt an Dubh-loch and round the south side of Carn an t-Sagairt Mor to return to Glen Callater.

**Cairn Bannoch;** 1012m; (OS Sheet 44; NO223826); M117; *peaked hill*
**Broad Cairn;** 998m; (OS Sheet 44; NO240815); M142

The glacial valley which bites into the eastern part of the Mounth plateau to the south of Lochnagar forms a deep trough containing Loch Muick, with an upper basin holding the Dubh Loch. Broad Cairn stands at the southern side of this basin and Creag an Dubh-loch, its northern extension, has a great face of overlapping slabs above the loch and is one of the most awe-inspiring features of the Mounth. Cairn Bannoch rises to the west and is distinguished from other neighbouring tops by its small, yet prominent, summit cone.

From the car park at the end of the Glen Muick road, go south-west past Spittal of Glenmuick and in 1km take the path to the right to reach the road on the west side of Loch Muick. Continue along the lochside past Glas-allt-Shiel with its bothy at the back and 100m beyond the wood take the right fork in the path and go up the glen of the Allt an Dubh-loch. On the right the Stulan Burn cascades down its rocky bed, while below on the left the Allt an Dubh-loch flows over a succession of red granite slabs.

Abruptly the Dubh Loch comes into view with the magnificent cliffs of Creag an Dubh-loch rising above it. Continue along the lochside, the path deteriorates half way along, and upstream until past the north-west end of Creag an Dubh-loch. After crossing the tributary that tumbles down from Eagle's Rock, cross to the south side of the Allt an Dubh-loch and ascend by the burn between Creag an Dubh-loch and Cairn Bannoch until it is easy to climb to the summit cone of the latter with its broken granite tor. (11.5km; 610m; 3h 40min).

Go south-east for 1km along the undulating plateau to Cairn of Gowal (991m), and then east across a wide col to the bouldery summit of Broad Cairn. (14km; 710m; 4h 20min).

Descend east down granite boulders to a rough path, which becomes a track, and in a further 1km reach a wooden shed at a flat col. Continue east for 300m, then bear left along the path which slants down to reach Loch Muick near its head. The path continues along the south shore of the loch and joins a track leading back to Spittal of Glenmuick. Alternatively, stay on the high-level track above Loch Muick until it drops in steep zigzags to the bridge over the Black Burn. Map on page 123.

Broad Cairn from the track above Loch Muick

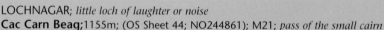
Lochnagar

## LOCHNAGAR; *little loch of laughter or noise*
### Cac Carn Beag;1155m; (OS Sheet 44; NO244861); M21; *pass of the small cairn*

### LOCHNAGAR

Cliff edge, Lochnagar

Located entirely in the Balmoral Estate, this fine and complex mountain lies south of the Dee, and north-west of Loch Muick. Its summit crowns the northern rim of the great Mounth plateau, which from there sweeps far southward to Glen Shee and the Angus glens. The grandeur of Lochnagar is best appreciated from the north, from Deeside or even better from the B976 road from Crathie to Gairnshiel, from where its sharp summit and flanking corries can be seen rising above the lower slopes, mantled by the ancient pinewoods of Ballochbuie.

The usual route to Lochnagar starts at the pay and display car park at the end of the public road up Glen Muick. Walk south-west over the bridge, past the toilets and along the estate road for 250m to Spittal of Glenmuick and turn right along the edge of the plantation to reach the other side of the glen at Allt-na-giubhsaich. Continue west along a path on the south side of the burn through the pinewoods to reach a track which is followed west for almost 3km to the col at the head of Glen Gelder.

From there take the path south-west across a slight dip and then uphill for 1.25km to the last water point at the Fox Cairn Well on the left side of the path. The slope relents for a short distance before the steep ascent known as The Ladder, where a short diversion west to the col just south of Meikle Pap gives a splendid view of the great north-east corrie of Lochnagar.

If there is old hard snow covering the steep slope of The Ladder it may be safer to keep to the right among the boulders near the edge of the corrie. At the top the summit ridge is reached where a short descent west across a wide col and a climb of 70m leads to the almost level roof of the mountain. Finally, an airy walk of 1km along

Lochnagar from Deeside

the rim of the great north-east corrie past the cairn of Cac Carn Mor and round the deep indentation of the Black Spout ends at the summit cone of Cac Carn Beag, as the highest point of Lochnagar is called, where the trig point stands on top of a granite tor. (9km; 800m; 3h 20min).

The quickest descent is by the route of ascent, but an enjoyable alternative is by the path down the Glas Allt past a fine waterfall and then by steep zigzags to the wood of Glas-allt-Shiel. From there return to Spittal of Glenmuick by the road along the north-west side of Loch Muick, and then either by the path across the outflow of the loch or by Allt-na-giubhsaich.

LOCHNAGAR

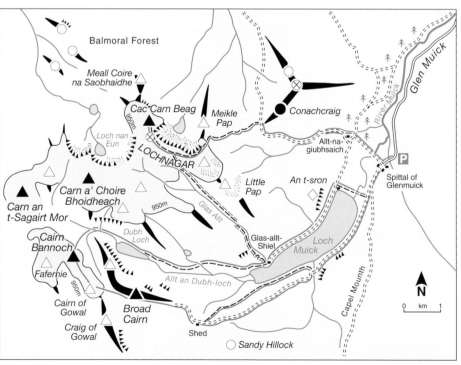

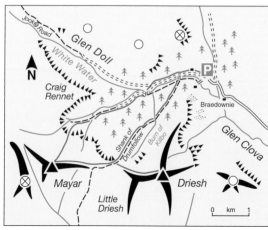

Driesh (right) across the head of Glen Clova from Capel Mounth

**Driesh;** 947m; (OS Sheet 44; NO271736); M219; *a thorn bush*
**Mayar;** 928m; (OS Sheet 44; NO241738); M253; *may be magh ard, high plain*

DRIESH

MAYAR

The straightest of the Angus glens, its sides scalloped by many corries, Glen Clova slices north-westwards into the Mounth. At its head it divides into two, the northerly glen leading to Bachnagairn, the southern one being Glen Doll. Both are hemmed in by steep slopes and rocky bluffs, and on its south side Glen Doll opens out to form the wide amphitheatre of Corrie Fee. These two hills stand above this corrie, Driesh to its south-east and Mayar to its south-west.

There are extensive plantations in upper Glen Clova and Glen Doll, and the route to Driesh and Mayar starts at the Forestry Commission Scotland pay and display car park in Glen Doll, located 500m past Braedownie farm. Go west along the road to the bridge at NO276763, cross it and reach the start of the old hill path to Kilbo in Glen Prosen. This path leads south-west across the Burn of Kilbo and out of the forest area at a deer fence. Continue up the path along the side of the Shank of Drumfollow to the col between Driesh and Mayar. Turn south-east then east to reach the summit of Driesh in 1.5km of easy walking over a subsidiary top. (5.5km; 700m; 2h 30min). From there one can see into the upper reaches of the Clova glens and identify the lines of the old drove roads crossing to Glen Muick and Braemar.

Return to the col and follow the line of the fence, then intermittent fence posts westwards over grassy tundra to Mayar. (9km; 860m; 3h 30min). On a clear day the position of this hill at the southern edge of the Mounth plateau is obvious, for to the north is its wide undulating expanse while to the south are the many rounded hills between Glen Isla and Glen Prosen.

Grassy slopes lead down north for 1km to the head of Corrie Fee where the Fee Burn tumbles down the steep headwall. Descend on the south side of the burn on a good path past small waterfalls and continue across the lovely flat-floored corrie into the Glendoll Forest. The path develops into a forest road which leads downhill across the White Water and back to the car park.

Adam Watson

Mount Keen with the plateau of Braid Cairn to its left

**Mount Keen;** 939m; (OS Sheet 44; NO409869); M235;
*from Gaelic monadh caoin, meaning gentle hill*

This is the most easterly Munro and one of the most solitary. Its pointed dome is on the spine of the Mounth between the Dee and Strathmore, and it is the highest summit east of Loch Muick. There are two commonly used approaches to Mount Keen, from Glen Esk to the south-east and Glen Tanar to the north-east. Both follow the old Mount Keen drove road, which is a right of way.

The Glen Esk route starts at the Invermark car park where the glen divides into its two upper reaches, Glen Lee and Glen Mark. Go west past the church to the road junction and take the right fork up Glen Mark, continuing for 3.5km to the Queen's Well, a monument which commemorates a visit by Queen Victoria. Bear right (north) past the last house in the glen and follow the track up the narrow defile of the Ladder Burn, climbing its west slope to emerge onto high moorland near the Knowe of Crippley. The blunt cone of Mount Keen rises to the north, and the track reaches a fork. The traditional Mounth Road goes due north and another path bears right to ascend Mount Keen. Just before the summit cairn there is a boundary stone with a large **B** carved on it. (9km; 680m; 3h 10min).

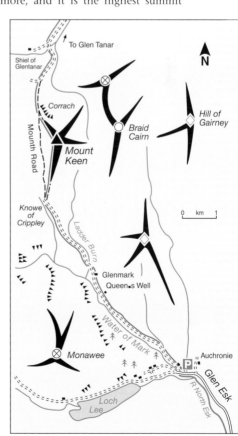

The other route to Mount Keen starts at the end of the public road up Glen Tanar. From the car park go along the private road up the north side of the Water of Tanar. This road passes through fine native pines for 6km, and for another 4km goes up the open glen, crossing the river three times before starting the climb of the Mounth Road southwards by a track up heathery slopes. After climbing for 2km, diverge south-east along the path which goes above the headwall of the Corrach to the top of Mount Keen. (13.5km; 760m; 4h 20min).

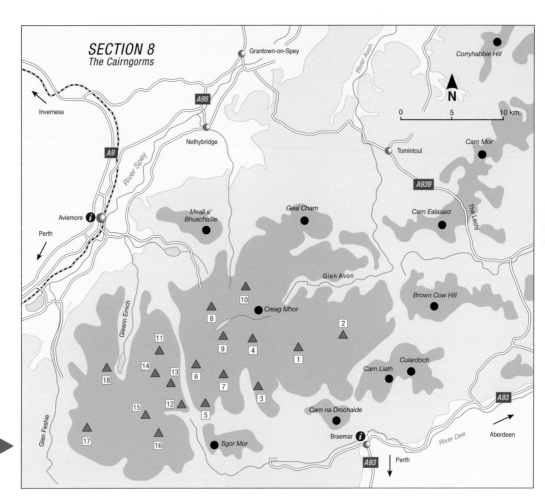

## SECTION 8

### The Cairngorms

*i* VisitScotland Information Centres
**Aviemore**; Grampian Road, Aviemore, PH22 1RH, (01479 810930), open Jan–Dec
**Braemar**; The Mews, Mar Road, Braemar, AB35 5YL, (01339 741600), open Jan–Dec

The Cairngorms from Morrone

# The Cairngorms

The vast high range of the Cairngorms is divided into three main blocks or massifs by two major passes, the Lairig Ghru and the Lairig an Laoigh, which go from north to south across the range through glacially-carved valleys. To the east of the Lairig an Laoigh are Beinn Bhreac, Beinn a' Chaorainn and the huge plateaux of Beinn a' Bhuird and Ben Avon. The middle block consists of the high ground above Strath Nethy and the deep basin of Loch Avon; it extends over Cairn Gorm to Ben Macdui and round to Beinn Mheadhoin in a great horseshoe, with off-shoots to Derry Cairngorm, Bynack More and Carn a' Mhaim. To the west of the Lairig Ghru, the largest of the three blocks extends from the rim of the mighty amphitheatre of An Garbh Choire across the grassy plateau of the Moine Mhor to Glen Feshie; it includes Braeriach and Cairn Toul which face Ben Macdui across the Lairig Ghru, and further south and west The Devil's Point, Beinn Bhrotain and Monadh Mor above Glen Geusachan, and Mullach Clach a' Bhlair and Sgor Gaoith overlooking Glen Feshie.

Largely of intrusive granites, the Cairngorms are characterised by poor acid soils and bleak stony tundra, albeit richer and grassier on the western massif. Consequently, the most obviously impressive features tend to be in the corries and penetrating valleys where cliffs, streams and lochans create variety and interest. The high plateaux might be thought at first sight to tend towards monotony, but it is there that one finds a little piece of the arctic in Scotland, a fascinating landscape with vast spacious views.

Many of the summits of the Cairngorms may be approached from either Deeside or Speyside. Since both approaches are frequently used, brief descriptions of access routes from the two directions are included where appropriate.

In Deeside the usual starting point for most of the peaks is Linn of Dee not far from the end of the public road, where there is a National Trust for Scotland pay and display car park. From there a rough estate road continues up the River Dee towards the Lairig Ghru and other distant passes leading to Glen Tilt and Glen Feshie. Another estate road leads north-west up Glen Lui to Derry Lodge and it is the most important access route on the south side of the Cairngorms. Both roads follow rights of way and bikes can be used along them.

From Speyside the Cairngorms appear as a great scarp, scalloped by corries and sliced through by the deep cleft of the Lairig Ghru, with the dark forests of Glenmore, Rothiemurchus and Inshriach in the foreground. There are a number of suitable starting points for the mountains, that most frequently used for the central massif being at the end of the road to the ski slopes on Cairn Gorm. Walkers should be sensitive to the fact that the car park is also provided for the ski area and the funicular tourist attraction. Its high altitude provides rapid access to a wild mountainous area where severe storms and very high winds arrive quickly.

The western mountains are reached by three possible routes. The first is from the car park at the end of the road up the east side of Glen Feshie 1km north of Achlean farm. The second is from Coylumbridge or Whitewell by the rough estate road up Gleann Einich; it is possible to bike along this road to its end at Loch Einich. The same two points and also the bridge across the River Luineag at the west end of Loch Morlich give access along tracks and paths through Rothiemurchus Forest to the Lairig Ghru. Another traditional starting point for reaching the Lairig Ghru and Braeriach is from the public road to Coire Cas near the upper edge of the forest, from where a path strikes south-west through the Creag a' Chalamain gap to join the Lairig Ghru path.

This vast mountain between Glen Quoich and Glen Avon has one of the biggest high tablelands in the Cairngorms, and although it sweeps down gently on its west side to lower peaty glens and plateaux, on the east and north-east it plunges in spectacular cliffs to great wild corries.

One possible approach is from Keiloch, close to Invercauld Bridge, a few kilometres east of Braemar, where there is a pay and display car park. It follows the estate road past Keiloch and Alltdourie and onwards up Gleann an t-Slugain by a bulldozed track past the ruined Slugain Lodge to reach Glen Quoich. There a path breaks off to the west towards Quoich Water, crosses the stream and on the far bank continues north-west high up past Carn Fiaclach, from where easy slopes of short heath and gravel lead up to the edge of the plateau of Beinn a' Bhuird.

Once on the plateau, it is a short distance to the South Top (1179m) close to the cliff edge. The walking along the plateau is excellent, on dry ground with grand views at times into the great east-facing corries - Coire na Ciche, Coire an Dubh Lochain and Coire nan Clach. In misty weather in summer the cliff-edge on the right can be useful for navigating, but remember that snow wreaths and unstable cornices sometimes remain along the edge long after the spring thaw. The cliff edge leads close to the North Top, which is the true summit, although marked by only a small cairn in the middle of the plateau. (16km; 980m; 5h 10min).

The bouldery top of Cnap a' Chleirich (1174m) rises from the grassy plateau to the east, and the return journey can be varied by crossing this Top, descending east to the saddle called The Sneck, and then turning south to reach Clach a' Chleirich and the path down Glen Quoich to Gleann an t-Slugain.

An alternative route to Beinn a' Bhuird starts at the Linn of Quoich, which can be reached by car from Braemar *via* the Linn of Dee. Walk up the track on the south-west side of the Quoich Water through fine stands of Old Caledonian pines, and after 6km cross the west tributary of the Quoich Water. Keep on north, following an old track through the highest trees and onto the ridge of An Diollaid. The track peters out on a broad shoulder which ends about 1.5km south of the summit, which is easily reached across the plateau. (14km; 870m; 4h 40min).

**BEINN A' BHUIRD**

Although shorter than the Gleann an t-Slugain route and having the merit of passing through the Old Caledonian forest in Glen Quoich, this route is rather spoiled by following a bulldozed track up the glen. This track was extended up to the plateau in the 1960s, but under the ownership of the National Trust for Scotland the upper section has been restored to its natural state.

Beinn a' Bhuird from the moors above Glen Quoich

Adam Watson

Coire an Dubh Lochain, Beinn a' Bhuird

*Greg Strange*

BEINN A' BHUIRD

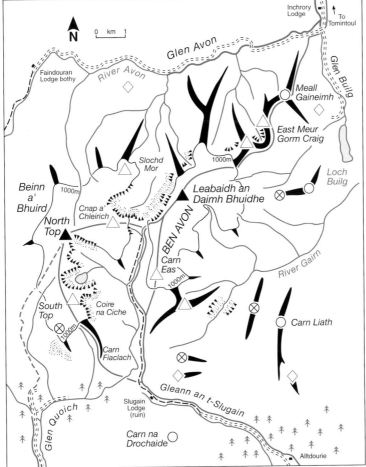

Ben Avon from the Garbh Choire of Beinn a' Bhuird

BEN AVON; *from the river name, probably Gaelic athfhionn, meaning the bright one*
**Leabaidh an Daimh Bhuidhe;** 1171m; (OS Sheets 36 and 43; NJ132018); M17; *bed of the yellow stag*

One of the most unusual mountains in Scotland because of the many strange granite tors along its skyline, Ben Avon is also one of the biggest in terms of its area of high ground, being a vast plateau stretching 12km from Glen Quoich in the south-west to Inchrory in Glen Avon far to the north-east. It is the most easterly mountain of the main Cairngorms range, and the most prominent of them when seen from lower Aberdeenshire or Banffshire.

Ben Avon can be reached from three points – Inchrory in Glen Avon to the north, Corndavon Lodge high up the River Gairn to the east, and Invercauld Bridge near Braemar to the south. All these routes are long, and the use of a bike along the estate roads will save some time and shorten walking distances.

The Invercauld Bridge route, which is probably the most frequently used, starts from the A93 road a few kilometres east of Braemar. Turn up the public road to Keiloch where there is a pay and display car park. Continue for 5.5km along the estate road past Alltdourie into Gleann an t-Slugain, and onwards by the bulldozed track past the ruins of Slugain Lodge to reach Glen Quoich. The path continues up the east side of this glen passing the huge boulder of Clach a' Chleirich. From there it is an easy climb up the narrowing grassy glen to the col at 970m called The Sneck, where a fine view opens out to the north into the wild corrie of Slochd Mor. Climb east up slopes of gravel and turf to the plateau of Ben Avon, and then go 1.5km north-east across the level tundra to the large summit tor, Leabaidh an Daimh Bhuidhe, whose top is reached by an easy scramble. (16km; 850m; 5h).

To vary the return route, keep high along the plateau on the east side of Glen Quoich, going south to Carn Eas (1089m), then descend south-west into Glen Quoich to rejoin the path 3km north of the ruined lodge in Gleann an t-Slugain.

The northern approach is from Tomintoul. Cars should be left 1km beyond the village at the Queen's View car park at NJ165176 and the old road along the east side of Glen Avon is followed for 12.5km past Inchrory Lodge to a point shortly before the Linn of Avon. From there a footpath goes south uphill past Carn Fiaclach to end at a height of 850m at the col west of Meall Gaineimh at the north-eastern corner of the vast tor-studded plateau of Ben Avon. Finally, the route goes south-west across this undulating plateau for another 5km to the summit. (20.5km; 870m; 6h). The return will take just as long, so obviously this is an expedition which will be greatly helped by cycling up Glen Avon to the foot of the mountain. Map on page 129.

**Beinn Bhreac;** 931m; (OS Sheets 36 and 43; NO058971); M249; *speckled hill*
**Beinn a' Chaorainn;** 1083m; (OS Sheets 36 and 43; NJ045013); M58; *hill of the rowan*

These two hills occupy a large area of high ground on the east side of Glen Derry with the flat expanse of the Moine Bhealaidh between them, a featureless plateau at about 850m. Seen from Derry Lodge or Luibeg, Beinn Bhreac stands out above the Old Caledonian pine wood of Derry, a broad heathery hill speckled with grey scree that obviously gives its Gaelic name. Beinn a' Chaorainn is a conical stony hill rising at the head of Glen Derry, just above the Lairig an Laoigh pass, towards which its western slopes drop steeply in broken crags.

The National Trust for Scotland pay and display car park at Linn of Dee (NO064898) is the starting point for this walk, as well as for others to the mountains round Glen Derry and the southern end of the Lairig Ghru. Gain an estate road by a path through the woods, or from its start just to the east, and follow this for 5km to Derry Lodge. From there head north-east uphill through the trees and over heather slopes, keeping above the boggy ground to the 673m col between Meall an Lundain and Beinn Bhreac. This point can also be reached by staying on the main path for 1.5km to a highpoint in the trees at NO045949 where a vague path may be found leading to the col. Climb north on heath to the summit of Beinn Bhreac. (10km; 590m 3h 10min).

Continue north-west then north across the grassy, peaty plateau of the Moine Bhealaidh. Stay near the watershed as this gives the driest ground. After 4km it becomes firmer and the going is easy on heath, gravel and stones up the broad ridge to Beinn a' Chaorainn. (15km; 820m; 4h 50min).

The easiest return to Derry Lodge goes south-west for 1.5km, then steeply down to the summit of the Lairig an Laoigh at 740m. There is a fine view northwards through the pass to the distant Barns of Bynack. Follow the path south down Glen Derry, where the Glas Allt Mor may be difficult to cross if it is in spate. In this state the uphill detour is considerable. Continue for 3km to just beyond the first trees where the path forks; either go right and cross the Derry Burn by a footbridge then go down the west side of the burn through the Old Caledonian pine wood, or go left and follow the higher path on the line of the track reinstated by the National Trust for Scotland. It may be better to go up Glen Derry to the summit of the Lairig an Laoigh at the start of the day and climb Beinn a' Chaorainn first. The 4km high-level walk south across the Moine Bhealaidh gives splendid views beyond the pine woods of the Dubh-Ghleann and Glen Quoich to Lochnagar. Map on page 132.

Since the National Trust for Scotland became owners of the Mar Lodge Estate in 1995, there has been a steady and welcome replacement of the estate tracks beyond Derry Lodge and elsewhere, with footpaths. However, bikes can be used as far as Derry Lodge (30mins) and this results in a significant time saving, especially on the longer rounds.

BEINN BHREAC

BEINN A'
CHAORAINN

131

Bynack More (left) and Beinn a' Chaorainn from the slopes of Derry Cairngorm above Glen Derry

*Adam Watson*

**Carn a' Mhaim;** 1037m; (OS Sheets 36 and 43; NN994952); M95; *cairn of the large rounded hill*
**Ben Macdui;** 1309m; (OS Sheets 36 and 43; NN989989); M2; *MacDuff's hill*
**Derry Cairngorm;** 1155m; (OS Sheets 36 and 43; NO017980); M20; *blue peak of the (oak) thicket*

The central group of the Cairngorms, lying between the defiles of the Lairig Ghru and the Lairig an Laoigh, has as its highest point the great dome of Ben Macdui. From it two long high ridges thrust southwards separated by Glen Luibeg. The eastern ridge includes Derry Cairngorm and ends above the woods of Glen Derry; the western one is Carn a' Mhaim, whose crest, one of the narrowest of Cairngorm ridges, is joined to Ben Macdui by a high col.

These three mountains can all be climbed from the Linn of Dee via Derry Lodge, either singly or together. The latter is a long day, which can be made easier by cycling to Derry Lodge (30mins).

Start from the National Trust for Scotland pay and display car park at Linn of Dee (NO 064898) and gain the estate road by a path through the woods, or from its start just to the east, and follow this for 5km to Derry Lodge. Cross the Derry Burn by a footbridge north of the lodge and go west by the path along the north side of the Luibeg Burn for 3km through splendid scattered native pines to the Robbers' Copse, where the Lairig Ghru and Glen Luibeg paths diverge. The direct route to Ben Macdui itself goes north along the path beside the Luibeg Burn and up the Sron Riach ridge. (15km; 950m; 5h)

The route to Carn a' Mhaim crosses the Luibeg Bridge upstream of boulder debris: evidence of the power of the flood which carried away the earlier bridge. In dry conditions it may be possible to ford the burn to short-cut the loop over the bridge. From the bridge, boggy ground leads back left beside a deer fence to a gate, drier ground and a good path, which is soon left to climb a path up the south-east ridge of Carn a' Mhaim. There is a slight drop between its two boulder-clad tops, of which the north-west one is the summit. (11.5km; 700m; 3h 50min).

Continuing to Ben Macdui, go north-west along the narrow ridge, crossing several rocky knobs and small tors until after 2km a wide col is reached at 800m. Beyond it climb the steep side of Ben Macdui up the broad shoulder south-east of Allt Clach nan Taillear (*the tailors' burn*) to reach the flatter summit dome and the huge cairn at its highest point. (16km; 1210m; 5h 40min).

CARN A' MHAIM

BEN MACDUI

DERRY
    CAIRNGORM

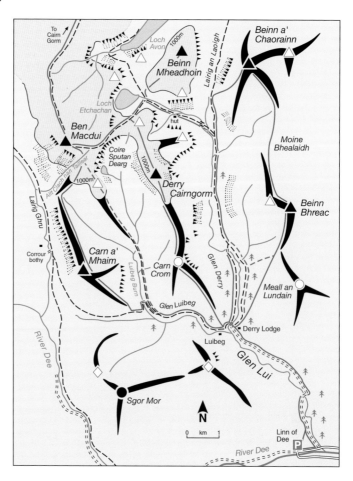

Carn a' Mhaim (left) and Ben Macdui from the south

Adam Watson

Descend 1km east to the edge of Coire Sputan Dearg and then north-east down the ridge along its edge to the col which forms the watershed between the Luibeg Burn and Loch Etchachan. This is an excellent point from which to appreciate the grandeur of the central Cairngorms, with their deep glaciated hollows, granite slabs, snow beds, streams and lochs.

From the col contour south-east round the side of Creagan a' Choire Etchachan (1108m) and descend a little to reach the saddle on its south side. Then go south-east up the boulder-strewn cone of Derry Cairngorm. (21km; 1350m; 7h). Continue down the broad ridge, keeping slightly on its east side above Glen Derry, and climb 50m to Carn Crom. From there descend south-east to the Derry woods and the road back to the Linn of Dee. See p134 for the northern approach to Ben Macdui.

Derry Cairngorm from Beinn Mheadhoin

Douglas Scott

Standing at the highest point on the northern edge of the central Cairngorms massif, Cairn Gorm itself is very prominent from Speyside. Its rounded summit rises above the bowl of Coire Cas, with the narrow Coire na Ciste to the north-east, and the fine Coire an t-Sneachda and Coire an Lochain, the Northern Corries, to the south-west.

Access provided by the ski road into Coire Cas makes Cairn Gorm one of the easiest and most climbed of all Munros. Although the funicular might seem a quick way to the summit of Cairn Gorm the top area is closed and there is no access to the summit or surrounding high plateau from there.

For the simple ascent of Cairn Gorm from the Coire Cas car park, climb steeply east for a short distance to the broad ridge of Sron an Aonaich. Go up the ridge alongside the snow fences to the hemispherical dome of the Ptarmigan restaurant, and continue for a further 1km south to the top of Cairn Gorm. (3km; 620m; 1h 50min).

There are several possibilities for continuing the day's walk rather than returning directly by the route of ascent. Descend 500m west by gravelly slopes to the broad col at the head of Coire Cas. From there a quick return to the car park may be made down the Fiacaill a' Choire Chais, the bounding ridge of Coire Cas, in little more than half an hour. Alternatively, continue south then south-west following a worn path across the plateau, along the rim of Coire an t-Sneachda and over Stob Coire an t-Sneachda (1176m) to the next col.

Climb from this col for 500m to Cairn Lochan (1215m), a fine summit right on the edge of the vertical cliffs of Coire an Lochain. The high-level circuit of the Northern Corries can be continued by going west along the edge of the corrie past spectacular cliff scenery and descending north-west then north down the ridge separating Coire an Lochain from the Allt Creag an Leth-choin. Finally, follow the path north-east below the corries back to the car park.

CAIRN GORM

Ben Macdui can also be climbed from the direction of Cairn Gorm, and this is probably the most popular route. The Coire Cas car park is considerably nearer to Ben Macdui than the Linn of Dee, and also much higher. However, this route goes for several kilometres across a high and exposed plateau and cannot be recommended in bad weather. Follow the route described above to the col between Stob Coire an t-Sneachda and Cairn Lochan and from there go south-west along a path which leads to Lochan Buidhe at the lowest point of the plateau. Continue south-south-east for another 2km, keeping just west of the rounded spine of the plateau to reach the summit of Ben Macdui. (From Coire Cas, 9.5km; 930m; 3h 40min.).

134

The south side of Cairn Gorm above Loch Avon

*Donald Bennet*

Coire an Lochain in spring

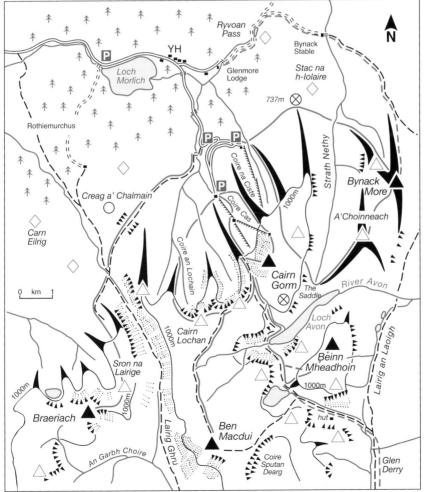

CAIRN GORM

Beinn Mheadhoin (right) above Loch Avon

**Beinn Mheadhoin;** 1182m; (OS Sheet 36; NJ024017); M13; *middle hill*

Beinn Mheadhoin lies on the east side of the central Cairngorms, separated from Ben Macdui by the hollow of Loch Etchachan, and from Cairn Gorm by the deep trough holding Loch Avon. It is a rather inaccessible mountain, in the centre of the massif as its name implies, and not easily seen from either Deeside or Speyside. There is a particularly fine view of the mountain from the northern approach to Ben Macdui, with the granite tors along its summit ridge giving it a distinctive appearance.

The nearest approach is from the car park at the foot of Coire Cas on Cairn Gorm, and the route from there involves first crossing the plateau south-west of Cairn Gorm and descending to Loch Avon before climbing Beinn Mheadhoin itself. There is a good deal of up and downhill effort and in winter the route is a serious one, calling for mountaineering experience.

From the Coire Cas car park ascend the Fiacaill a' Choire Chais ridge on the south-west side of the corrie to reach the plateau 500m west of Cairn Gorm. From there descend south down the wide upper bowl of Coire Raibert and follow a rough path steeply down the east side of the stream to reach Loch Avon.

This is the 'heart of the Cairngorms' and the Loch Avon basin is a magnificent place, ringed by precipitous slopes and high crags with the streams at its upper end cascading from the plateau down granite slabs in a profusion of white torrents. Continue round the head of Loch Avon where the crossing of the Feith Buidhe may be difficult, particularly if it is swollen by meltwater. There are also stepping stones at the head of the loch, though paddling across the sands may end up being the best option.

Pass below the Shelter Stone and the great cliffs of The Sticil and Carn Etchachan, then climb south-east up a slanting path towards the hollow containing Loch Etchachan. Either continue to the far end of this loch to ascend the good path up the shoulder and reach the south-west top of Beinn Mheadhoin (1163m), or break off earlier and head more directly up to this top. The broad crest leads past several granite tors 'The Barns of Beinn Mheadhoin' to reach the largest of these, which forms the summit. A short scramble from the north-east with an exposed move gains the top. (9km; 960m; 3h 40min). Return the same way with a further 410m of ascent from Loch Avon.

A longer alternative is from the Linn of Dee via Derry Lodge, made easier by cycling as far as the Lodge (30mins). Continue up the glen for 6km to a fork in the paths then follow the path over a bridge at NO032995 to climb north-west up Coire Etchachan past the Hutchison Memorial Hut to reach Loch Etchachan where the path of the above route leads to the top. (17km; 860m; 5h 20min). See maps on pages 132 and 135.

Bynack More from Beinn a' Chaorainn

**Bynack More;** 1090m; (OS Sheet 36; NJ042063); M54; *possibly means large cap*

Bynack More forms the north-eastern outpost of the central Cairngorms, separated from Cairn Gorm by Strath Nethy. When seen from Nethybridge or other nearby viewpoints in Strathspey it appears as a shapely pointed mountain rising above the dark pinewoods of Abernethy, rather isolated from the rest of the Cairngorms.

Two interesting and popular direct routes to Bynack More start from the car park at the foot of Coire na Ciste, off the Cairn Gorm access road. They cross generally rough and fairly demanding terrain and can be combined to give a good traverse of the mountain.

The lower route heads east across the heather-clad hillside below Coire Laogh Mor for 1.5km to the col just south of Pt.737m. Descend steeply east to Strath Nethy, cross the river and climb the north-west ridge of Bynack Beg (970m). Continue south-east across boulders and granite outcrops to the upper slopes of Bynack More. (6km; 790m; 2h 40min).

The higher route climbs the ridge flanking Coire na Ciste on its east side to reach the flat col between Cairn Gorm and its north-east top, Cnap Coire na Spreidhe (1150m). Descend south-east down steep slopes to reach The Saddle at the head of Strath Nethy. Continue north-east over A' Choinneach (1016m) to a grassy plateau leading to the upper slopes of Bynack More. On the ridge crest above are the granite tors of the Little Barns, and beyond them, 40m down on the east side at NJ045058, are the Barns of Bynack. They are impressive granite castles, well worth the short diversion required to visit them before going on to the summit. (9.5km; 960m; 3h 50min).

The traditional approach to Bynack More is from Loch Morlich through the Ryvoan Pass, and it is possible to drive to Glenmore Lodge and start from there. Continue on foot through Ryvoan Pass past An Lochan Uaine and 500m further take the track going east to Bynack Stable. Cross the River Nethy and climb south-east over the lower shoulder of Bynack More towards the Lairig an Laoigh. Follow the path for 3km almost to its highest point and then bear south up the north ridge to the summit. (10km; 750m; 3h 30min). Map on page 135.

A Little Barn of Bynack

Braeriach from Ben Macdui

**Braeriach;** 1296m; (OS Sheets 36 and 43; NN953999); M3; *the brindled upland*

Mighty Braeriach forms a high peninsula of the Cairngorm plateau, joined to Cairn Toul around the rim of An Garbh Choire. When seen from the vicinity of Aviemore, it appears as the western half of the plateau, lying to the right of the cleft of the Lairig Ghru, its northern slopes scalloped by three graceful corries. The hidden south-east face of the mountain is even more impressive, for on that side the precipices of Coire Bhrochain drop from the summit sheer into the depths of An Garbh Choire.

Although the mountain can be climbed from Gleann Einich or Glen Feshie, the usual route is from the road to Coire Cas on Cairn Gorm. Start from the Sugar Bowl car park near the edge of the trees at NH985074 and descend south along a good path to a footbridge over the Allt Mor. Cross this stream and continue south then south-west along a path high on the opposite bank.

The path leads south-west to the prominent notch of the Chalamain Gap and through this little gorge. Continue south-west downhill to reach the Lairig Ghru path and cross the stream. To the south-west a path leads up the hillside to the broad base of the Sron na Lairige ridge which is climbed for 400m, steeply at first, then less so. A line along the east edge of this ridge gives some striking views down into the Lairig Ghru. Traverse the gravelly tundra of the crest over the summit of Sron na Lairige (1184m), then descend south to a wide col and finally climb 140m, south-west at first to reach the cliff-top of Coire Bhrochain, and finally west along the edge of the corrie to the summit. (10.5km; 1000m; 4h).

The cairn stands on the brink of the 200m granite cliffs of Coire Bhrochain, and looks out across the great amphitheatre of An Garbh Choire to Cairn Toul and Sgor an Lochain Uaine, with between them the high hanging corrie holding the Lochan Uaine. To the south-west the plateau stretches for many kilometres, gradually dropping towards the Moine Mhor.

The alternative route by Gleann Einich is 11km from Whitewell, the nearest point on a public road, but the first 7km can be biked. The combination of cycling makes this a faster, but less adventurous route. Starting from Whitewell, follow the rough estate road up Gleann Einich, possibly by bike, as far as the Beanaidh Bheag, the stream which flows down to Gleann Einich from the northern corries of Braeriach. Cross the stream, possibly difficult if in spate, and go up its south side, gradually diverging from it and bearing south-east towards the foot of the ridge between Coire an Lochain and Coire Ruadh. This ridge gives a fine, but perfectly easy route up to the plateau of Braeriach, and finally a walk of 600m across this boulder-strewn expanse leads to the summit. (11km; 1000m; 4h 10min).

Braeriach from the Baird & Barrie cairn near Whitewell at the foot of Gleann Einich

The route from Glen Feshie is 14km long. The going is good on paths and across the smooth expanse of the Moine Mhor, but most of it is at high altitude which calls for accurate navigation in bad weather, and may be slow going in winter. Start from the car park 1km north of Achlean farm and follow the path which starts near the farm and goes east up the north side of Coire Fhearnagan to pass just south of Carn Ban Mor. Descend south-east along the path and across the grassy tundra of the Moine Mhor to Loch nan Cnapan. From there climb north-east up long featureless slopes to Carn na Criche (1265m) and finally go for 2km across the plateau, crossing the infant River Dee, to reach Braeriach. (14km; 1130m; 5h). Maps on pages 135 and 145.

BRAERIACH

Ben Macdui from Braeriach

Cairn Toul and Sgor an Lochain Uaine from Braeriach

*Donald Bennet*

**The Devil's Point;** 1004m; (OS Sheets 36 and 43; NN976951); M130;
*from bod an deamhain, the demon's penis*
**Cairn Toul;** 1291m; (OS Sheets 36 and 43; NN963972); M4; *hill of the barn*
**Sgor an Lochain Uaine;** 1258m; (OS Sheets 36 and 43; NN954976); M5;
*peak of the little green loch*

THE DEVIL'S
POINT

CAIRN TOUL

SGOR AN
LOCHAIN UAINE

The west side of the deep glen of the Lairig Ghru is dominated by the plateau of Braeriach which curves round the huge amphitheatre of An Garbh Choire before continuing southwards over the shapely peaks of Sgor an Lochain Uaine (The Angel's Peak) and Cairn Toul, whose corries hang high above the glen. South from Cairn Toul a broad ridge drops to the col at the head of Coire Odhar before thrusting outward to The Devil's Point. This remarkable feature is a spur truncated by the streams of ice which once flowed down Glen Dee and Glen Geusachan, and it now forms a prominent landmark with its great headland of granite slabs.

The southern approach to Cairn Toul and The Devil's Point starts from the National Trust for Scotland Linn of Dee pay and display car park and follows the same route as that for Ben Macdui and its neighbours, (see p132), namely the estate road up Glen Derry to Derry Lodge, followed by the path up Glen Luibeg to the Luibeg bridge. From there the way to Cairn Toul continues west, rising slightly round the southern base of Carn a' Mhaim along a path which is initially boggy, then well-constructed. After a few more kilometres the path descends to join the path in Glen Dee leading north to the Lairig Ghru.

Continue only about 200m beyond the path junction and then diverge west to cross the River Dee by a bridge and reach Corrour Bothy. A path leads west behind the bothy up the grassy banks of the Allt a' Choire Odhair and reaches the col at the head of this corrie by steep zigzags. Any potentially dangerous snow slope is probably best avoided on the south side of the corrie. From the col an easy walk heading south-east then east leads to The Devil's Point. (15.5km; 700m; 4h 40min). It is a splendid viewpoint above the River Dee.

Return to the col from where a broad grassy ridge rises north along the top of the shallow bowl of Coire Odhar, then swings north-west, becoming stonier, to Stob Coire an t-Saighdeir (1213m). Beyond this Top the ridge curves round Coire an t-Saighdeir, dropping slightly and then climbing more steeply up the last 120m to the summit of Cairn Toul. (18.5km; 1120m; 6h).

Sgor an Lochain Uaine is less than 1 km north-west along the ridge round the edge of the corrie of the Lochan Uaine, and it is a fine point from which to appreciate the grandeur of An Garbh Choire and its wild recesses. (19.5km; 1230m; 6h 30min). Returning along the outward route to the head of Coire Odhar, it is possible to traverse below Cairn Toul at about 1150m and thus avoid some climbing.

Adam Watson

Sgor an Lochain Uaine

Alan O'Brien

Cairn Toul from the River Dee near Corrour bothy

**CAIRN TOUL**

The alternative approach to Cairn Toul and Sgor an Lochain Uaine is from the car park 1km north of Achlean farm in Glen Feshie. Follow the path eastwards from the farm into the Nature Reserve and up the north side of Coire Fhearnagan. Continue past Carn Ban Mor and downhill south-eastwards across the Moine Mhor as far as Loch nan Cnapan. From there bear east-north-east across the plateau and up the long slopes to Sgor an Lochain Uaine on the edge of An Garbh Choire. (11km; 1100m; 4h 20min). Descend south-east for 120m to the col and climb the west ridge of Cairn Toul. (12km; 1250m; 4h 50min). This may be a shorter route than the one from the Linn of Dee, but it goes for a long way over high ground where accurate navigation is essential in bad visibility and conditions may be very severe in winter storms.

**142**

**SGOR AN LOCHAIN UAINE**

The Devil's Point

Hamish Brown

**Monadh Mor;** 1113m; (OS Sheet 43; NN938942); M40; *big hill*
**Beinn Bhrotain;** 1157m; (OS Sheet 43; NN954923); M19; *hill of Brotan (the mastiff)*

These two rounded mountains are the southern extension of the great Braeriach – Cairn Toul plateau, separated from it by Glen Geusachan, and separated by the River Eidart from the Glen Feshie hills. Their grandest features are the steep faces overlooking Glen Geusachan which form a discontinuous line of slabby buttresses and gullies extending for several kilometres. At its north end, Monadh Mor merges into the undulating expanse of the Moine Mhor, the great moss, a vast lonely basin of peat and tundra which sweeps across from below Braeriach and Cairn Toul to the edge of Glen Feshie.

Two routes are possible for the ascent of these two mountains, from the Linn of Dee and from the public road near Achlean farm in Glen Feshie. The first of these is longer, but it is possible to use a bike for a long way up the Dee to the foot of the mountains.

From the National Trust for Scotland Linn of Dee pay and display car park, walk or bike up the right of way along the north side of the River Dee to reach White Bridge. Continue along the south-west side of the river, past the Chest of Dee where it plunges over granite slabs, to reach a conifer plantation and some ruined shielings. After Whitebridge the road is rough and stony, but it is still bikeable. However, it then deteriorates and ends 500m north of the crossing of the Allt Garbh at the boundary of the National Nature Reserve.

Continue up the west bank of the River Dee, choosing the best line possible over rough ground, and enter Glen Geusachan. This remote and enchanting glen is flanked by the imposing slabs of Beinn Bhrotain and The Devil's Point, and directly ahead rises Monadh Mor with a prominent plaque of slabs below and to the right of its summit. These may be outflanked on the right by following the stream up to Loch nan Stuirteag, and then heading south to the summit of Monadh Mor. (18km; 750m; 5h 20min). From the summit cairn continue south for 750m to another cairn and south-east by grassy tundra for 1km, then descend quite steeply to reach a narrow col at 975m. From there climb south-east up a boulder-strewn slope for about 750m to reach the summit of Beinn Bhrotain. (21km; 930m; 6h 20min).

The return journey goes south-east over or round Carn Cloich-mhuilinn (942m) and down its long east ridge. Before the glen is reached, drop down on the south flank of this ridge to avoid slabs and boulders at its foot, and reach the road back to the Linn of Dee at the conifer plantation. This route, in reverse, is an alternative to the ascent route described above and is

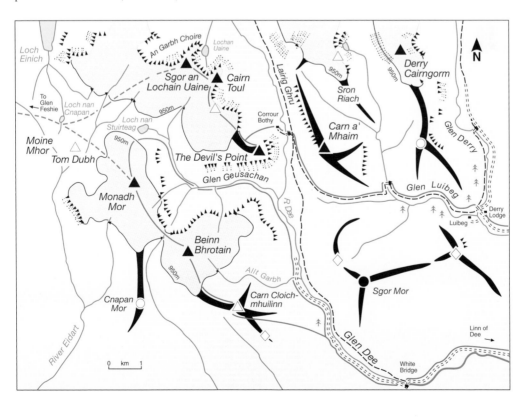

Beinn Bhrotain from the north across the head of Glen Geusachan

## MONADH MOR

probably an easier option, being shorter and avoiding the very rough going in Glen Geusachan.

The route from Achlean in Glen Feshie is the same as that for Braeriach and Sgor an Lochain Uaine as far as Loch nan Cnapan at the centre of the Moine Mhor. From there bear south-east across the Allt Luineag, or go a little further south to climb the knoll of Tom Dubh (918m), which is a very remote and insignificant Top of Monadh Mor. The rounded north ridge of Monadh Mor is reached and followed to the summit. (11km; 950m; 4h 10min). Continue to Beinn Bhrotain as above (14km; 1130m; 5h 10min), and return by the same route.

## BEINN BHROTAIN

Beinn Bhrotain and Monadh Mor from Ben Macdui

# The Glen Feshie Hills

To the west of the main Cairngorms, the Moine Mhor, or great moss, extends for several kilometres, forming a wide shallow basin whose western edge is the long broad ridge of the Glen Feshie hills. This range rises in the north above the pine woods of Loch an Eilein and Inshriach, and extends 18km south to end above the desolate upper reaches of Glen Feshie. At its north end the ridge is well defined, particularly on its east side which falls steeply into Gleann Einich in a long series of buttresses and gullies from Sgoran Dubh Mor and Sgor Gaoith down to Loch Einich. Further south the crest broadens out to form a plateau between Coire Garbhlach and the River Eidart in the south-west corner of the Moine Mhor.

From the west and south-west the range of the Glen Feshie hills looks like a long level plateau, the dips between the summits being almost imperceptible, and on that side the deep gash of Coire Garbhlach is the most prominent feature. This corrie is particularly interesting because it lies on the geological boundary between the granites of the Cairngorms and the schistose rocks into which they have been intruded. The north side of the corrie is of granite with screes and an inner recess formed by the typically bowl-shaped Fionnar Choire. The rest of the corrie is cut in schist, with a narrow V-shaped entrance, steeply sloping stream bed with waterfalls and a botanical variety derived from lime-rich soils.

Despite its length and height, there are only two Munros in this group: Sgor Gaoith and Mullach Clach a' Bhlair. Both are usually climbed from Glen Feshie, where a narrow public road goes south from Feshiebridge up the east side of the glen to end at Achlean farm. Cars should be parked 1km north of the farm.

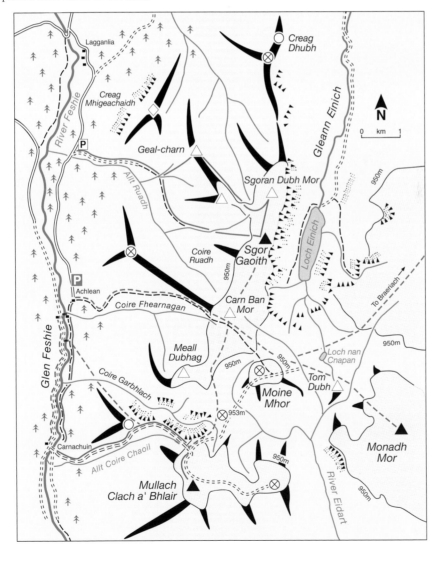

Mullach Clach a' Bhlair across the River Feshie

**Mullach Clach a' Bhlair;** 1019m; (OS Sheets 35, 36 and 43; NN882927); M114;
*summit of the stone of the plain*

Between the indentations of Coire Mharconaich on the east and Coire Garbhlach on the west, the Moine Mhor extends south in a featureless tableland of grassy tundra. At its southwest corner it rises slightly to reach its highest point at the summit of Mullach Clach a' Bhlair.

The ascent starts from a car park 1km before the road up the east side of Glen Feshie ends at Achlean. Walk to the road end (the summit dome can be seen ahead above Coire Garbhlach) and go left around the farm to follow the main path along the floor of the glen. About 500m beyond Achlean, go through a gate and ford the Allt Fhearnagan; normally straightforward. Pass a footbridge across the River Feshie over to the right and a kilometre beyond this drop down and cross the Allt Garbhlach; the sides have been washed away but the crossing is straightforward when the water is low.

Continue on a good path crossing over a track right then left and after a kilometre drop down onto a track leading to the river again. The track has been washed away here and a short section of path links with the track beyond which is followed to a cross roads. The track on the right used to link with a bridge and the surfaced estate road up the west side of Glen Feshie at Carnachuin. Together with the lower bridge across the River Feshie this used to provide an alternative high water route avoiding the Allt Fhearnagan and Allt Garbhlach crossings, however the bridge was washed away in 2009 and a replacement may not happen.

Turn left and follow the track uphill above the Allt Coire Chaoil to pass just below a saddle overlooking Coire Garbhlach where a detour is worthwhile for the view into the corrie. Continue uphill to the plateau and take the right fork in the track which curves across the tundra to pass within 300m of the summit of Mullach Clach a' Bhlair where a rough path leads to the small cairn marking the top (10.5km; 700m; 3h 30min).

Return the same way, although from the base of the narrow ridge overlooking Coire Garbhlach it is worth making the detour out to Meall nan Sleac for the view. It is possible to descend Meall nan Sleac's north-west ridge to cross higher up the Allt Garbhlach then cut across to rejoin the path about 1km from Achlean. However, despite being shorter the going is tiring on rough and pathless ground.

Another option is to return to the track junction then follow the track north-east across the Moine Mhor, first to Pt.953m then to Pt.957m; Meall Dubhag and Tom Dubh are outlying Tops to the west and east here. Leave the track and follow a path north-west onto the shoulder just below the summit of Carn Ban Mor, also a Top (16.5km; 850m; 5h). Descend the engineered path down Coire Fhearnagan to Achlean. This second option opens up the possibility of including Sgor Gaoith to the north, since this sits temptingly close to Carn Ban Mor and can be climbed by an easy 5km there and back route taking 1h 25min.

The summit of Sgor Gaoith, looking towards the northern corries of Braeriach

## Sgor Gaoith; 1118m; (OS Sheets 36 and 43; NN903989); M35; *windy peak*

This is the highest point of the ridge which extends from Carn Ban Mor to Sgoran Dubh along the west side of the Einich glacial trough. The east side of this ridge between Sgor Gaoith and Sgoran Dubh Mor forms a magnificent series of ridges, buttresses and gullies above Loch Einich in a wild and remote setting, but the approach from that side of the mountain is long and there are no easy routes up the steep slopes above the loch. The usual routes of ascent are from Glen Feshie, either up Coire Ruadh or from Achlean.

The Coire Ruadh route starts from the road on the east side of Glen Feshie at NN852013 near the bridge over the Allt Ruadh and goes east along a forest track which leads uphill through pine trees high on the north side of the narrow glen of the Allt Ruadh. After crossing a small side stream and passing through the last scattered pines, the path continues south-east across the open hillside. Cross the Allt Coire na Cloiche and follow the path south, at first over rather boggy ground, but as it climbs gradually round the lower slopes of Meall Tionail the path gives good going. Eventually it reaches the Allt a' Chrom-alltain and disappears in rough heathery ground. Cross to the south side of the burn and ascend east for 400m up fairly steep slopes of heather, grass and heath, becoming easier as height is gained, to reach the ridge. The summit of Sgor Gaoith is finely situated on a little promontory at the edge of the crags which plunge for 500m to Loch Einich far below. (7km; 830m; 3h).

The descent may be varied by going north for 1.5km along the ridge across the col at 1053m and climbing to Sgoran Dubh Mor (1111m). From the rocks of its summit tor descend south-west for 750m to reach the start of a broad ridge which projects north-west. Follow the undulating crest of this ridge for 2.5km over Meall Buidhe (976m) to the stony summit of Geal-charn (920m), once classified as a Munro but now just a Top. Descend south-west down slopes of boulders, grass and heather to rejoin the Coire Ruadh path above the tree-line.

The alternative route starts from the car park 1km north of Achlean at the end of the public road on the east side of Glen Feshie. Follow the path east from Achlean to Coire Fhearnagan and continue along the path which climbs gradually across the north side of the corrie to reach the plateau just south of Carn Ban Mor (1052m). Leave the path near its highest point to climb this hill. From there go north for 2km across the grassy plateau, dropping only slightly to the col between Carn Ban Mor and Sgor Gaoith. (7.5km; 820m; 3h 10min). Although it is slightly longer, this route gives easier walking than the previous one, being on a good path and short grass the whole way.

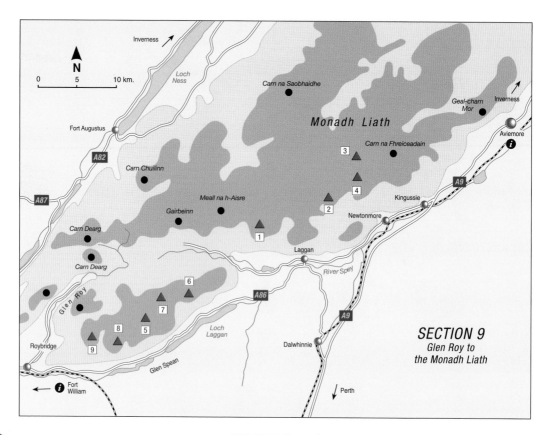

## SECTION 9

### Glen Roy to the Monadh Liath

---

ⓘ VisitScotland Information Centres

**Fort William**; 15 High Street, Fort William PH33 6DH, (01397 701801), open Jan–Dec
**Aviemore**; Grampian Road, Aviemore, PH22 1RH, (01479 810930), open Jan–Dec

The approach to Geal Charn at the head of the Piper's Burn

## Geal Charn; 926m; (OS Sheet 35; NN561988); M260; *white hill*

Geal Charn is the westernmost of the Monadh Liath Munros, and has all the characteristics of these hills. Its most interesting feature is the eastern corrie, with its high lochan above Glen Markie and the ice-carved window in its innermost recess forming a steep-sided col between Geal Charn and its neighbour Beinn Sgiath. To the north-west the hill merges into the vast undulating moorland typical of the western Monadh Liath.

The approach to the hill is along the narrow public road west from Laggan Bridge on the north side of the River Spey. This road leads towards the Corrieyairack Pass, a famous right of way and military road of the 18th century.

One route to Geal Charn is up Glen Markie from the Spey Dam, there being a track up the glen for 5km on the east side of the Markie Burn. On-going works at the dam may complicate parking. There is restricted room for cars south of the bridge over the Spey or at the bends 300m south. Follow the track to where a grassy track goes left to the Markie Burn at a point opposite the foot of the Piper's Burn, the stream descending from Lochan a' Choire. Cross over and follow the burn into the lip of the corrie, where paths veer north-east to the broad ridge west of Bruach nam Biodag. If the Markie Burn is in spate there is a bridge across the burn further north at (NN588983). Go south-west round the corrie rim to the huge, finely built summit cairn. (9km; 650m; 2h 50min).

Geal Charn can also be climbed from Garva Bridge. Follow a track north for 750m to cross a steel bridge, then aim for the footbridge over the Feith Talagain at NN525959 from where a path continues on the south-east side of the stream. At the end of the path cross the Allt Coire nan Dearcag and climb the heathery south-west ridge of Geal Charn direct to its summit. (7.5km; 630m; 2h 50min).

GEAL CHARN

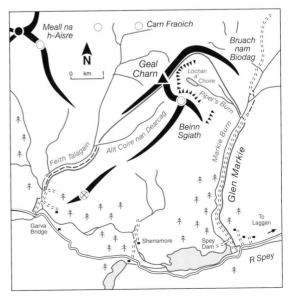

Carn Dearg from the head of Gleann Ballach

**Carn Dearg;** 945m; (OS Sheet 35; NH635024); M225; *red hill*
**Carn Sgulain;** 920m; (OS Sheet 35; NH684058); M271; *hill of the basket*
**A' Chailleach;** 930m; (OS Sheet 35; NH681042); M251; *the old woman*

CARN DEARG

CARN SGULAIN

A' CHAILLEACH

The Monadh Liath range is an extensive undulating plateau on the north-west side of Strathspey above Newtonmore and Kingussie. This desolate high moorland extends a long way north and west across the headwaters of the River Findhorn towards Loch Ness, but it is mainly the south-east corner near Glen Banchor that holds any interest for the hillwalker and cross-country skier, for it is there that the four Munros of the Monadh Liath are to be found. Of the four, Geal Charn on the west side of Glen Markie is described separately.

From a viewpoint on the A9 road opposite Newtonmore, Carn Dearg and A' Chailleach show up clearly, for they have well-defined summits and prominent east-facing corries. Carn Sgulain on the other hand is rather inconspicuous, appearing as little more than a high point on the horizon, almost hidden behind A' Chailleach. The starting point for all three hills is 2km from Newtonmore where the narrow road up Glen Banchor changes from being public to private at the foot of the Allt a' Chaorainn.

The route to Carn Dearg continues up Glen Banchor for 1km and then takes the rough track north-west up the Allt Fionndrigh. Go for 3.5km up this track, then cross the stream by a footbridge and follow a path south-west through a gap onto the broad ridge above Gleann Ballach. Continue north-west up rough heathery ground on the north-east side of the glen for 2km towards its head. Cross the stream and climb an easy grassy slope above broken rocks (appearing from below as a slanting shelf) in a south-westerly direction to reach the broad ridge of Carn Dearg 500m north of the top. A short climb up this ridge leads to the summit cairn which is perched right on the edge of the east face. (9km; 650m; 3h 10min). This face is mostly steep grass and broken crags, and a shorter and more direct route might possibly be made up it from Gleann Ballach, but it is too steep to be regarded as a sensible route of ascent.

The way to A' Chailleach and Carn Sgulain goes up the estate road on the east side of the Allt a' Chaorainn. Leave this track at a small cairn at NH692015 to cross a footbridge which is not visible from the track and climb north-west to a small stalkers' hut on the slopes of A' Chailleach. Keep on uphill in the same direction to reach the broad south-west ridge of the hill and climb this easy-angled slope to the big cairn at the edge of the east corrie. (6km; 630m; 2h 30min).

Descend north into the deep little glen of the Allt Cuil na Caillich and climb rough tussocky grass and peat to Carn Sgulain. A line of fence posts across its flat summit makes finding the cairn easy, even in thick weather. (8km; 750m; 3h 10min).

On the Monadh Liath plateau between A' Chailleach and Carn Sgulain

The most direct return to Glen Banchor goes down the Allt Cuil na Caillich, on its right (south) bank at the point where it cascades down through crags to join the Allt a' Chaorainn. Cross this stream to its east side where there is a path down the glen.

It is quite possible to traverse these three hills in a single expedition. The plateau between Carn Dearg and Carn Sgulain is an undulating featureless expanse of grass, moss and stones, giving fairly easy walking past a series of minor tops and cairns and at least one tiny lochan. Others may appear in wet weather. Even in the thickest weather there are no route finding problems, for a line of fence posts goes all the way from Carn Ban, 750m north of Carn Dearg, to Carn Sgulain. The distance for the complete circuit, starting at and returning to the road at the foot of the Allt a' Chaorainn, is 24km.

CARN DEARG

A' CHAILLEACH

CARN SGULAIN

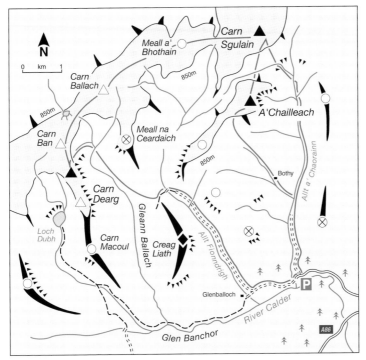

The approach to Coire Ardair and Creag Meagaidh

**CREAG MEAGAIDH**

**Creag Meagaidh;** 1128m; (OS Sheets 34 and 42; NN418875); M30; *possibly bogland rock*

This is a massive and magnificent mountain with a rather complicated topography. From its high central plateau several steep-sided ridges radiate outwards enclosing some very fine corries, of which Coire Ardair to the north-east is the most impressive. This corrie provides a superb approach to the mountain, home to some of the best winter climbing in Scotland. It is quite difficult to get a good impression of Creag Meagaidh from the south, for example from the A86 road along the side of Loch Laggan, and one has to walk up towards Coire Ardair from Aberarder to appreciate the grandeur of the mountain. There are two walking routes to the summit which can be combined into a traverse to make a fine mountain expedition. However, as the finishing point of this traverse is 8km from the start, two cars would be useful.

The first route starts at the Creag Meagaidh National Nature Reserve car park at Aberarder, half way along Loch Laggan. Follow the new path past Aberarder climbing high above the Allt Coire Ardair through scattered birches. In about 3km the corrie bears round towards the west and as the path passes through the highest group of birch trees the great cliffs of Coire Ardair come into view. Continue along the path on the north side of the burn to the outlet of Lochan a' Choire which is in a superb situation under the cliffs. Bear west, climbing across grassy slopes, then up screes and boulders into the steepening, narrow upper corrie leading to the obvious bealach called The Window, which separates Creag Meagaidh from Stob Poite Coire Ardair. From there climb south up steep slopes to reach the grassy plateau of Creag Meagaidh and cross this, south at first, then south-west past a massive cairn on the rim overlooking Lochan Uaine, then finally west to the summit. (9km; 880m; 3h 30min).

The return to Aberarder may be made by the same route, but a better way is to go east across the plateau, first to the Top of Puist Coire Ardair (1071m), then along the narrower ridge with good views on the left down into Coire Ardair. Bear north-east and cross the flat-topped dome of Sron a' Choire (1001m) and descend east down a wide shallow corrie towards Aberarder. There is a footbridge across the Allt Coire Ardair at NN476875 from where a path leads back to the car park.

The second route starts at Moy, 2km west of the west end of Loch Laggan and 8km from Aberarder. Leave the A86 road on the west side of the Moy Burn and cross gradually rising moorland to the steep craggy ground below Creag na Cailliche. Climb easily through the broken rocks and reach the crest of the long ridge on which there is a substantial stone wall. This ridge is followed all the way to the summit. (6km; 880m; 2h 50min).

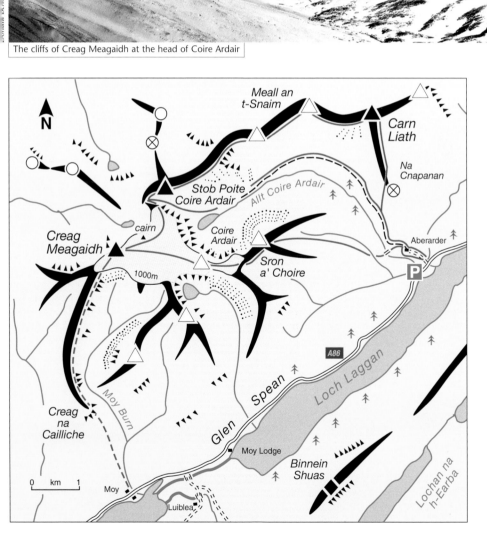

The cliffs of Creag Meagaidh at the head of Coire Ardair

CREAG
MEAGAIDH

Meall an
t-Snaim

Carn
Liath

Na
Cnapanan

Stob Poite
Coire Ardair

Allt Coire Ardair

Aberarder

Creag
Meagaidh

cairn

Coire
Ardair

Sron
a' Choire

1000m

A86

Loch Laggan

Creag
na
Cailliche

Moy Burn

Glen Spean

Lochan na
h-Earba

Moy Lodge

Binnein
Shuas

0    km    1

Moy

Luiblea

N

Stob Poite Coire Ardair

CARN LIATH

STOB POITE
COIRE ARDAIR

**Carn Liath;** 1006m; (OS Sheet 34; NN472903); M126; *grey hill*
**Stob Poite Coire Ardair;** 1054m; (OS Sheet 34; NN428888); M76; *peak of the pot of the high corrie*

These two mountains lie on a long, fairly level ridge which forms the north bounding wall of Coire Ardair. They are best combined in an east to west traverse which gives a fine high-level walk with excellent views of the impressive cliffs at the head of the corrie. The traverse can in fact be easily combined with the ascent of Creag Meagaidh.

The best starting point is the Creag Meagaidh National Nature Reserve car park at Aberarder, half way along Loch Laggan. Follow the new path past Aberarder climbing high above the Allt Coire Ardair towards the shoulder of Na Cnapanan. At the edge of a dense area of birches a cairned path goes off right, beside a ditch. Zigzag up through the trees to open ground and the col between Na Cnapanan and the broad south ridge of Carn Liath. Ascend the ridge over grass, heather and patches of boulders to the flat stony summit of Carn Liath. (4km; 750m; 2h).

Turn west and follow the broad mossy ridge, gradually descending to a col and climbing again to the Top of Meall an t-Snaim (969m). Continuing west-south-west, the ridge narrows and drops to a well-defined notch followed by a short steep rise to the next Top, Sron Coire a' Chriochairein (993m). Thereafter the ridge continues around the edge of this corrie to the level crest of Stob Poite Coire Ardair, the summit cairn being at the west end. (8.5km; 980m; 3h 30min).

Continue south-west down the smooth ridge for barely 500m and then turn south to descend more steeply to the narrow bealach called The Window. From that point Creag Meagaidh can be climbed and the return to Aberarder by the ridge over Puist Coire Ardair and Sron a' Choire as described on the previous page completes an excellent traverse.

Alternatively, the direct return from The Window to Aberarder goes east from the bealach, at first quite steeply down a bouldery corrie, then more easily across grassy slopes above Lochan a' Choire to reach the path down Coire Ardair to Aberarder. Map on page 153.

**Beinn a' Chaorainn;** 1052m; (OS Sheets 34 and 41; NN386851); M79; *hill of the rowan*
**Beinn Teallach;** 915m; (OS Sheets 34 and 41; NN361859); M282; *forge hill*

These two mountains are north of the Laggan Dam on opposite sides of the glen of the Allt a' Chaorainn. Beinn a' Chaorainn, which is much the finer of the two, has three tops of similar height on its north-south spine, the highest being the middle one. Its western slope is uniformly steep, but not rocky, while the eastern face is steep and rocky, forming

Beinn a' Chaorainn from Luiblea in Glen Spean

the fine Coire na h-Uamha. The eastern and northern corries of Beinn Teallach are steep, but to the south and west there are long, easy-angled slopes which give the mountain an uninteresting appearance from those directions.

Start the traverse from the A86 road at Roughburn, 500m north-east of the Laggan Dam, there is limited parking at the entrance to a forestry track with an additional layby 200m further east. Follow the forest track north-west for 1km to a junction where a road runs across the hill-side in both directions. Turn west for 100m to a firebreak which is marked by a small cairn. Walk north up the firebreak to reach the upper deer fence where there is a stile. From the stile climb north-west then north-east, passing Meall Clachaig to the west, then ascend north-east up easy slopes to the South Top (1049m), and thence 500m along the broad ridge to the summit of Beinn a' Chaorainn. (4.5km; 800m; 2h 20min). In winter the summit ridge is often heavily corniced above Coire na h-Uamha, so keep well away from its edge in bad visibility.

Continue along the narrower ridge to the North Top (1045m) and from there descend north-west to the bealach at the source of the Allt a' Chaorainn, which is marked by a large cairn. Climb the slopes to the west to reach the north-east ridge of Beinn Teallach, which is followed to the top. The cairned summit is the north-east-erly of two bumps some 100m apart. (9km; 1100m; 3h 50min).

The descent from Beinn Teallach goes south down wide, easy-angled grassy slopes towards the northern edge of the forest. Bear left lower down to look for a suitable place to cross the Allt a' Chaorainn, which may be difficult when in spate. In such conditions cross the stream high up and continue along its east bank. Otherwise follow the path on the west bank and cross lower down. Continue down to the flat ground where the stream joins the Feith Shiol and reach the forest road which leads back to Roughburn.

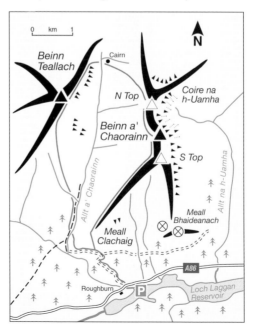

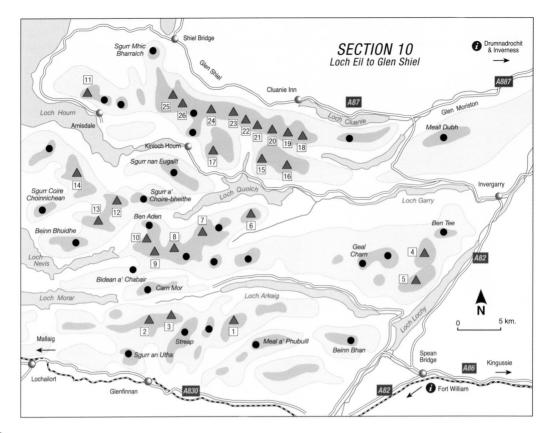

# SECTION 10

## Loch Eil to Glen Shiel

**ⓘ VisitScotland Information Centres**
**Fort William**; 15 High Street, Fort William, PH33 6DH, (01397 701801), open Jan–Dec
**Drumnadrochit**; The Car Park, Drumnadrochit, IV63 6TX, (01456 459086), open Jan–Dec

The summit of Gulvain from the South Top

**Gulvain;** 987m; (OS Sheets 40 and 41; NN003876); M161;
*from Gaelic, either gaorr, filth or gaoir, noise*

Gulvain, or Gaor Bheinn, is a secretive mountain hidden in the jumble of hills between Loch Eil and Loch Arkaig. It is rather a remote peak and, apart from the route described below, it is quite complicated to reach. Gleann Fionnlighe gives a pleasant approach, much of which can be biked, with the mountain in view ahead for a long way.

Start from the A830 Fort William to Mallaig road almost opposite the A861 Strontian junction. Cross the old bridge to follow the rough track up the east side of the Fionn Lighe river. After 2km this track crosses to the west bank, passes Uachan cottage and continues for another 4km to a bridge over the Allt a' Choire Reidh. On the other side of this stream the ascent of the south-west ridge of Gulvain begins. It is unrelentingly and uniformly steep and as long as the crags on the west of the ridge are avoided, it is a straightforward ascent with a path all the way.

A craggy knoll (855m) is passed, and beyond it the South Top, the trig point, is reached just over 500m further on. Continue north from there, dropping 60m to a saddle, and climb the narrowing ridge to the summit, which has a substantial cairn. (10.5km; 1050m; 4h 10min). Return by the route of ascent.

Other approaches to Gulvain are much longer and less attractive scenically. From the east end of Loch Arkaig a long and rather uninteresting walk up the rough track in Glen Mallie leads to the north-east ridge of the mountain. It is, however, possible to bike for a long way up the glen. From Strathan at the head of Loch Arkaig one has to cross an intermediate ridge and drop down into Gleann Camgharaidh before reaching the steep flank of the north ridge, all across rough trackless terrain.

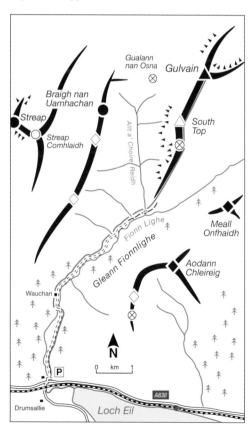

Streap (left) and Sgurr Thuilm (right) from Fraoch Bheinn

**Sgurr Thuilm;** 963m; (OS Sheet 40; NM939879); M193; *peak of the rounded hillock*
**Sgurr nan Coireachan;** 956m; (OS Sheet 40; NM903880); M206; *peak of the corries*

SGURR NAN
    COIREACHAN

SGURR THUILM

These Munros are just two of many peaks in an area of unusually rough and steep complexity, belonging in character if not geographically to the Rough Bounds of Knoydart further north-west. The approach from Glenfinnan has been rather tamed by afforestation and road-making, but it is still the easiest and most popular route.

The National Trust for Scotland's Visitor Centre at Glenfinnan is worth a visit, and it is interesting to recall that after his defeat at Culloden the fugitive Prince Charles spent a night out on Sgurr Thuilm, an unlikely Munroist.

Park in a small car park just off the A830 on the road to Glen Finnan Lodge and go up the estate road on the west side of the River Finnan. The road passes under the spectacular railway viaduct and continues well up the glen which is extensively tree-planted. In 3.5km pass below the lodge and reach Corryhully bothy <www.glenfinnanestate.co.uk> beside the river. It is possible to bike to this point and save on the stated timings.

Continue along the track northwards for 1km and then take the stalkers' path on the left up onto the south ridge of Sgurr nan Coireachan. This ridge becomes quite steep-sided and rocky and the best way is along the crest of Sgurr a' Choire Riabhaich (852m), followed by a short descent before the final climb to Sgurr nan Coireachan. (8km; 990m; 3h 30min).

Traverse east along the rough undulating ridge over the tops of Meall an Tarmachain and Beinn Gharbh. There are many ups and downs over rocky knolls and across peaty hollows, but the best way is always near the crest where a line of fence posts shows the way even in the worst of weather. Eventually the ridge rises over the last knoll (858m) and leads to Sgurr Thuilm. (12km; 1400m; 5h 30mins).

Descend the long easy ridge of Druim Coire a' Beithe south then south-west to reach Glen Finnan 1.5km above Corryhully bothy.

An alternative and equally fine traverse of these two mountains can be made from the head of Loch Arkaig, and this route takes one into the wild corries on the south side of Glen Pean. The narrow public road along Loch Arkaig ends 1km from Strathan, and although there is a good car park it can get busy. Continue west along the private road past Strathan and up Glen Pean for 1km, cross the River Pean by the footbridge at NM968906 and climb directly up the long north-east ridge of Sgurr Thuilm. (6km; 960m; 3h 10min).

Coming back from Sgurr nan Coireachan, return to Meall an Tarmachain and descend the

The ridge from Sgurr Thuilm to Sgurr nan Coireachan seen from the north

ridge on the west side of Coire nan Gall to Glen Pean at the Pean bothy. In spate conditions the crossing of the River Pean may be difficult or impossible, as also may be the crossing of the Allt a' Chaorainn at the foot of Sgurr Thuilm's north-east ridge, so this traverse should probably not be attempted when the burns are full.

SGURR THUILM

SGURR NAN
COIREACHAN

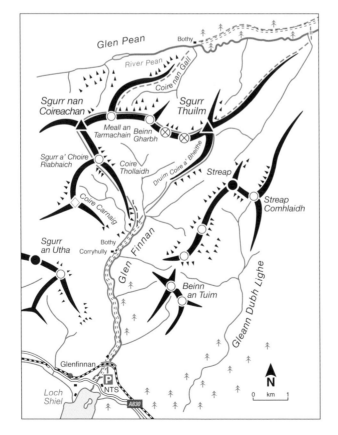

Sron a' Choire Ghairbh from the head of Gleann Cia-aig

**Sron a' Choire Ghairbh;** 937m; (OS Sheet 34; NN222945); M239; *nose of the rough corrie*
**Meall na Teanga;** 918m; (OS Sheet 34; NN220925); M276; *hill of the tongue*

SRON A' CHOIRE
GHAIRBH

MEALL NA
TEANGA

These two bold, deeply-corried hills are situated west of Loch Lochy in the Great Glen, and dominate the view across that loch from the A82 north of Spean Bridge. The two hills are usually climbed together, and the traverse can be started either at Kilfinnan near Laggan Locks at the north-east end of Loch Lochy, or at the foot of Gleann Cia-aig near the east end of Loch Arkaig, and this route is described first. The times and distances for both routes are approximately the same.

The Gleann Cia-aig start is from the narrow B8005 near the east end of Loch Arkaig. From the car park at the Eas Chia-aig waterfalls follow the signposted 'Forest Walk' footpath up through the trees until it reaches a forestry road (about 15 minutes). Turn north and follow this road, then a path up Gleann Cia-aig to a footbridge across the Abhainn Chia-aig at NN188929. Beyond this point the footpath shown on the 1:50,000 map is indeterminate, so continue up the Allt Cam Bhealaich to reach another path just west of the Cam Bhealach. From this pass (615m) climb the stalkers' path which zigzags northwards up the steep grassy hillside (further than the 1:50,000 map shows) to end almost on the ridge. Finally an easy walk for a few hundred metres north-west along this broad mossy ridge leads to Sron a' Choire Ghairbh. (9.5km; 880m; 3h 40min).

Having returned down the stalkers' path to the Cam Bhealach, climb south below the screes of Meall Dubh to gain the col between that hill and Meall na Teanga. A steep climb leads to the crest of Meall na Teanga at a small cairn, and the larger summitcairn is a few hundred metres further south. (11.5km; 1200m; 4h 40min). It is a splendid viewpoint.

To return to Gleann Cia-aig, descend south-west from Meall na Teanga and climb a narrow rocky ridge to Meall Coire Lochain, whose top is reached suddenly at the edge of a broad grassy ridge. Go west along the crest of the Meall Odhar crags and descend easy grassy slopes, still heading west, to reach the path in Gleann Cia-aig 3.5km north of the day's starting point.

For the northern approach, drive along the narrow public road from Laggan Swing Bridge to Kilfinnan and park just before reaching the farm. Continue on foot or by bike along the forestry road and after 1km take the upper track at a junction. 3km further take a path which climbs west through the forest and emerges into a steep-sided glen leading to the Cam Bhealach, where the preceding route is joined. Unless a complete traverse to Gleann Cia-aig is intended, it is

*Richard Wood*

Meall na Teanga and Meall Coire Lochain from Sron a' Choire Ghairbh

necessary to return from Meall na Teanga to the Cam Bhealach on the way back to Kilfinnan.

The best expedition on these hills is the complete traverse from Kilfinnan to Gleann Cia-aig or vice versa, but this requires the assistance of a friendly car driver. If doing this traverse from north to south, the descent from Meall Coire Lochain can be shortened by going south-west down the broad ridge of Leac Chorrach and over the 585m knoll to the edge of the Clunes Forest at NN200890. At that point it is easy to reach the end of a forest road which leads down to Clunes.

SRON A' CHOIRE
GHAIRBH

MEALL NA
TEANGA

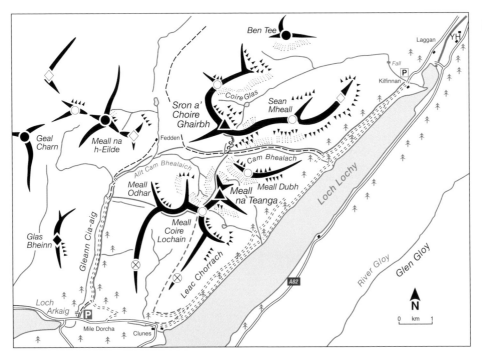

Gairich from the west

## Gairich; 919m; (OS Sheet 33; NN025995); M272; *roaring*

Gairich is the isolated peak which looks fine in the view westwards along Loch Garry. It stands boldly on the south side of Loch Quoich, with lonely Glen Kingie to its south, and it gives an easier day's climb than most peaks in the wild westland.

The starting point for the ascent is the dam at the east end of Loch Quoich, reached along the road which branches off the A87 beside Loch Garry and goes west past Tomdoun to Kinloch Hourn. From the south end of the dam follow a path south and after 600m join the old stalkers' path whose first few hundred metres are now submerged by the raised water level of Loch Quoich.

Take this path south over wet and boggy moor, dropping a little to the upper limit of the Glen Kingie forest where another stalkers' path leads west up the Druim na Geid Salaich. This path, which is becoming increasingly eroded by many hillwalkers, continues along the broad ridge over Bac nam Foid. The lochan shown on the map does not seem to exist, except in the wettest of weather.

At the foot of the final steep rise to Gairich an old stalkers' path goes leftwards onto the south face. However, ignore it and keep further right up the hillwalker's path on the crest of the ridge, which gives a steep climb with some rocky steps. The spacious summit dome has a large cairn. (8km; 730m; 3h).

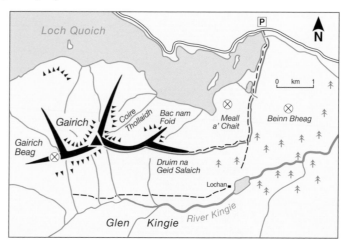

Sgurr Mor and Sgurr na Ciche from Loch Quoich

**Sgurr Mor;** 1003m; (OS Sheets 33 and 40; NM965980); M132; *big peak*

This mountain is part of the long ridge from Gairich to Sgurr na Ciche which runs from east to west on the south side of Loch Quoich. South of Sgurr Mor is desolate Glen Kingie, and one has to pass through the hills on the south side of this glen to find the nearest point of access at the western end of Loch Arkaig. On its north side Sgurr Mor is protected by Loch Quoich, and access from that direction is only possible if you have a boat or canoe in which to cross the loch.

The approach is from the end of the public road at the west end of Loch Arkaig, where there is limited space for cars, so please park considerately. This is the nearest point of access by car to all the mountains west and north-west from Loch Arkaig towards Loch Nevis and Knoydart.

Walk up the estate road almost to Glendessarry Lodge and take the stalkers' path north up to the pass at about 360m between Druim a' Chuirn and Fraoch Bheinn. Follow the path down into Glen Kingie, and at the point where it goes north-east towards Kinbreack bothy descend north-west to cross the River Kingie. From there the most direct ascent of Sgurr Mor is straight uphill, but it is a long steep pull of 500m to the col south-east of the peak, from where a stalkers' path leads up the ridge to the summit. (9km; 1100m; 3h 50min).

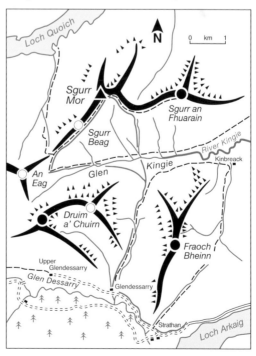

In spate conditions it may be necessary to go up Glen Kingie to find a safe crossing place. Once across the river, follow the stalkers' path on its north side westwards, then back north-east up to the col (662m) between An Eag and Sgurr Beag. Continue along the ridge over Sgurr Beag (890m), down to the col at 750m and steeply up again to Sgurr Mor. (10km; 1240m; 4h 20min).

The return should be made by the ascent route, depending on the state of the River Kingie. If conditions are suitable, a good circular traverse is up the stalkers' path over Sgurr Beag to Sgurr Mor, and down from the col to its south-east.

Sgurr na Ciche from Garbh Chioch Mhor

Jim Renny

**Sgurr nan Coireachan;** 953m; (OS Sheets 33 and 40; NM933958); M213; *peak of the corries*
**Garbh Chioch Mhor;** 1013m; (OS Sheets 33 and 40; NM909961); M116; *big rough place of the breast*
**Sgurr na Ciche;** 1040m; (OS Sheets 33 and 40; NM902966); M92; *peak of the breast*

SGURR NAN
COIREACHAN

GARBH CHIOCH
MHOR

SGURR NA CICHE

These grand mountains are in the heart of the remote wilderness between Loch Arkaig, Loch Quoich and Loch Nevis, an area which fully lives up to the name and character of The Rough Bounds of Knoydart. The day spent traversing them will be a memorable one, and one calling for Munro experience for it is a serious expedition in rugged terrain.

The approach is from the end of the public road at the west end of Loch Arkaig, where there is limited space for cars, so please park considerately. Walk or bike up the estate road, which is the right of way to Inverie, on the north side of Glen Dessarry <www.glendessarry.info> provides information on the estate and access. From Upper Glendessarry continue along a path which climbs the hillside behind the house for a short way, then contours along the glen just above the forest.

There is a footbridge across the Allt Coire nan Uth, well hidden from sight and not shown on the OS map, which is essential if the burn is in spate. The bridge lies below the line of the main path on the line of the fence along the top edge of the forest. This point can also be reached along the forest road past A' Chuil bothy on the south side of Glen Dessarry, across the river by a bridge at NM930934, which can be biked to in 1hr, then uphill through the forest by a rough path.

Once across the Allt Coire nan Uth leave the main path to go north up the steep grassy ridge to Sgurr nan Coireachan, an unrelenting 750m climb. There is a path on the right side which crosses left higher up, dodging around the small outcrops of rock. The ridge narrows and is edged with crags near the top, but there is no difficulty if the crest is followed. (8km; 900m; 3h 20min). 1hr 30mins from the bridge where bikes can be left.

The continuation of the traverse goes west then south-west steeply down to the Bealach Coire nan Gall (733m). Westwards from there, the Garbh Chiochs live up to their name, for the ridge is a succession of rocky outcrops, and Coire nan Gall on its north side is one of the roughest corries outside Skye. However, navigation along the ridge is simplified by there being a well-built dry stone dyke to follow. Garbh Chioch Bheag (968m) is passed on the way to the summit of Garbh Chioch Mhor. (l0.5km; 1200m; 4h 20min).

Keep following the wall west then north-west down to the col (845m) below Sgurr na Ciche. This pass is called Feadan na Ciche, the 'whistle' or 'chanter' of the peak; an apt description on a windy day. The upper slopes of Sgurr na Ciche are a maze of crags and boulders, and a faint path zigzags up this very rough ground initially following a shelf left, then up the right side of a boulder slope to reach the summit ridge just east of the top. (11.5km; 1400m; 5h).

To return to Loch Arkaig, retrace the route to the Feadan na Ciche col and descend the narrow boulder-filled gully south-west towards Coire na Ciche. At the foot of this gully (about

Sgurr na Ciche from Druim a' Ghoirtein

166

SGURR NAN
COIREACHAN

GARBH CHIOCH
MHOR

SGURR NA CICHE

670m) traverse south-east almost horizontally below the crags of Garbh Chioch Mhor and descend grassy slopes by the right side of a streamway to the Bealach an Lagain Duibh, the pass at the head of Glen Dessarry; an ATV (all-terrain-vehicle) track which cuts across this slope from the right is joined and this crosses the stream further down. Follow the path (often very wet and muddy) down this glen, then along the top edge of the forest to rejoin the outward route at the Allt Coire nan Uth. If bikes have been left at the bridge at NM930934, then a boggy ATV track offers an alternative route through the forest from where it starts.

Another well trodden route to Sgurr na Ciche, particularly for those staying at Sourlies bothy, is the Druim a' Ghoirtein, the ridge which rises direct from the head of Loch Nevis to the summit. Those embarking on this test of stamina during the stalking season might be best staying on the crest of this ridge to avoid the deer gathering grounds of Coire na Ciche.

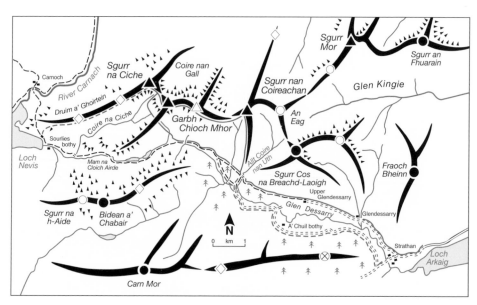

Beinn Sgritheall across Loch Hourn

**Beinn Sgritheall;** 974m; (OS Sheet 33; NG836127); M183; *probably scree hill*

This grand peak, rising steeply above Loch Hourn, dominates the Glenelg peninsula and gives fine views across the loch to Knoydart, and beyond the Sound of Sleat to Rum and Eigg. Its best features, the northern ridges and corries, are remote and hidden, and the southern flanks above Loch Hourn present a steep expanse of rotten crags and scree slopes that would deter the bravest. However, Beinn Sgritheall proves to be one of the best of the solitary Munros.

The approach by road from Glen Shiel goes over the Mam Ratagan and through Glenelg village to reach the north shore of Loch Hourn. The ascent from there starts near Creag Ruadh, 2.5km before reaching Arnisdale village. The hillside above the road gives rough going at first, but head north-west through the open woods of Coille Mhialairigh where traces of a path lead steeply up through the trees to a little lochan on the level crest of the west ridge. From there turn east and climb this ridge direct to the summit of Beinn Sgritheall. (3km; 930m; 2h 20min).

To make a traverse of the mountain, continue east along the summit ridge over the 900m east top and go down steep stony slopes to the Bealach Arnasdail. Descend steeply south-west from the bealach beside the stream on a rough path and follow this as it heads down and across to the west end of Arnisdale village, reaching the road just west of a bridge over a stream. A signpost indicates this point if you are starting the ascent from the village.

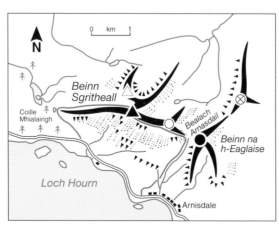

Looking up the south-east ridge of Meall Buidhe from Sgurr Sgeithe

## The Knoydart Hills

The next three mountains to be described are in the Knoydart peninsula, one of the wildest and least accessible parts of the Scottish Highlands. No roads penetrate into this area so access is either by boat or on foot along one of the rights of way which go west from the nearest road ends. Because of the remoteness of Knoydart, the climbing of its mountains entails finding overnight accommodation in the area. Wild camping is possible almost anywhere except near the habitations at Inverie, Barrisdale and Camusrory.

Access by boat: 1) Via Knoydart Sea Bridge who operate regular crossings from Mallaig/ Inverie (as well as charters) with times accommodating to walkers. <www.knoydartferry.com>. Tel. 01687 462916. 2) Via the mail boat from Mallaig to Inverie on Mondays, Wednesdays and Fridays. Contact Bruce Watt Cruises, The Pier, Mallaig, Inverness-shire. Tel. 01687-462233, <www.knoydart-ferry.co.uk>.

Access on foot: 1) From the road end at the head of Loch Arkaig by the right of way through Glen Dessarry to the head of Loch Nevis, and then over the Mam Meadail to Inverie. A good day's walk. 2) From the road end at Kinloch Hourn (pay car park and seasonal cafe) by the right of way along Loch Hourn to Barrisdale (10.7km; 3-3hr 30mins) and then over the Mam Barrisdale to Inverie. This is shorter and easier than the previous route.

Accommodation is available in and around Inverie village <www.knoydart-foundation.com> and <www.road-to-the-isles.org.uk/knoydart.html> and there is a bothy and campsite. There is accommodation at Barrisdale, including a bothy and campsite, Tel. 01764 684946 <www.baris-dale.com>. There is also a small open bothy at Sourlies at the head of Loch Nevis.

---

**Luinne Bheinn;** 939m; (OS Sheet 33; NG869008); M234; *probably swelling hill*
**Meall Buidhe;** 946m; (OS Sheets 33 and 40; NG849990); M222; *yellow hill*

---

LUINNE BHEINN

MEALL BUIDHE

These two fine and complex mountains are in the heart of Knoydart. Luinne Bheinn overlooks Loch Hourn and Meall Buidhe to its south rises a short distance north of the head of Loch Nevis, and between them is Coire Odhair, a remarkably rough corrie of glaciated slabs and an impressive example of the effects of the last ice age. The extremely wild nature of these two mountains and the corries surrounding them well justify the name given to this corner of the Highlands - the Rough Bounds of Knoydart.

The traverse of the two mountains can be made either from Barrisdale on Loch Hourn or from Inverie on Loch Nevis. Inverie is more easily reached by a regular boat service from Mallaig, and accommodation is available in the village, so it is probably the better starting point.

Going clockwise round the traverse, walk from Inverie along the rough road up the Inverie River past Loch an Dubh-Lochain, and up the path to the Mam Barrisdale. From there climb the north-west ridge of Luinne Bheinn. It is tempting to take the obvious path which contours round the right side of the hill but the better route is to break off this line to climb the crest

Luinne Bheinn from Meall Buidhe across the head of Coire Odhair

itself, where there is a rough path, separated by a more level section at 665m. A big cairn is passed before reaching the summit. (12km; 940m; 4h 20min).

The south face of Luinne Bheinn is steep and rocky and it is advisable to continue to the East Top (937m) and descend from there, south-east at first then south-west along the ridge round the head of Coire Odhair. This ridge gives rough going over the knoll of Druim Leac a' Shith and down to the Bealach Ile Coire, from where the narrow north-east ridge of Meall Buidhe leads to its South-east Top (942m). The summit is a short distance further. (16km; 1400m; 6h).

The most direct return to Inverie is down the long west ridge to the foot of Gleann Meadail. Drop down bracken covered slopes before reaching the rocky termination of this ridge to gain the path in Gleann Meadail then the bridge at NM813988 and continue past Druim Bothy to rejoin the main track to Inverie. A path of sorts continues all the way down the ridge but ends up in flat boggy ground, although there are footbridges where the rivers join.

Alternatively, descend the south-east ridge towards Sgurr Sgeithe and go south to the Mam Meadail, where the right of way from Loch Arkaig to Inverie is joined and followed down Gleann Meadail to reach the road to Inverie.

MEALL BUIDHE

LUINNE BHEINN

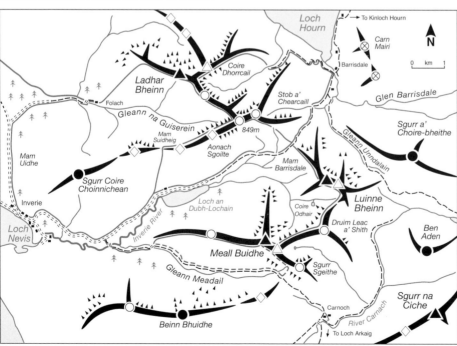

Ladhar Bheinn from Stob a' Chearcaill

**Ladhar Bheinn;** 1020m; (OS Sheet 33; NG824040); M111; *hoof hill*

Ladhar Bheinn rises in the northern part of the Knoydart peninsula, overlooking Loch Hourn. It is one of the finest mountains in Scotland, with narrow rocky ridges and spectacular corries. The summit and fine northern side of the mountain from Coire Dhorrcail down to Li on the side of Loch Hourn is owned by the John Muir Trust, which aims to maintain the wild character of this outstanding area. Restoration of native woodlands on the lower slopes of the mountain and path maintenance has been carried out by the Trust.

The northern circuit of Coire Dhorrcail is the finest traverse of Ladhar Bheinn, but it is rather difficult of access from Inverie, being on the Loch Hourn side of the mountain. From Inverie the direct approach by Gleann na Guiserein is easier, but less interesting. However, a longer route up Gleann an Dubh-Lochain and the Aonach Sgoilte ridge or from the Mam Barrrisdale is finer and includes the traverse along the headwall of Coire Dhorrcail. The ascent by this route and descent by Gleann na Guiserein is the best circuit of the mountain from Inverie.

From Inverie take the track up the Inverie River to Loch an Dubh-Lochain. It is possible to ascend steep slopes here to reach the Mam Suidheig col on the ridge above then follow the fine Aonach Sgoilte ridge to reach Pt.849m above the south-east corner of Coire Dhorrcail. This ridge becomes progressively narrower and at one point is split into two parallel rocky ridges, thereby living up to its name, the split ridge. However, attainting the ridge is not the most pleasant of slopes especially when the bracken is high and perhaps the better route is to continue on the track to the high pass of the Mam Barrisdale. From here climb grassy slopes up the side of Coire a' Phuil and continue up the obvious grassy spur which descends from Stob a' Chearcaill. The upper slopes consist of wet vegetated slabs which should be avoided. The key is a grassy ramp, gained after a short steep step, which slants up left towards the col to the southwest of the peak; from where the summit can be obtained if desired. An easy short ascent southwest gains Pt.849m above the south-east corner of Coire Dhorrcail.

From Pt.849m descend north-west to the Bealach Coire Dhorrcail and traverse over a series of rocky knolls and past the tops of the steep gullies that plunge down to the corrie. Finally, climb to the junction of ridges at the western corner of Coire Dhorrcail and reach the top of Ladhar Bheinn a short distance along the nearly level summit ridge. (12km; 1250m; 4h 50min).

Continue along the summit ridge to the 1010m trig point and descend the grassy ridge of An Diollaid to the shallow bealach at NG811045. Here a useful 'baggers' path descends the slope

The approach to Ladhar Bheinn at the foot of Coire Dhorrcail

steeply south-west towards Folach in lonely Gleann na Guiserein. Cross the bridge and follow a track west, then swing south through the Mam Uidhe pass to return to Inverie.

The northern traverse of Ladhar Bheinn round Coire Dhorrcail is best done from Barrisdale. From there walk up the right of way to Inverie as far as the summit of the Mam Barrisdale and climb north-west towards Stob a' Chearcaill as for the previous route to gain Pt.849m, continuing as described to gain Ladhar Bheinn (7.5km; 1180m, 3h 40min).

Descend the north-east ridge over Stob a' Choire Odhair (960m) and continue down to a more level part of the ridge at about 400m where one should turn south-east and drop down into Coire Dhorrcail to reach the path which leads back to Barrisdale. Map on page 169.

LADHAR BHEINN

Spidean Mialach (left) and Gleouraich from Creag a' Mhaim

**Gleouraich;** 1035m; (OS Sheet 33; NH039053); M97; *roaring noise*
**Spidean Mialach;** 996m; (OS Sheet 33; NH066043); M146; *peak of deer*

GLEOURAICH

SPIDEAN
MIALACH

The road westwards along the north side of Loch Quoich passes close below three fine mountains whose ascents are among the easiest in the Western Highlands. Distances from road to summits are short and stalkers' paths give fast and easy walking onto the high ridges. Gleouraich and Spidean Mialach are separated from Sgurr a' Mhaoraich to the west by the deep trough of Glen Quoich into which the raised waters of Loch Quoich thrust a narrow arm.

These two mountains have two quite distinct aspects, dark rocky corries and steep spurs on their north side, and more gentle grassy slopes to the south. Their traverse is a delightful expedition combining good stalkers' paths and a splendid undulating high-level ridge.

The start is from the road on the north side of Loch Quoich at a point about 4.5km west of the Loch Quoich dam NH029030. A cairn on the west side of the Allt Coire Peitireach marks the start of a fine stalkers' path which climbs to 850m on Gleouraich. This is one of the most impressive of all such paths, particularly high up where it traverses along the edge of the steep-sided south-west ridge, giving a feeling of exposure as one looks down to Loch Quoich hundreds of metres below. Beyond the end of the path, continue up the ridge to its junction with the north ridge, then turn south-east up the crest to the summit of Gleouraich. (3.5km; 830m; 2h 10min).

Spidean Mialach and Gleouraich

Continue along the ridge to Craig Coire na Fiar Bhealaich (1006m). Beyond this Top a stalkers' path zigzags down to the Fiar Bhealaich (740m), and from this col the ascent of Spidean Mialach is straightforward, following the scalloped cliff-edge of three successive corries. (7km; 1150m; 3h 30min).

Descend south-west down easy slopes towards the west side of Loch Fearna. During the stalking season the stalkers' path down the lower part of Coire Mheil is a favourite gathering ground for red deer and can be avoided by climbing over Pt.614m to descend the broad ridge on the east side of the Allt a' Mheil to the road, 1.5km south-east of the starting point.

Sgurr a' Mhaoraich from Sgurr an Doire Leathain

## Sgurr a' Mhaoraich; 1027m; (OS Sheet 33; NG984065); M104; *peak of the shellfish*

Sgurr a' Mhaoraich is an isolated mountain which bulks large in the view up Loch Hourn, although to Loch Quoich it shows only its grassy side. Its hidden northern and western aspects hold vast flanks of dark rock and a complex of ridges and steep corries. However, the ascent is most commonly made from the Kinloch Hourn road on the south side of the mountain.

Leave the road 1km south-west of the bridge which spans the northern extension of Loch Quoich at the start of a stalkers' path (NH010035) where there is limited space for parking. There is additional parking 700m further west and 700m back towards the bridge.

Follow this path north up the Bac nan Canaichean ridge to Sgurr Coire nan Eiricheallach (891m), and a short distance further across a slight dip to its north-west top. There is another drop and then a rather contorted ridge leads to the summit of Sgurr a' Mhaoraich. There are outcrops of rock to either circumvent or scramble over, and at one point iron spikes driven into the rock are evidence of early fence building. (5km; 910m; 2h 40 min).

To continue the traverse, descend the knobbly south ridge of the mountain to Leac nan Gaidhseich and reach the road about 2km west of the starting point via an ATV track which takes the line of a path shown on the map. Rocks on the lower slopes bear much evidence of glacial action. The lower part of Coire nan Eiricheallach has been planted with trees, and the corrie should be avoided.

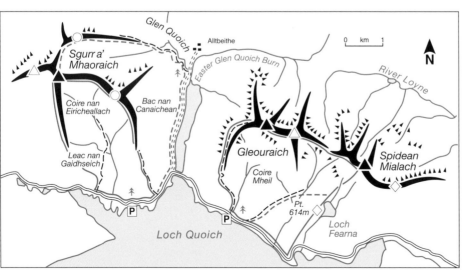

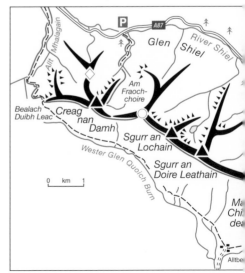

Aonach air Chrith from the west

**Creag a' Mhaim**; 947m; (OS Sheet 33; NH088078); M218; *rock of the large rounded hill*
**Druim Shionnach**; 987m; (OS Sheet 33; NH074085); M160; *ridge of foxes*
**Aonach air Chrith**; 1021m; (OS Sheet 33; NH051083); M109; *ridge of trembling*
**Maol Chinn-dearg**; 981m; (OS Sheet 33; NH032088); M168; *bald red head*

174

CREAG A' MHAIM

DRUIM
   SHIONNACH

AONACH AIR
   CHRITH

MAOL CHINN-
   DEARG

The eastern half of the South Glen Shiel ridge lies to the south of Cluanie Inn across the headwaters of the River Cluanie and gives a good traverse over its four peaks, whether climbed as described below, or as the prelude to the magnificent longer traverse of the whole 14km ridge. Start just east of the inn at the junction of the old road from Cluanie to Tomdoun, and walk up this road for 6km to a point about 1km beyond its highest point. From there a stalkers' path is followed west then north-west virtually all the way the summit of Creag a' Mhaim. (7.5km; 730m; 3h).

A broad grassy ridge leads down to the first col, and on the way up to Druim Shionnach there is one surprisingly narrow section of ridge before the flat summit is reached. (9km; 850m; 3h 30min). Navigation along the ridge is simplified by the very obvious path. An alternative way to reach the east end of the ridge which reduces the road walking is to leave the road 500m after the bridge across the Cluanie and go up the stalkers' path to Loch a' Mhaoil Dhisnich. From there continue up the north ridge of Druim Shionnach. This would involve an out and back ascent of Creag a' Mhaim.

The next 2.5km section of the ridge to Aonach air Chrith is bounded by the slabby crags of Coire an t-Slugain. (11.5km; 1020m; 4h 20min). Beyond, the crest of the ridge is narrower; crags on right side drop steeply into the north-facing corries and on the left bare grassy slopes fall away towards Glen Quoich, but the traverse to Maol Chinn-dearg is perfectly easy. (13.5km; 1180m; 5h).

The descent is down the north-east ridge, the Drum Coire nan Eirecheanach. It is steep at first, but becomes a very pleasant grassy crest with lower down a stalkers' path leading back to the road in Glen Shiel 4km west of the day's starting point.

Sgurr an Lochain

**Sgurr an Doire Leathain;** 1010m; (OS Sheet 33; NH015099); M122; *peak of the broad oak grove*
**Sgurr an Lochain;** 1004m; (OS Sheet 33; NH005104); M131; *peak of the little loch*
**Creag nan Damh;** 918m; (OS Sheet 33; NG983112); M275; *rock of the stags*

The west half of the South Glen Shiel Ridge has two lower summits to cross as well as its three Munros, so this traverse is as long as the eastern section. The views are better, particularly to the south and west where Ladhar Bheinn and Beinn Sgritheall dominate the horizon.

The start is a few hundred metres east of the summit of the A87 road on the watershed between the Shiel and Cluanie rivers. Follow the stalkers' path south across the Allt Coire a' Chuil Droma Bhig, and follow its west branch onto the Druim Tholaidh. Climb up this ridge to reach Sgurr Coire na Feinne. The first Munro, Sgurr an Doire Leathain, is 1.5km north-west along the main ridge with its summit on a grassy spur about 100m north of the ridge. (4.5km; 800m; 2h 20min).

**SGURR AN DOIRE LEATHAIN**

**SGURR AN LOCHAIN**

**CREAG NAN DAMH**

The next corrie is the only north-facing one to hold a lochan, hence the name of the shapely Sgurr an Lochain, the most distinctive peak on the ridge. (6km; 910m; 3h). Sgurr Beag (896m) is the next peak, a smaller one as the name implies, and not a Munro. Drop to the next col, the lowest on the ridge at 729m and climb the last Munro, Creag nan Damh. (9km; 1210m; 4h 10min).

To return to Glen Shiel, two routes are possible. One goes north-east down a steep but quite easy ridge leading to the lower part of Am Fraoch-choire where a stalkers' path is reached at about 400m, leading down to the plantation in Glen Shiel near the site of the 1719 battle. The other route continues west along the main ridge to the Bealach Duibh Leac (725m). From there a vague path descends in zigzags to the Allt Coire Toteil and on its opposite side continues downhill beside the Allt Mhalagain to reach Glen Shiel.

The Saddle from the north-east ridge of Faochag

*Donald Bennet*

**The Saddle;** 1010m; (OS Sheet 33; NG936131); M121
**Sgurr na Sgine;** 946m; (OS Sheet 33; NG946113); M223; *peak of the knife*

THE SADDLE

SGURR NA SGINE

The Saddle combines in one mountain a complex of narrow ridges and deep corries that makes it one of the great Highland hills. With its neighbouring sharp peak Faochag (*the whelk*), it forms the classic view down Glen Shiel from the site of the 1719 battle. Sgurr na Sgine is another fine peak, with a very steep south-east face, but it is hidden behind Faochag in views from Glen Shiel. The traverse of The Saddle by the Forcan Ridge, followed by Sgurr na Sgine and Faochag is one of the best mountain expeditions in Kintail.

Start in Glen Shiel from the A87 road at NG968143, 500m south-east of the old quarry at Achnangart. There is a layby 200m away. A good stalkers' path is followed west to the col between Biod an Fhithich and Meallan Odhar. Continue south then south-west to the foot of the narrow east ridge of The Saddle, the Forcan Ridge. This superb rock ridge involves some exposed scrambling, and a short tricky pitch to descend on the far side of Sgurr na Forcan, but it is not technically difficult. Nervous or inexperienced hillwalkers may prefer the alternative route described below.

The crest of the Forcan Ridge sweeps up, narrowing to a rocky knife-edge above the slabs of Coire Mhalagain before reaching Sgurr na Forcan (963m). Continue west, descending a short steep pitch with good holds and traversing the narrow ridge over the East Top (958m) to the summit cairn on top of a rocky crag. (5km; 1080m; 3h). The OS trig point is about 100m west along a level ridge.

The alternative route avoiding the Forcan Ridge is to traverse below its south flank, following a dry stone dyke across the rough hillside to the little lochan at the Bealach Coire Mhalagain (696m). From there climb north-west on a rising traverse towards The Saddle, aiming for a point a short distance south of the summit to avoid steep ground below the summit itself. Finally, climb north up a steep but easy slope to the trig point.

*Gill Nisbet*

The upper part of the Forcan Ridge of The Saddle

To continue to Sgurr na Sgine, descend this easy route from the trig point to Bealach Coire Mhalagain and climb south to the North-west Top of Sgurr na Sgine (942m). Continue south-east along the rocky ridge to the summit cairn perched right at the edge of the steep south-east face of the mountain. (7.5km; 1330m; 4h).

Return past the North-west Top and continue north then east to Faochag along a narrow crest. Descend the north-east ridge, a continuously steep but otherwise easy route, with steep slopes on both sides, leading down to Glen Shiel 500m up the road from the day's starting point.

The south-east face of Sgurr na Sgine

*Hamish Brown*

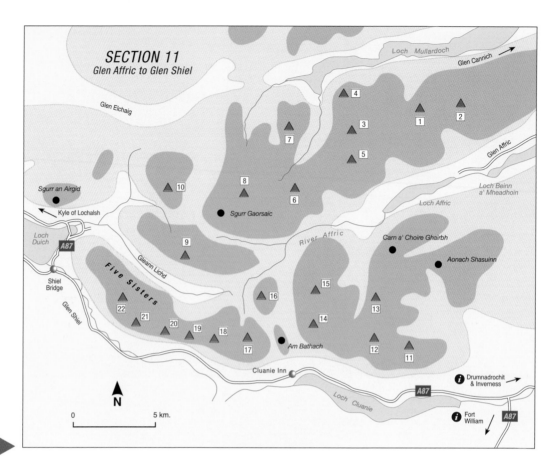

Glen Elchaig

Loch Mullardoch

Glen Cannich

Sgurr an Airgid

Kyle of Lochalsh

Glen Affric

Loch Beinn
a' Mheadhoin

Loch Affric

Sgurr Gaorsaic

River Affric

Carn a' Choire Ghairbh

Aonach Shasuinn

Loch
Duich

A87

Gleann Lichd

Shiel
Bridge

Five Sisters

Glen Shiel

Am Bathach

Cluanie Inn

Drumnadrochit
& Inverness

A87

Fort
William

A87

Loch Cluanie

N

0        5 km.

# SECTION 11

## Glen Affric to Glen Shiel

*i* VisitScotland Information Centres
**Fort William**; 15 High Street, Fort William, PH33 6DH, (01397 701801), open Jan–Dec
**Drumnadrochit**; The Car Park, Drumnadrochit, IV63 6TX, (01456 459086), open Jan–Dec
**Inverness**; Castle Wynd, Inverness, IV2 3BJ, (01463 252401), open Jan–Dec

Looking up the south-east ridge of Tom a' Choinich

**Tom a' Choinich;** 1112m; (OS Sheet 25; NH163273); M41; *hill of the moss*
**Toll Creagach;** 1054m; (OS Sheet 25; NH194283); M77; *rocky hollow*

These two hills are at the eastern end of the long range of mountains on the north side of Glen Affric, a range which stretches 25km from the forested lower reaches of Glen Affric and Cannich westwards to the Glomach chasm above Glen Elchaig. Toll Creagach is a hill of rounded outlines and a fairly level summit ridge 2km long, with the highest point at the east end. Tom a' Choinich has a more distinctive outline with a crescent-shaped ridge enclosing its east corrie. Between the two hills is the Bealach Toll Easa, once a well used crossing between Glen Affric and Glen Cannich.

Although it is possible to climb these hills from Glen Cannich, this way is not recommended as the going on the south side of Loch Mullardoch is very rough. It is better to approach from Glen Affric, leaving the road at the foot of Gleann nam Fiadh near the west end of Loch Beinn a' Mheadhoin. Walk up the track in this glen for 4km and continue along the stalkers' path up the west side of the Allt Toll Easa until fairly level ground is reached. Then go west to reach the foot of the south-east ridge of Tom a' Choinich. As height is gained on this ridge, it becomes quite rocky and narrow and gives a fine route to the summit. (7.5km; 870m; 3h 10min)

Go a short distance from the cairn to the edge of the corrie where the east spur drops steeply. Descend it to the Bealach Toll Easa and climb the west ridge of Toll Creagach to its West Top (951m). Continue north-east along a broad level ridge, then descend very slightly to a col before the easy climb to Toll Creagach. (11km; 1000m; 4h 10min).

Go due south down easy slopes for about 2km and then descend more steeply to Gleann nam Fiadh, which is reached near the end of the track 3km from the road at Loch Beinn a' Mheadhoin.

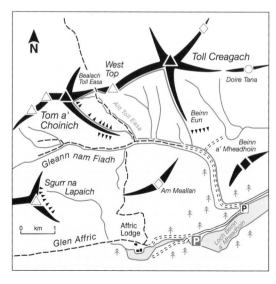

Scott Johnstone

Mam Sodhail and Carn Eige from the ridge to Sgurr na Lapaich

**Carn Eige;** 1183m; (OS Sheet 25; NH123262); M12; *file hill*
**Beinn Fhionnlaidh;** 1005m; (OS Sheet 25; NH115282); M128; *Finlay's hill*
**Mam Sodhail;** 1181m; (OS Sheet 25; NH120253); M14; *hill of the barns*

CARN EIGE

BEINN
FHIONNLAIDH

MAM SODHAIL

Carn Eige and Mam Sodhail, almost identical twins in height and appearance, are the highest mountains north of the Great Glen and dominate the high ground between Glen Affric and Loch Mullardoch. They form a great horseshoe around Gleann nam Fiadh, both having long ridges to the east to enclose this glen. From Carn Eige another important ridge goes north to end at Beinn Fhionnlaidh, a very remote mountain overlooking the head of Loch Mullardoch. The most familiar view of this group is from Glen Affric, from where Sgurr na Lapaich (one of the Tops of Mam Sodhail) is the most prominent peak, projecting far in front of its two higher neighbours. These are not particularly rocky mountains, but their ridges are steep-sided and their corries wild and craggy enough to make this a fine group whose traverse gives a long and serious mountain expedition. Beinn Fhionnlaidh is included as it is more difficult to reach by any other way.

The closest starting point is the car park at the end of the public road in Glen Affric, 1.5km east of Affric Lodge. From there go west along the road on the north side of the loch for 1km and follow the stalkers' path north across the moorland between Sgurr na Lapaich and Am Meallan to reach Gleann nam Fiadh. Go west along the path on the north side of the burn for 2km and uphill towards the lochans in Coire Mhic Fhearchair. From the upper lochan climb north to the Garbh-bhealach and traverse west along the ridge by a stalkers' path, which at one point has been so well constructed as to resemble a flight of stone steps, to reach Sron Garbh (1131m). Continue west along the nearly level ridge over the narrow rocky crest of Stob Coire Dhomhnuill (1137m) and the more rounded top of Stob a' Choire Dhomhain (1147m) to reach Carn Eige. (11km; 1120m; 4h 20min).

To include Beinn Fhionnlaidh in this long day, descend the north ridge of Carn Eige over the intermediate Top of Stob Coire Lochan (917m) to reach Beinn Fhionnlaidh in 2km. (13km; 1290m; 5h 10min). Return to Carn Eige, descend its south-west ridge to the col at about 1044m and climb to Mam Sodhail, whose large cairn is a reminder that this peak was once a key point in the survey of Scotland. (16.5km; 1790m; 6h 40min).

The return route to the starting point may depend on time and fitness. The easiest way is to go down the south-west ridge of Mam Sodhail for 500m to the col at 1086m and then follow the path all the way down Coire Leachavie to the right of way on the north side of Loch Affric, which leads back past Affric Lodge to the car park at the end of the public road. A slightly more direct route, but one involving a bit more climbing, goes along the south-east ridge of Mam Sodhail for almost 4km to Sgurr na Lapaich (1036m), then down its south-east

181

Carn Eige from the ridge to Beinn Fhionnlaidh

Beinn Fhionnlaidh and An Socach beyond from Carn Eige

ridge to regain the stalkers' path of the outward route.

The easiest way to climb Beinn Fhionnlaidh is to hire a boat at the Loch Mullardoch dam and sail up the loch to land near the foot of the hill and make a direct ascent up its north-east side. Enquiries about boat hire should be made locally. Another way to Beinn Fhionnlaidh is up Glen Elchaig by bike from Killilan for 12km to Iron Lodge, followed by a walk along the track over the pass to the head of Loch Mullardoch and the ascent of the north-west side of the hill.

CARN EIGE

BEINN
FHIONNLAIDH

MAM SODHAIL

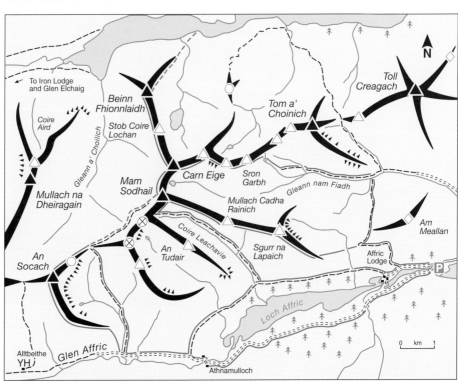

Looking west along Loch Affric

**An Socach;** 921m; (OS Sheets 25 and 33; NH088230); M269; *the snout*

This Munro is the lowest on the long chain of mountains on the north side of Glen Affric, and it is overshadowed by its big neighbours Mam Sodhail and Sgurr nan Ceathreamhnan. In shape it has three broad ridges converging at a flat summit, and the east-facing Coire Ghaidheil has some small crags around its rim, but lower down it is eroded peat bog.

An Socach is very isolated, lying 12km from the end of the public road in Glen Affric, nearly the same distance over the hills from Cluanie Inn to the south, and 3km from Glen Affric's remote Alltbeithe youth hostel, the loneliest in Scotland. As a consequence, the effort required to climb An Socach is more in the approach march to the hill, than in the ascent of the hill itself.

The approach from the car park at the west end of Loch Beinn a' Mheadhoin in Glen Affric is either along the right of way on the north side of Loch Affric, or along the Forestry Commission road which crosses to the south side of the loch. It is quite possible to bike along this road for 7km to Athnamulloch, where the River Affric is recrossed to join the right of way on the north side. Whichever way one chooses, the approach up Glen Affric is scenically the best part of the day.

Beyond Athnamulloch the glen becomes bare, but the track continues and in 2.5km the footbridge over the Allt Coire Ghaidheil is reached. On the west side of the stream bear north-west up easy slopes of grass and heather leading to the broad flat ridge which continues round the edge of Coire Ghaidheil. After a long level section, a final short rise leads to the summit. (l3.5km; 680m; 4h 10min).

To vary the descent, go down the north-east ridge to the Bealach Coire Ghaidheil and follow the stalkers' path down the east side of the corrie to the track in Glen Affric. From this bealach one can also traverse to Mam Sodhail along another stalkers' path which climbs diagonally north-east to reach the south-west ridge of Mam Sodhail near a prominent cairn 1km from its summit.

If a bike is used to Athnamulloch and beyond, then An Socach can be combined with Beinn Fhionnlaidh by cutting around the back of Mam Sodhail and Carn Eige, then returning over their tops.

AN SOCACH

**Mullach na Dheiragain;** 982m; (OS Sheets 25 and 33; NH081259); M167; *summit of the kestrels*
**Sgurr nan Ceathreamhnan;** 1151m; (OS Sheets 25 and 33; NH057228); M22;
*peak of the quarters*

The long range on the north side of Glen Affric culminates at its western end in the great massif of Sgurr nan Ceathreamhnan, a superb and complex mountain of many ridges, peaks and corries. In size it is the equal of several normal peaks, and from its summit long ridges radiate out to the north and east. The longest of these goes for 7km towards the head of Loch Mullardoch, and rises near its mid-point to Mullach na Dheiragain, classified as a separate Munro, though very much a part of its higher neighbour.

Sgurr nan Ceathreamhnan is in a remote situation, surrounded by other mountains and a long way from the nearest public road. This remoteness adds to its character and makes it one of the great prizes for the hillwalker, involving a long approach from any direction, unless one happens to be staying at Alltbeithe youth hostel in Glen Affric.

The Glen Affric approach starts from the end of the public road at Loch Affric, from where it is possible to bike for 13km along the south side of the loch past Athnamulloch and up the glen by a rough track to the youth hostel. From there follow the stalkers' path north up Coire na Cloiche to the bealach at its head and make a descending traverse across steep ground to Loch Coire nan Dearcag. Go north-west up to the Bealach nan Daoine (840m) and traverse the long north-east ridge of Sgurr nan Ceathreamhnan over Carn na Con Dhu (967m) to Mullach na Dheiragain. (From the youth hostel; 7.5km; 860m; 3h 10min).

Return along the ridge to the Bealach nan Daoine and climb the final narrow rocky part of the north-east ridge of Sgurr nan Ceathreamhnan. (11km; 1240m; 4h 40min). Descend along the east ridge over Stob Coire na Cloiche (915m) to the bealach at the head of Coire na Cloiche and go down the path to the youth hostel.

It is also possible to bike up the private road in Glen Elchaig and this is a fine approach for the traverse of these mountains, with a visit to the Falls of Glomach to complete a superb expedition.

If biking, go for 8km to the outflow of Loch na Leitreach and leave your bike near there. Continue up the glen to Iron Lodge, and take the track east through the pass towards Loch Mullardoch until 500m beyond Loch an Droma. There branch south along the path to Gleann Sithidh and cross the Abhainn Sithidh via a bridge.

From the end of the path climb steeply east up a grassy slope onto the north-west ridge of Mullach Sithidh (974m) and continue up to this Top and 500m further to Mullach na Dheiragain. (From Loch na Leitreach; 10.5km; 930m; 4h). The long ridge is followed over

Mullach na Dheiragain and Beinn Fhionnlaidh from the east ridge of Sgurr nan Ceathreamhnan

Carn na Con Dhu to the Bealach nan Daoine and up to Sgurr nan Ceathreamhnan. (14.5km; 1310m; 5h 30min).

Traverse the narrow summit crest to the West Top (1143m) and descend west, then north-west along the broad grassy ridge round the rim of Coire Lochan. Continue down to Gleann Gaorsaic, across the Abhainn Gaorsaic and along its left bank to reach the path near the Falls of Glomach. The Falls may be visited by a short diversion, and the descent continues along the path which traverses across the precipitous south-west flank of the Glomach chasm before dropping to the Allt a' Ghlomaich and Glen Elchaig at Loch na Leitreach

The shortest all-walking route to Sgurr nan Ceathreamhnan, about 11km, is from Morvich in Strath Croe over the Bealach an Sgairne (see page 186) and up the south side of Sgurr Gaorsaic.

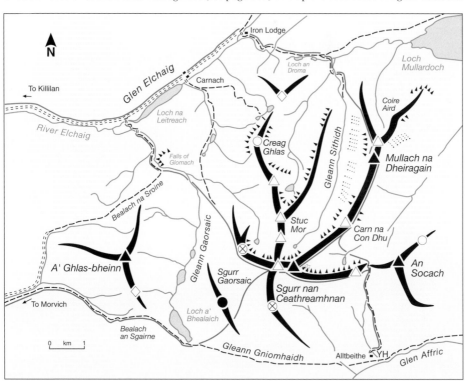

Sgurr a' Choire Ghairbh from Strath Croe

**Beinn Fhada;** 1032m; (OS Sheet 33; NH018192); M100; *long hill*
**A' Ghlas-bheinn;** 918m; (OS Sheet 33; NH008231); M274; *the greenish-grey hill*

186

BEINN FHADA

A' GHLAS-BHEINN

To the north of the Five Sisters of Kintail a single great mountain, Beinn Fhada, extends from Glen Affric to the head of Loch Duich. It is well named the long mountain, for it extends from east to west for almost 9km, and occupies an area equal to all the Five Sisters. The only roadside view of the mountain is from Loch Duich, from where the knobbly ridge of Sgurr a' Choire Ghairbh is seen. The summit, however, is hidden behind this ridge. The south and west sides of Beinn Fhada above Gleann Lichd are uniformly steep and in places craggy, and the north side of the mountain is a succession of wild corries. By contrast, A' Ghlas-bheinn is a rather small and insignificant hill rising at the head of Strath Croe. Beinn Fhada is in National Trust for Scotland property, and is accessible at all times of the year; A' Ghlas-bheinn is in the Inverinate estate.

The traverse of these two mountains starts from the end of the public road just beyond the National Trust for Scotland camp site at Morvich in Strath Croe. Follow the right of way east across the bridge over the River Croe and round the foot of Beinn Bhuidhe, the north-western end of Beinn Fhada. Continue along the path east up Gleann Choinneachain below the steep and craggy north face of Sgurr a' Choire Ghairbh. Cross the stream which comes down from Coire an Sgairne and a few hundred metres further, above the zigzags in the path, take the stalkers' path southwards up this corrie onto the ridge of Meall a' Bhealaich at NH011206. Go south along this ridge, which merges into the great summit plateau of Beinn Fhada, the Plaide Mhor, and continue south-east along the edge of this plateau to the big summit cairn. (7km; 980m; 3h 20min).

Return by the same route along the Meall a' Bhealaich ridge and go north to this outlying top. The direct descent from there to the Bealach an Sgairne is steep and rocky, and an easier way is to the east of the direct line to the pass, descending north-east at first then down to the pass. An alternative which may be preferable in bad conditions of visibility or rain is to return down Coire an Sgairne by the stalkers' path of the uphill route to the junction with the main path in Gleann Choinneachain, and then to climb 1km up this path to the pass. This is a longer but absolutely certain route.

From the Bealach an Sgairne climb the knobbly south-east ridge of A' Ghlas-bheinn, passing to the east of Loch a' Chleirich. (12km; 1380m; 5h). Descend west along a broad grassy ridge which steepens lower down near the forest. Keep on the crest of the ridge and aim for the point where the path from Strath Croe to the Bealach na Sroine emerges from the

Sgurr a' Choire Ghairbh from the south ridge of A' Ghlas-bheinn

forest, and from there continue south through the forest to the clearing where the house at Dorusduain once stood. Cross to the south side of the Abhainn Chonaig by a footbridge hidden in its wooded gorge and return along the path to Morvich.

An alternative and better route of ascent from Morvich to Beinn Fhada, but with one slightly difficult section, is to climb east from the bridge over the River Croe up the grassy ridge of Beinn Bhuidhe. Towards the top of this ridge climb steeper, rockier slopes to the northern point of Sgurr a' Choire Ghairbh. This western outlier of Beinn Fhada forms a fine undulating ridge with steep cliffs on its east side. Traverse south along it and descend steeply to The Hunters' Pass down a rocky pitch which may be awkward when wet or in winter conditions.

Beyond the pass climb south-east up a narrow ridge to Meall an Fhuarain Mhoir (954m) which is at the western end of the Plaide Mhor. Cross this featureless plateau eastwards for 2km to the summit of Beinn Fhada.

BEINN FHADA

A' GHLAS-BHEINN

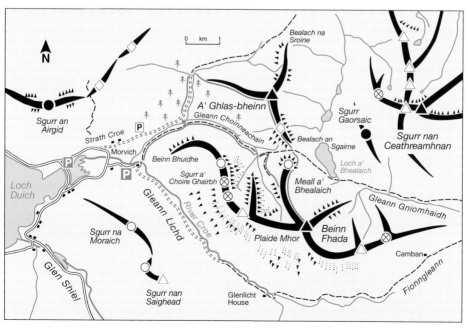

Sgurr nan Conbhairean from Carn Ghluasaid

**SGURR NAN CONBHAIREAN**

**Carn Ghluasaid;** 957m; (OS Sheet 34; NH146125); M203; *hill of movement*
**Sgurr nan Conbhairean;** 1109m; (OS Sheet 34; NH130139); M44; *peak of the hound keepers*
**Sail Chaorainn;** 1002m; (OS Sheet 34; NH133154); M133; *hill (literally heel) of the rowan*

188

These three mountains are on the north side of Loch Cluanie mid-way between Loch Ness and Loch Duich. From the A87 road they do not look very impressive, for their southern slopes and corries are featureless and their tops hidden. Only when one is on the summits can their true character be appreciated, in particular the great wild eastern corrie in which rise the headwaters of the River Doe.

CARN GHLUASAID

SAIL CHAORAINN

Start the traverse at Lundie, 4km west of the Loch Cluanie dam. Follow the old military road west for 500m, then turn north along a stalkers' path and follow this up to the flat plateau of Carn Ghluasaid The summit cairn may be hard to find in the mist; it is about 50m away from the precipitous north face of the hill and there is another cairn 50m to the west of it. (4km; 720m; 2h 10min).

Traverse west then north-west along a broad ridge to Creag a' Chaorainn (998m), then west to the Glas Bhealach over a smooth expanse of grass, and finally climb north-west to Sgurr nan Conbhairean. (7km; 990m; 3h 20min). Descend north along a narrow ridge overlooking Lochan Uaine, one of the sources of the River Doe, to the col at 914m and reach Sail Chaorainn by its easy-angled south ridge. (8.5km. 1100m; 4h).

Return to just below the top of Sgurr nan Conbhairean and traverse beneath its summit on a path, to descend the narrowing south-west ridge to the col above Gorm Lochan. Climb a short distance further to Drochaid an Tuill Easaich (1001m), turn south and descend the grass ridge which leads to the shoulder of Meall Breac. When the descent steepens, bear south-east across the Allt Coire Lair to reach the path on its east side and go down it to the old military road which leads east back to Lundie.

**N**

0 km 1

Gleann na Ciche

Tigh Mor na Seilge

Sail Chaorainn

Sgurr nan Conbhairean

Drochaid an Tuill Easaich

Allt Coire Lair

Meall Breac

Carn Ghluasaid

P Lundie

A87

Loch Cluanie

Mullach Fraoch-choire from Ciste Dhubh

**A' Chralaig;** 1120m; (OS Sheets 33 and 34; NH094148); M34; *the basket or creel*
**Mullach Fraoch-choire;** 1102m; (OS Sheets 33 and 34; NH095171); M49;
*summit of the heathery corrie*

These two peaks are the high points of an 8km-long ridge between the west end of Loch Cluanie and Glen Affric. When seen from Loch Cluanie, A' Chralaig gives the impression of being a massive mountain with long grassy slopes. Mullach Fraoch-choire is more elegant, its summit being the meeting point of three narrow ridges, and it looks particularly fine seen from the pine woods round Loch Affric. The east side of the high ridge between these two peaks drops in a series of large grassy corries draining towards Glen Affric, while the west side is more uniformly steep above the deep glen of An Caorann Mor.

Park below a felled area at the foot of the south-east ridge of Am Bathach, about 1.5km east of the Cluanie Inn. Walk 350m east along the road to where the track through An Caorann Mor starts. Go up this for about 100m to a small path which climbs steeply north-east up grassy slopes for 500m until the angle eases on the south ridge of A' Chralaig. Continue up this ridge to the summit, which is crowned by a large cairn. (3.5km; 900m; 2h 20min).

Traverse north along a grassy ridge to a col at 952m and climb the outlying Top, Stob Coire na Cralaig (1008m). The ridge becomes narrower, dropping north-east across another col (949m), then turning north to Mullach Fraoch-choire. The ascent to this peak involves the traverse of a narrow ridge by an eroded path which avoids several rock towers first on the right, then the left before leading without difficulty to the summit. Taking the towers direct offers some tricky scrambling. The path is quite exposed in winter when banked-out with snow. (6km; 1110m; 3h 20min).

The return to Loch Cluanie may well be made by the outward route over the summit of A' Chralaig. However, if circumstances dictate a quick descent to lower ground, the best route is back to the 949m col 250m north-east of Stob Coire na Cralaig, then down north-west into Coire Odhar. Lower down this corrie bear south-west to reach the path near the pass at the head of An Caorann Mor, and descend this to the road.

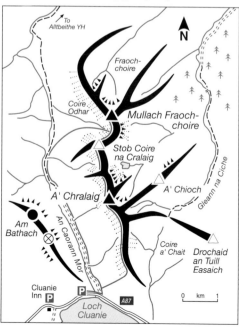

Ciste Dhubh from the south ridge

**Ciste Dhubh;** 979m; (OS Sheet 33; NH062166); M173; *black chest*

AONACH
MEADHOIN

SGURR A'
BHEALAICH DHEIRG

SAILEAG

Ciste Dhubh is a fine peak rising about 5km north of Cluanie Inn. 2km to the south of the peak the wide grassy Bealach a' Choinich separates it from its two neighbours, Sgurr an Fhuarail and Am Bathach. The south ridge of Ciste Dhubh rises above this bealach and continues as a fine narrow arete which leads to the steep rocky summit of the peak. On its north side, three steep ridges drop from the summit towards the Fionngleann, and the west face of Ciste Dhubh is remarkably steep.

The ascent of Ciste Dhubh from Cluanie Inn is a straightforward and fairly short climb. From the car park opposite the Inn walk east for 100m and follow the track and path up the west side of the Allt Chaorainn Bhig to the Bealach a' Choinich.

A finer, but rather longer route to this col is via the narrow grassy ridge of Am Bathach. Park about 1.5km east of Cluanie Inn below felled forest at the foot of the south-east ridge. From a gate just west of the bridge over the Allt a' Chaorainn Mhoir, follow an old stalkers' path up onto the south-east ridge and over its delightful undulating crest to the summit and down to the Bealach a' Choinich. A bit of extra effort, but well worthwhile.

The south ridge of Ciste Dhubh rises abruptly from the Bealach a' Choinich. A wet and eroded path takes a line immediately right of the crags up and left of the bealach. A pleasanter ascent is via the steep grass slope further right which is followed for 150m until the gradient eases and the little rocky top of An Cnapach is reached. From there the ridge goes north for 1km, level and very narrow, but perfectly easy and with a well-defined path. There is a slight drop before the final rise to the summit of Ciste Dhubh. (5.5km 740m; 2h 30min).

**Aonach Meadhoin;** 1001m; (OS Sheet 33; NH049137); M135; *middle ridge*
**Sgurr a' Bhealaich Dheirg;** 1036m; (OS Sheet 33; NH035143); M96; *peak of the red pass*
**Saileag;** 956m; (OS Sheet 33; NH018148); M205; *little heel*

The broad grassy ridge which rises from the side of the A87 road at Cluanie Inn is the start of a very fine mountain range which extends westwards along the north side of Glen Shiel for about 15km to end at the head of Loch Duich. The western half of this range is the Five Sisters of Kintail, and the eastern half is a group of three mountains, known as the Three Brothers which are linked to the Five Sisters by a high col, the Bealach an Lapain.

Going from east to west, the first of the eastern group is Aonach Meadhoin, which with its slightly lower Top, Sgurr an Fhuarail (987m), looks very imposing from the east along the side

Sgurr an Fhuarail from the east with Aonach Meadhoin just visible behind

of Loch Cluanie. A narrow ridge links Aonach Meadhoin to Sgurr a' Bhealaich Dheirg, the highest of this group and a fine peak whose long northern spurs enclose remote corries at the head of Gleann Lichd. To its west is Saileag, a more modest hill described by one writer as 'a mere swelling on the ridge', and from it a grassy ridge drops to the Bealach an Lapain. The lower slopes of these mountains along Glen Shiel have been extensively forested, but felling of the trees has begun and the appearance of the glen will be changed again.

The traverse of these mountains may be started from the A87 road 2km west of Cluanie Inn. from a small layby next to the bridge over the Allt Coire Tholl Bhruach. Follow a path up the east side of the Allt Coire Tholl Bhruach to a sheepfank and continue north up Coire na Cadha. High up the corrie, but well below its headwall, go west to reach the crest of the short steep south ridge of Aonach Meadhoin and climb this to the summit. (3km; 750m; 2h). An alternative and longer route goes up the east side of Coire na Cadha onto the south-east ridge of Sgurr an Fhuarail and over this peak to Aonach Meadhoin.

AONACH
MEADHOIN

SGURR A'
BHEALAICH DHEIRG

SAILEAG

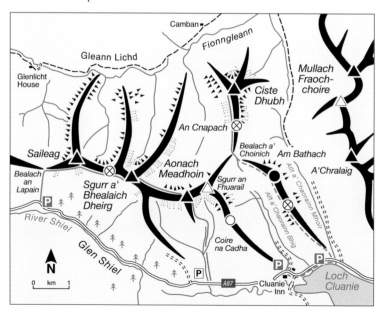

Looking up the north ridge of Sgurr a' Bhealaich Dheirg

**SAILEAG**

**192**

**SGURR A'
BHEALAICH DHEIRG**

Continue down the fine narrow west ridge of Aonach Meadhoin to a col at 827m and climb to the level crest of Sgurr a' Bhealaich Dheirg. From it traverse about 70m along the narrow north-east spur, following a dry stone dyke to the fine tall cairn which stands astride the narrow ridge and marks the summit. (5km; 950m; 2h 50min). Return to the level crest and go north-west then west along the ridge to Saileag. (7km; 1030m; 3h 20min).

Descend west along a grassy ridge to the Bealach an Lapain and go down from there by a steep path to reach the A87 road in Glen Shiel 5.5km west of the starting point.

Saileag and Sgurr a' Bhealaich Dheirg from the west

*Roger Robb*

The Five Sisters of Kintail

**Sgurr na Ciste Duibhe;** 1027m; (OS Sheet 33; NG984149); M105; *peak of the black chest*
**Sgurr na Carnach;** 1002m; (OS Sheet 33; NG977159); M134; *rocky peak*
**Sgurr Fhuaran;** 1067m; (OS Sheet 33; NG978167); M70; *peak of the wolf*

For most of its length Glen Shiel is enclosed on its north-east side by a mountain range of awe-inspiring height and steepness, the Five Sisters of Kintail. They rise from glen to summit crests in uninterrupted slopes of heather, grass, scree and crag, riven by great gullies. The best known view of the group is from the south side of Loch Duich, from where the mountains have a remarkable simplicity and symmetry of outline

A classic hillwalking expedition is the traverse of the three Munros and two Tops, preferably from south-east to north-west. It is not an unduly strenuous day, but is does end at least 8km away from the starting point, so some suitable transport arrangement will be needed if a long walk through Glen Shiel is to be avoided. Possibly the bus services through the glen might help.

The start from the A87 road in Glen Shiel is directly below the Bealach an Lapain (725m), and a steep unrelenting climb up the zigzag path on this slope leads to the ridge in little more than an hour of hard work. Turn west and traverse the ridge which climbs gradually to Sgurr nan Spainteach (990m). For a few hundred metres down to the next col the ridge is a bit more rocky and there is one very short pitch where a little very easy scrambling is needed. The ridge up to Sgurr na Ciste Duibhe has a curious double crest with a hollow in between. This might be confusing in bad visibility, however in good weather the shape of the ridge is quite clear and a path can be followed up to the big cairn. (4km; 950m; 2h 30min).

Descend stony slopes west then north-west to the Bealach na Craoibhe (849m) and climb a broad ridge to Sgurr na Carnach. (5.5km; 1100m; 3h 10min). A direct escape to Glen Shiel can be made down the very steep west-north-west ridge. The top of this ridge is quite rocky and is steep enough to have a sense of exposure high above the glen, but careful route-finding enables any difficulties to be negotiated and lower down the ridge becomes grassy, though still very steep, and leads to the River Shiel 1.5km downstream from Achnangart. In ascent, this ridge is a steep and continuous slog whose only merit is that it leads direct to the cairn of Sgurr na Carnach without any diversions.

The traverse of the Five Sisters continues from Sgurr na Carnach down to the Bealach na Carnach (867m) and steeply up a zigzag path on the south face of Sgurr Fhuaran. (6.5km; 1300m; 3h 40min). A quick if fairly brutal direct descent to Glen Shiel is possible down the long west-north-west ridge, but a more satisfactory end to the traverse continues over the fine

SGURR
NA CISTE DUIBHE

SGURR
NA CARNACH

SGURR FHUARAN

Sgurr na Ciste Duibhe from Sgurr nan Spainteach

pointed Top of Sgurr nan Saighead (929m), notable for its steep slabby east face, and along the narrow rocky ridge to its north-west peak; Beinn Bhuidhe. This is a fine viewpoint, south-east to the peaks of the Five Sisters and north-west to Loch Duich and the western seaboard. The main ridge divides at Beinn Bhuidhe and the shorter of two possible descent routes goes down the west ridge to the wide col before Sgurr an t-Searraich and from there south-west steeply down rough grassy slopes to cross the River Shiel just upstream from Loch Shiel. The bridge which used to exist at NG948181 has gone and if the river cannot be waded, then the north

**SGURR
NA CISTE DUIBHE**

**SGURR
NA CARNACH**

**SGURR FHUARAN**

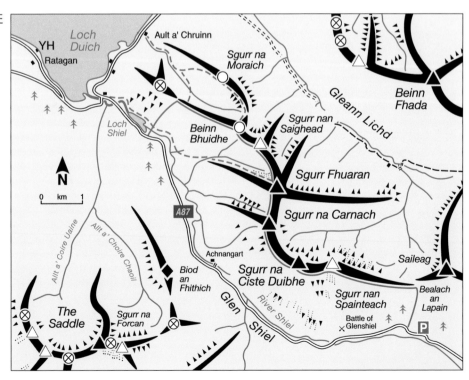

Sgurr nan Saighead and Sgurr Fhuaran from Beinn Bhuidhe

side of Loch Shiel will have to be followed back to Shiel Bridge. An alternative descent is to veer right from the col before Sgurr an t-Searraich to gain the path from Sgurr na Moraich beside the Allt a' Chruinn.

Purists who want to traverse the fifth of the Five Sisters should descend north-east from Beinn Bhuidhe to a col and then climb north-west along the ridge to Sgurr na Moraich (876m). Go down its north-west ridge for about 500m, then bear west down to the Allt a' Chruinn and follow a path along its steep right bank to reach the head of Loch Duich.

Beinn Bhuidhe, the north-west peak of Sgurr nan Saighead

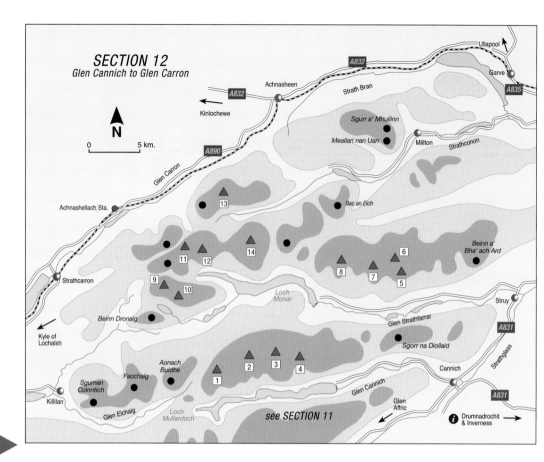

# SECTION 12

## Glen Cannich to Glen Carron

*i* VisitScotland Information Centres

**Drumnadrochit**; The Car Park, Drumnadrochit, IV63 6TX, (01456 459086), open Jan–Dec

**Inverness**; Castle Wynd, Inverness, IV2 3BJ, (01463 252401), open Jan–Dec

Donald Bennet

An Socach from Glen Elchaig

## An Socach; 1069m; (OS Sheet 25; NH100333); M67; *the snout*

Situated in the remote hinterland of Ross-shire between the upper reaches of Glen Cannich and Glen Elchaig, An Socach is a very inaccessible hill, many kilometres from the nearest public road. It is a westward extension of An Riabhachan, the col between the two being low enough to give An Socach the character of a separate mountain. Its summit ridge is an east-facing crescent enclosing Coire Mhaim, whose lower level is an extensive area of eroded peat bog. Around its western perimeter An Socach is grassy, and a curving ridge goes out to enclose Coire Lungard.

There are two long access routes to the mountain, from the Loch Mullardoch dam to the east, and from Glen Elchaig to the south-west.

From the Mullardoch dam, walk along the north shore of the loch following a fairly good path for most of the way for 8km to the lodge at the foot of the Allt Socrach. It may be possible to hire a boat to reach the lodge; enquiries should be made locally. From there continue west up a stalkers' path towards Coire Mhaim and climb the south-east ridge of An Socach, thereby avoiding the rough ground in the corrie. (13.5km; 870m; 4h 30min).

It is not possible to drive up Glen Elchaig from Killilan and a bike is very useful for the 12km of estate road, which is a right of way, to Iron Lodge. Beyond the road end continue along the path beside the Allt na Doire Gairbhe leading towards Pait Lodge. From the south-west end of Loch Mhoicean climb east to the level ridge round the head of Coire Lungard, go north along it and finally up the south-west face of An Socach to the summit. (19.5km; 1070m; 6h 10min. About 2h less by bike).

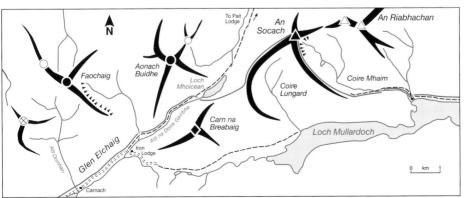

Melanie Nicoll

Sgurr na Lapaich from An Riabhachan

**An Riabhachan;** 1129m; (OS Sheet 25; NH134345); M29; *the grey or streaked one*
**Sgurr na Lapaich;** 1150m; (OS Sheet 25; NH161351); M24; *peak of the bogland*
**Carn nan Gobhar;** 992m; (OS Sheet 25; NH182344); M152; *hill of the goats*

AN RIABHACHAN

SGURR NA
LAPAICH

CARN NAN
GOBHAR

These three mountains, together with An Socach further west, form the main range between Glen Strathfarrar and Glen Cannich along the north side of Loch Mullardoch. An Riabhachan is a 4km-long ridge with open grassy corries on all sides except at the north-east end where there are steep rocky crags above Loch Beag and Loch Mor. Sgurr na Lapaich is a more defined peak, visible from a long distance down Strath Glass, and having some steep corries on its east side. Carn nan Gobhar is a rounded and rather undistinguished hill with an outlying top, Creag Dubh (945m), 2km to its east.

The closest approach to these mountains is from Glen Strathfarrar, provided it is possible to drive along the estate road up this glen to the little power station in Gleann Innis an Loichel. (see access notes on page 201). If this approach is impossible, the alternative starting point is the road end in Glen Cannich at the Loch Mullardoch dam.

From the power station continue west along a track for 1km and then up the stalkers' path for a further 1.5km before branching left. Cross the stream, possibly difficult if in spate, and climb south-west up a stalkers' path which ends at the lip of An Riabhachan's north-east corrie, the Toll an Lochain, which is a grand wild place with dark crags overlooking two high lochans. Beyond the end of the path go along the level ridge between the two lochans, then south-east on a gradually rising traverse among huge fallen boulders towards the Bealach Toll an Lochain, the col (820m) at the head of the corrie.

From this col the ridge to An Riabhachan rises at a fairly easy angle with one short narrow section to the North-east Top and then across level mossy ground to the summit. (8.5km; 950m; 3h 30min).

Return to the col and climb the steep grassy south-west shoulder of Sgurr na Lapaich to the large circular cairn enclosing the trig point. (11.5km; 1280m; 4h 50min). The east ridge is a narrow rocky crest which gives some scrambling, and an easier descent goes down the slope of grass and boulders on its south side direct to the next col, the Bealach na Cloiche Duibhe (796m).

The first part of the broad ridge leading to Carn nan Gobhar is littered with huge boulders, and higher up the angle steepens to the small cairn on the summit. (14km; 1480m; 5h 40min). The top of Carn nan Gobhar is a wide level ridge running south to north, with a big cairn about 200m south of and slightly lower than the small summit cairn.

To return to the day's starting point, descend north, at first down steep grassy slopes, then across several streams in the very rough and peaty Garbh-choire and finally over a little col to drop down through scattered birches on the steep hillside above the power station.

An Riabhachan from the south-west ridge of Sgurr na Lapaich

The traverse of Carn nan Gobhar and Sgurr na Lapaich from the Loch Mullardoch dam is a good day without being unduly long. Take the path for 1.5km along the north side of the loch. Then climb the south-east ridge of Mullach na Maoile and continue to Carn nan Gobhar, passing the large cairn shortly before reaching the summit. Continue to Sgurr na Lapaich up its rocky east ridge or by easier ground on its left.

From its summit descend south to Sgurr nan Clachan Geala (1095m). From this peak the most direct return is down the south-east ridge to the Glas Toll, across the Allt Taige and on down the grassy hillside on a descending traverse south-east to join the path near the loch.

The inclusion of An Riabhachan in this traverse makes a very long day. An alternative and easier option is to hire a boat to sail from the Loch Mullardoch dam to the lodge at the foot of the Allt Socrach, this would also make it feasible to include An Socach. The ascent of An Riabhachan goes up the stalkers' path on the east side of this burn and the grassy corrie higher up. Return along the ridges of Sgurr na Lapaich and Carn nan Gobhar.

AN RIABHACHAN

SGURR NA
LAPAICH

CARN NAN
GOBHAR

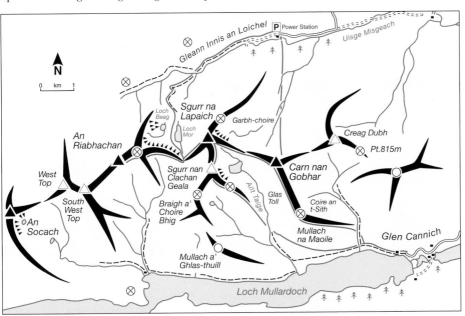

Looking west from Sgurr a' Choire Ghlais to Sgurr Fuar-thuill

Bill Brooker

**Sgurr na Ruaidhe;** 993m; (OS Sheet 25; NH289426); M151; *peak of the redness*
**Carn nan Gobhar;** 992m; (OS Sheet 25; NH273439); M153; *hill of the goats*
**Sgurr a' Choire Ghlais;** 1083m; (OS Sheet 25; NH259430); M60; *peak of the grey-green corrie*
**Sgurr Fuar-thuill;** 1049m; (OS Sheet 25; NH236437); M82; *peak of the cold hollow*

200

SGURR NA
RUAIDHE

CARN NAN
GOBHAR

SGURR A' CHOIRE
GHLAIS

SGURR FUAR-
THUILL

The four Munros on the north side of Glen Strathfarrar form a well-defined ridge several kilometres long which can be traversed in a single day, the only drawback being that the starting and finishing points on the road are about 7km apart. However, if a bike is left where the descent meets the road at NH224393, at a track next to the Allt Toll a' Mhuic, then it is an easy and pleasant cycle back to the start.

The two eastern hills, Sgurr na Ruaidhe and Carn nan Gobhar, are smooth and rounded and of no great distinction. Sgurr a' Choire Ghlais at the centre of the ridge is distinctly higher, steeper and more impressive, and at the west end Sgurr Fuar-thuill and its two adjacent Tops form an undulating crest with steep faces to the north. South-west of these, Sgurr na Muice (891m) can justifiably be regarded as the finest peak in this group by virtue of the great slabby face above the dark waters of Loch Toll a' Mhuic.

The Glen Strathfarrar road leaves the A831 at the north side of Struy Bridge across the River Farrar, 500m south of The Cnoc Hotel. From the locked gate at Inchmore, follow the tarmac road for 12.5km (7.8miles) to where a zigzag track can be seen above, beside the Allt Coire Mhuillidh. Park on the grass some 20m up the track but don't block it as it is used for access. Climb the track, followed by a stalkers' path on the east side of the stream, for 2km. Beyond the first side stream climb north-east up the grassy shoulder of Sgurr na Ruaidhe, which gives easy going all the way to the summit. (5km; 850m; 2h 40min). The upper slopes of this hill on its north and west sides are very smooth and mossy. Descend these slopes to a col at 770m and climb north then west to Carn nan Gobhar, which has a boulder-strewn summit with the cairn at its north edge. (7.5km; 1070m; 3h 20min).

Continue south-west along the level mossy ridge, then descend west to the next col at 860m. From there climb Sgurr a' Choire Ghlais along the steep ridge on the edge of its northern corrie. The summit is crowned by two cairns and a trig point. (9km; 1290m; 4h). The ridge drops again to 900m before rising over Creag Ghorm a' Bhealaich (1030m), dropping to 900m again, and continues, now with a steep drop on the north side, to Sgurr Fuar-thuill. (11.5km; 1570m; 4h 50min).

At the next col, just before Sgurr na Fearstaig (1015m), the top of a stalkers' path is reached and it may be followed downhill. However, it is worth continuing along the ridge to the last Top for the westward view, and then going south along the ridge towards Sgurr na Muice for a few hundred metres until a short easy descent can be made east to join the stalkers' path lower down. This path tends to disappear in the grassy corrie, but it reappears near Loch Toll a' Mhuic and thereafter gives a good fast descent to the glen to meet a track, then the road.

It is only slightly longer, and on a fine evening would certainly be worthwhile, to continue

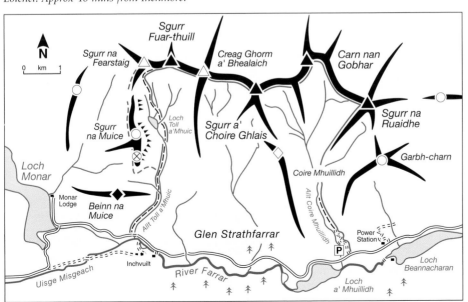

Richard Wood

Sgurr a' Choire Ghlais from Creag Gorm a' Bhealaich

along the southward running ridge to Sgurr na Muice, from where there is a splendid view westwards along the length of Loch Monar. From there descend south to the narrow col before Carn an Daimh Bhain and go down a path below the south end of the Sgurr na Muice crags to join the main path by the Allt Toll a' Mhuic.

*While access on foot and by bike is unaffected, a locked gate at Inchmore, 1km west of Struy Bridge, restricts vehicle access to the private road up Glen Strathfarrar. There is a dedicated parking area on the left at Inchmore. In 2012 vehicle access was possible from March 28 to October 31 through an arrangement between Scottish Natural Heritage and the landowners. The gatekeeper, whose cottage is beside the gate, will unlock it for a maximum of 25 vehicles as follows: April (9am-6pm), May (9am-7pm); June, July and August (9am-8pm); September (9am-7pm); October (9am-6pm). The glen is closed to vehicles Tuesday and Wednesday until 1.30pm. Last access one hour before closing. During the rest of the year vehicle access can ONLY be arranged by ringing the Mountaineering Council of Scotland during office hours on 01738 493942, in advance of your visit. See <www.mcofs.org.uk>. At present it is possible to drive to the Loch Monar dam, across it and 3km further to the little power station in Gleann Innis an Loichel. Approx 40 mins from Inchmore.*

SGURR NA
   RUAIDHE

CARN NAN
   GOBHAR

SGURR A' CHOIRE
   GHLAIS

SGURR FUAR-
   THUILL

Lurg Mhor from the col below Bidein a' Choire Sheasgaich

## The Loch Monar Hills

Five grand mountains lie to the south-east of Glen Carron in a remote setting round the head of Loch Monar. Two of them, Lurg Mhor and Bidein a' Choire Sheasgaich, are among the least accessible and hence most highly prized of the Munros. The easiest approach to all five is from the A890 road at Craig in Glen Carron, 3.5km east of Achnashellach. An estate road crosses the railway at a level crossing there and goes east along the north side of the Allt a' Chonais through the Achnashellach Forest, much of which has been felled.

Beyond the forest the road continues for several kilometres to Glenuaig Lodge, following the right of way to Strathconon. It is possible to bike along this road, which is quite a help in view of the long distance to these mountains. 5.5km from Craig, at the point where the glen turns east, the climber reaches the parting of the ways: east to Maoile Lunndaidh, south to Sgurr Choinnich and Sgurr a' Chaorachain, and south-west to Bidein a' Choire Sheasgaich and Lurg Mhor.

**Bidein a' Choire Sheasgaich;** 945m; (OS Sheet 25; NH049412); M224;
*pinnacle of the corrie of the farrow cattle*
**Lurg Mhor;** 986m; (OS Sheet 25; NH065404); M163; *big shank*

These two mountains are the remotest of the group on the south-east side of Glen Carron, and there is a sense of a real expedition to climb them. Some might prefer to take two days and stay in the remote and lonely Bearnais bothy at NH021430. Bidein a' Choire Sheasgaich is a very fine peak indeed, its sharp pointed summit being an easily recognisable landmark from many distant hills. Lurg Mhor is a long ridge, steep on the north side and narrow to the east where it joins Meall Mor (974m). This east end of the ridge extends for a long way above the west end of Loch Monar to lonely Pait Lodge. One of the best views of these two mountains is had from the east, looking along Loch Monar from the west end of the Glen Strathfarrar ridge.

The start from Craig in Glen Carron goes for 5.5km up the Allt a' Chonais, possibly by bike. Ford the burn at NH076465 (there is no bridge) and follow the stalkers' path south-west to the Bealach Bhearnais. Continue south-west, climbing onto the ridge of Beinn Tharsuinn and following its undulating crest to the summit (863m). Descend past the lochan on the crest of the ridge to the col between the two tops of Beinn Tharsuinn. From there descend steeply south-west to the Bealach an Sgoltaidh, the pass at the foot of the north ridge of Bidein a' Choire Sheasgaich.

This ridge rises very steeply and looks rather intimidating, being encircled by crags. Climb

Bidein a' Choire Sheasgaich from Beinn Tharsuinn

directly uphill close to a dry stone dyke and scramble easily up the first band of rocks to a more continuous cliff. The most direct way up this is by an open gully directly above; it is steep, but grassy rather than rocky, and the way is obvious, trending slightly rightwards. An alternative route lies further east, following a steeply-inclined grassy ledge which narrows near its top.

These routes both lead to a level section of the ridge where there is a tiny lochan. Continue south over a knoll to a larger lochan and finally climb more steeply, following a path up the narrowing ridge to the summit of Bidein a' Choire Sheasgaich. (From Craig: 12.5km; 1300m; 5h).

Go south at first for a short distance along the summit ridge, then descend south-east down a wide grassy slope to the next col at 740m. The ridge to Lurg Mhor is broad and bouldery, bounded on its north side by steep crags, and it leads directly to the summit. (From Craig: 14.5km; 1550m; 5h 50min). Only the most dedicated of 'Top baggers' are likely to continue the extra 750m east to Meall Mor; but it is worthwhile for the intervening ridge is narrow and rocky and gives a good scramble with one short pitch that cannot be easily avoided.

The return from Lurg Mhor to Craig is just as long and strenuous as the outward journey. One way is to reverse the traverse over Bidein a' Choire Sheasgaich and Beinn Tharsuinn, with all the climbing that that involves. The alternative is to descend north-east from the col between Lurg Mhor and Bidein and lose a lot of height to about 350m, then traverse round below the rocky lower nose of Beinn Tharsuinn's south-east ridge and climb the long grassy slopes on the east side of that hill to the Bealach Bhearnais. From there follow the outward route back to Craig. Altogether, it is a hard day's hillwalking that can be made easier with a bike.

An altogether less arduous option is to bike in from Attadale on Loch Carron to the west, past Ben Dronaig Lodge bothy and on to the shore of Loch Calavie NH044393 where an ascent up the Allt Coire Calavie gains the bealach between these two peaks.

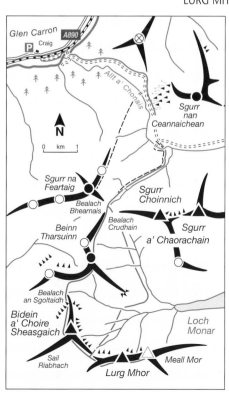

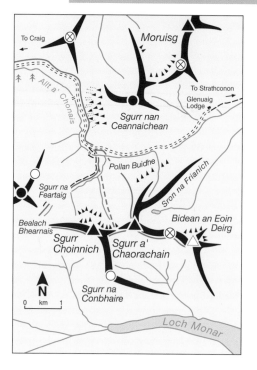

These two mountains are fairly accessible from Craig in Glen Carron and can be clearly seen as one approaches up the track along the Allt a' Chonais above the Achnashellach Forest. Sgurr Choinnich presents a steep rocky front, and it has a level summit ridge, while Sgurr a' Chaorachain appears as a more rounded mountain. Between them is a fine little corrie, very rocky on its west side below the cliffs of Sgurr Choinnich, but less so on the east side. Not seen from this viewpoint is the third peak in this group, Bidean an Eoin Deirg (1046m). It has a pointed summit 2km east of Sgurr a' Chaorachain, and it appears as the finest of the group when seen from the east, for example in the view westwards along Loch Monar.

To reach this pair, cross the Allt a' Chonais by the footbridge at NH074467 or by the two-wire bridge a short distance upstream and take the stalkers' path leading to the Bealach Bhearnais. A good traverse of Sgurr Choinnich, although not the shortest ascent, can be made by continuing up this path to the bealach, and then heading back east up the west ridge of the peak. This is a pleasant grassy ridge with a few little rocky steps, and it leads to the narrow level crest where the summit is perched on the edge of the steep north-east face. (From Craig: 9.5km; 950m, 3h 50min).

Continue south-east along the nearly level crest for about 200m, then turn north-east down the steep rocky ridge to the Bealach Coire Choinnich (860m). From there climb up the broad ridge to the level stony summit of Sgurr a' Chaorachain. (From Craig: 11km; 1050m; 4h 20min).

On a good day it is worthwhile going to Bidean an Eoin Deirg. The first 1km is along a

Sgurr a' Chaorachain from the summit of Sgurr Choinnich

*Bill Brooker*

Sgurr a' Chaorachain from the east

fairly level ridge which gives easy going on moss and flat stones. Then there is a short drop before the climb to Bidean, from where there is a good view east along Loch Monar and Glen Strathfarrar. The north face of the peak drops very steeply for 400m and is not a good route of descent unless one is intent on including Maoile Lunndaidh in this traverse. Otherwise it is best to return along the ridge to Sgurr a' Chaorachain.

From there the quickest descent is by the north ridge for about 750m, then north-west down steep but easy grassy slopes which lead to the Allt a' Chonais. Alternatively, return to the Bealach Coire Choinnich and go north down the corrie, keeping to the east side of the stream to avoid the small bands of rock below Sgurr Choinnich.

SGURR A'
CHAORACHAIN

205

SGURR CHOINNICH

Bidean an Eoin Deirg from the west

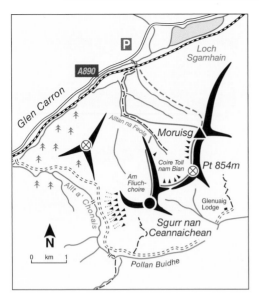

Moruisg is a long, flat-topped hill which lies on the south side of Glen Carron close to its upper reaches. Its northern corries look out over featureless moorland towards Achnasheen whilst its northwest flank drops in concave grassy slopes to the River Carron. To the south-west, on the other side of Coire Toll nam Bian, a deep hollow with a steep headwall, lies the adjoining Corbett of Sgurr nan Ceannaichean (913m); demoted from Munro status in 2009.

Both hills are normally climbed together especially since the descent down the west side of Coire Toll nam Bian begins close to the summit of Sgurr nan Ceannaichean. Start in Glen Carron some 11km to the south-west of Achnasheen where there is a layby on the A890 about 1.5km west of the outflow from Loch Sgamhain. Cross a bridge over the River Carron (NH082520) then pass beneath a low bridge carrying the railway to gain open moorland. The most direct route lies ahead up steepening grass slopes north of the obvious gullies however it is better and easier underfoot to follow the stalkers' path which heads south-west then south alongside the Alltan na Feola towards Coire Toll nam Bian. After about 2km turn left off the path and go east well below a cliff, the Creag nan Calman, to climb the grassy slopes on its left, steeply at first then more easily to the top (4.5km; 780m 2h 20min).

From here it is about 2.5km to Sgurr nan Ceannaichean following a broad mossy ridge south over Pt.854m, then descending more steeply south-west to the col at the head of Coire Toll nam Bian. Climb west up a broad grassy ridge for 500m then head south-west for another 500m to reach the summit of Sgurr nan Ceannaichean (NH 087481); the smaller cairn at the south-east edge would appear to be the highpoint. (7.5km; 978m; 3h 30min).

Retrace the last part of the ascent route for 500m down the north-east ridge, then bear north down a steep broad ridge, avoiding a rocky bluff halfway down on its left. Cross the Alltan na Feola to reach the stalkers' path on its north-east bank and follow this back to the start (12km; 5hs 30mins).

Moruisg from Sgurr nan Ceannaichean

Dave Snadden

Bidean an Eoin Deirg and Maoile Lunndaidh from Loch Monar before it was dammed

## Maoile Lunndaidh; 1005m; (OS Sheet 25; NH135458); M127; *bare hill of the wet place*

Another very remote Munro, Maoile Lunndaidh rises to the north of Loch Monar in the wild hinterland between Glen Carron, Glen Strathfarrar and Strathconon, and it is roughly equidistant from starting points in these three glens. In appearance it is a flat-topped, almost Cairngorm-like hill, with a level plateau ending abruptly in deep corries. This appearance is particularly evident looking along Loch Monar from its east end. From Glen Carron the hill is invisible, and one has to go several kilometres up the Allt a' Chonais before seeing it and reaching the foot of its north face, cleft by the deep Fuar-tholl Mor.

Of the three approaches, the one from Craig in Glen Carron is the shortest and has the advantage that one can bike most of the 10km to the foot of the hill. From the Forestry Commission Achnashellach Forest car park in Craig, cross the railway on the opposite side of the A890 and take the track up the Allt a' Chonais to the watershed. Continue for about 1.5km further past a small plantation almost to Glenuaig Lodge before turning off east across rough ground. Cross An Crom-allt and climb south towards Carn nam Fiaclan up the steepening hillside, keeping to the crest, then along the edge of the Fuar-tholl Mor, with grand views down to the lochans cradled in this fine corrie. Pass over the top of Carn nam Fiaclan (996m) and from this Top continue east then north-east across the plateau over the rounded bump between the corries of Fuar-tholl Mor and Toll a' Choin to reach the summit of Maoile Lunndaidh (From Craig: 14km; 980m; 4h 40min).

The descent may be varied by going north down to a col at 750m, then turning west to descend across the foot of Fuar-tholl Mor. Once fairly flat ground is reached, bear north-west across An Crom-allt to return to the track near Glenuaig Lodge.

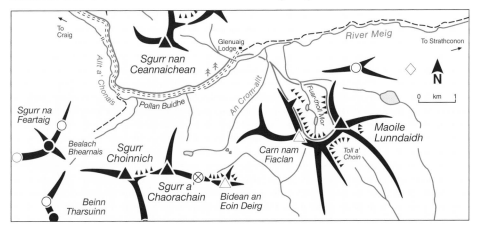

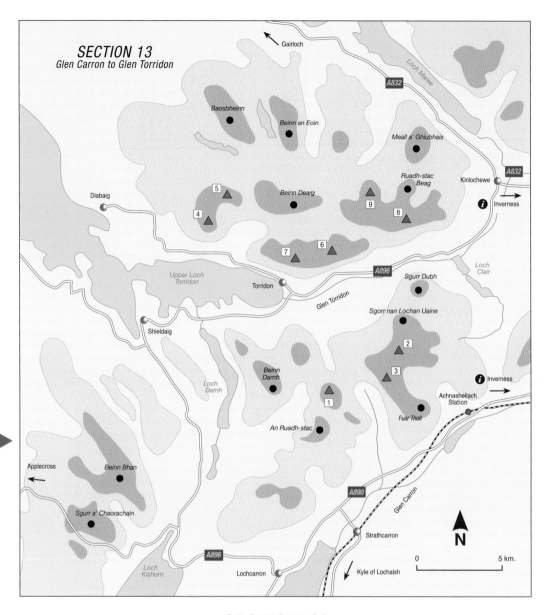

## SECTION 13

### Glen Carron to Glen Torridon

*i* VisitScotland Information Centre
**Inverness**; Castle Wynd, Inverness, IV2 3BJ, (01463 252401), open Jan–Dec

*Donald Bennet*

Looking west from Fuar Tholl to Maol Chean-dearg

## Maol Chean-dearg; 933m; (OS Sheet 25; NG924499); M247; *bald red head*

Maol Chean-dearg is one of three Munros on the north-west side of Glen Carron. It can be seen from the glen near Coulags, from where it is most frequently climbed, partly hidden behind the nearer and lower Meall nan Ceapairean. It is an isolated mountain whose summit is a great dome of bare rock and sandstone boulders, making its name, bald red head, particularly apt.

From the A890 road bridge just west of Coulags follow the right of way up the east side of the Fionn-abhainn, crossing to the west bank after 2.5km. Continue past the MBA Coire Fionnaraich bothy to the Clach nan Con-fionn, the stone to which the legendary Fionn tethered his hunting dogs. In a further 500m take the path which climbs more steeply west to the bealach at about 590m between Maol Chean-dearg and Meall nan Ceapairean.

From there climb north-west by a rough path up quartzite screes and grassy patches to reach a level shoulder. Continue along it and climb the final dome of Maol Chean-dearg, which resembles a great pile of sandstone boulders. The summit is a little plateau, with the large cairn near its north-west edge. (7.5km; 900m; 3h 10min). From a point a few metres beyond the cairn there is a spectacular view down the steep north face to Loch an Eoin. The best descent is by the uphill route, any other way up or down Maol Chean-dearg being much steeper.

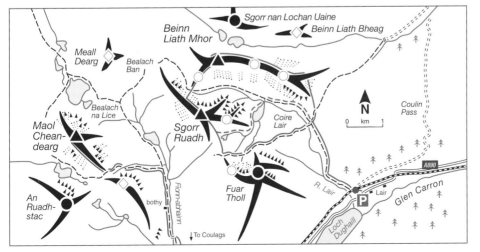

The east top of Beinn Liath Mhor

**Beinn Liath Mhor;** 926m; (OS Sheet 25; NG964519); M258; *big grey hill*
**Sgorr Ruadh;** 962m; (OS Sheet 25; NG959505); M195; *red peak*

BEINN LIATH
MHOR

SGORR RUADH

Coire Lair above Achnashellach is an impressive place surrounded by three fine mountains: Fuar Tholl (907m) is very much a climbers' peak with its great Mainreachan Buttress; Sgorr Ruadh is the shapely highest summit of the group with big sandstone cliffs towering above Loch Coire Lair, and Beinn Liath Mhor is the long ridge on the north side of Coire Lair whose white quartzite screes are in striking contrast with the dark sandstone cliffs of the other two peaks on the opposite side of the corrie. The approach to the Coire Lair peaks is up the right of way from Achnashellach to Torridon.

Park beside the A890 road near the end of the private road leading to Achnashellach station. Walk up to the station, cross the line and go through the gate opposite along a track through rhododendrons for 100m, then turn left along a forest road and follow it for several hundred metres until a path on the left leads to a gate and the path up Coire Lair. This path continues through the forest and onto the more open hillside where scattered pines cling to the steep sides of the ravine through which the River Lair plunges. At a height of 370m, with Coire Lair opening out ahead, there is a junction of paths. If the river is in spate, it is worth going along the left-hand path for a short distance to inspect the crossing which may have to be made at the end of the day. There are no better crossing places lower down.

Continue up the corrie for 100m and then go along the right-hand path which goes to Loch Coulin. In about 300m, at the high point of this path, go left up a faint path which climbs north-north-west across a boulder slope to reach the broad ridge leading to the 876m east top of Beinn Liath Mhor. From there traverse 2km along the undulating ridge of quartzite scree and grassy patches to the main summit. (7km; 1030m; 3h 20min).

Some care is needed on the descent to the Bealach Coire Lair. Go south-west down the ridge, at first over rough bouldery ground where the rock changes from quartzite to sandstone. Scramble down a low sandstone crag which crosses the ridge; it may be necessary to search for an easy way down. Then go past a small lochan and climb over a knoll (769m) to reach the path across the bealach, where there is another lochan.

From the Bealach Coire Lair (c 650m) climb south-west to the tiny lochan on the north-west ridge of Sgorr Ruadh, and follow this ridge to the summit. (9.5km; 1380m; 4h 30min). The descent goes south-east down an open slope of grass and boulders and leads to the broad col where there are several lochans, Loch a' Bhealaich Mhoir being the largest. Continue south beyond this loch past a few smaller ones to reach a stalkers' path. It would be quite possible to

The north-eastern buttresses of Sgorr Ruadh from Coire Lair

climb Fuar Tholl from there by its west ridge, thereby completing the traverse of the Coire Lair peaks. The direct return to Achnashellach, however, goes east down the stalkers' path below the imposing crags of Fuar Tholl to the crossing of the River Lair.

If previous inspection has shown this crossing to be difficult or dangerous, then descend east from Loch a' Bhealaich Mhoir to Loch Coire Lair. Go round the west side of this loch to reach the path down the corrie to Achnashellach. Map on page 209.

Sgorr Ruadh (left) and Maol Chean-dearg from Beinn Damh

*Douglas Scott*

Beinn Alligin seen across Loch Torridon

**BEINN ALLIGIN;** *possibly jewelled hill*
**Tom na Gruagaich;** 922m; (OS Sheet 24; NG859601); M268; *hill of the maiden*
**Sgurr Mhor;** 986m; (OS Sheet 24; NG866613); M162; *big peak*

212

BEINN ALLIGIN

The Torridonian triptych of Beinn Alligin, Liathach and Beinn Eighe is rightly regarded as one of the finest mountain groups in Scotland. They rise in castellated tiers and battlements of red Torridonian sandstone, in places crowned with white quartzite. Their long narrow ridges give serious expeditions with some difficult scrambling. Of the three, Beinn Alligin is the least complex, and is possibly the one which should be tackled first by visiting climbers.

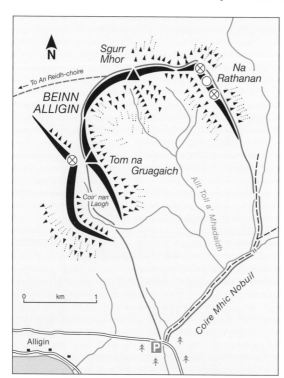

The road from the head of Loch Torridon to Inveralligin passes below Beinn Alligin, and the most convenient starting point is at the car park on the west side of the bridge over the Abhainn Coire Mhic Nobuil. Going to Tom na Gruagaich first, go north-north-west across the very rough and boggy moor by an eroded path towards the foot of Coir' nan Laogh, and climb up the east side of the stream in the corrie to reach Tom na Gruagaich, whose cairn is right on the edge of the plunging cliffs of Toll a' Mhadaidh Mor. (3km; 870m; 2h 10min).

Descend steeply north down a narrow rocky crest to the col at 766m and beyond there climb a broader ridge, still precipitous on its east side, to Sgurr Mhor, passing the spectacular cleft of the Eag Dhubh, the black cleft, just before reaching the summit. (4.5km; 1090m; 2h 50min).

Tom na Gruagaich from the north

The quickest and easiest return is by the route of ascent, and an escape route in bad weather is westwards down An Reidh-choire followed by a long walk round the west side of the mountain. However, the best continuation of the traverse is to continue along the castellated crest of Na Rathanan, the Horns of Alligin. Descend steeply east down a narrow ridge to the col at 757m, and traverse the three Horns. There is a very obvious path over these rocky tops, which give some easy, but in places exposed scrambling. From the third top continue south-east down the ridge to the moor below, where a stalkers' path is joined and followed across the Abhainn Coire Mhic Nobuil and along its left bank to the road.

On the summit ridge of Beinn Alligin at the top of the Eag Dhubh

Liathach from Loch Clair

## LIATHACH; *the grey one*
**Spidean a' Choire Leith;** 1055m; (OS Sheet 25; NG929580); M75; *peak of the grey corrie*
**Mullach an Rathain;** 1023m; (OS Sheet 25; NG912577); M108; *summit of the row of pinnacles*

LIATHACH

The central, highest and most awesome of the Torridonian trio is Liathach. Its great terraced wall rising above Glen Torridon is unique among Scottish mountains in conveying the impression of impregnability, an impression which is quite correct for there are few chinks in Liathach's armour. The mountain is a huge 7km-long ridge with two principal summits: Spidean a' Choire Leith near the eastern end and Mullach an Rathain towards the west. The ridge between them is narrow, and for almost half its length is a succession of pinnacles.

The traverse of this pinnacled ridge is an exposed and in places difficult scramble, so the complete traverse of Liathach, one of the great mountaineering expeditions in Scotland, is reserved for those with some scrambling experience and a good head for heights. In winter conditions the traverse is a major undertaking calling for a high level of mountaineering ability; however, the two main summits themselves can each be climbed quite easily, although they may be quite serious climbs requiring skill and proper equipment.

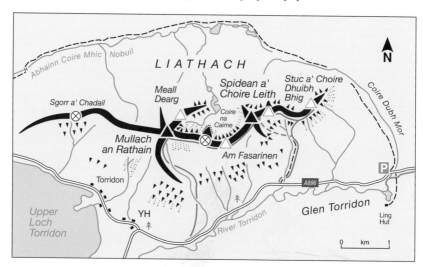

Spidean a' Choire Leith from Stuc a' Choire Dhuibh Bhig

The traverse is usually done from east to west, and the route to Spidean a' Choire Leith starts from the A896 road in Glen Torridon about 600m east of Glen Cottage. The path begins about 50m west of the Allt an Doire Ghairbh, crosses this stream and climbs steeply up its east bank into the Toll a' Meitheach by a well engineered path. High up at about 550m the stream forks and straight ahead are the dark cliffs at the head of Coire Liath Mhor. One route bears right up steep ground following a tenuous path to reach the col on the main ridge at 833m. From there a short diversion leads to Stuc a' Choire Dhuibh Bhig (915m), the easternmost peak of Liathach and a fine viewpoint.

Returning to the 833m col, the traverse continues along the crest of the ridge, north-west at first, then west over the two tops of Stob a' Coire Liath Mhor (983m) to the final bouldery summit cone of Spidean a' Choire Leith. (3km; 1120m; 3h).

LIATHACH

Mullach an Rathain from the east

The Liathach ridge from Am Fasarinen to Mullach an Rathain

An alternative and more direct route from Toll a' Meitheach bears left from the stream junction on a rising traverse north-west. There are several small sandstone cliffs which can be avoided with the exception of one which requires a short scramble. Above it a steep scree slope leads to the main ridge just below the bouldery cone of Spidean a' Choire Leith. If this is your objective, return by the ascent route.

To continue the traverse, descend south-west down quartzite boulders and easier grassy slopes to the col at the beginning of the narrow pinnacled section of the ridge. This gives excellent scrambling along the crest, with a few more serious pitches and considerable exposure on the north side overlooking Coire na Caime. There are usually easier alternatives on the south side of the ridge and for much of the way there is a narrow path several metres below the crest. However, it also is exposed, slippery when wet and eroded at places where it crosses some steep little gullies, so it is probably better to stay on firm rock. In winter this 'path' may be hidden under snow and any attempt to traverse along it may be more difficult than staying on or near the crest. Eventually the difficulties end at the peak of Am Fasarinen (927m), the ridge becomes broad and easy and leads over a minor point to Mullach an Rathain. (5km; 1300m; 4h 30min).

An exposed pinnacle above Coire na Caime

The most direct descent to Glen Torridon goes down the Toll Ban, the corrie immediately to the south. It is best to go west from the cairn for about 100m, then south down the stony ridge on the west side of the Toll Ban for a short distance before dropping down into the corrie itself. A path will be found near the Allt an Tuill Bhain, but it gives rather rough going down to Glen Torridon near the small pine woods. This descent route, in reverse, gives the most straightforward ascent to Mullach an Rathain.

*Douglas Scott*

Beinn Eighe from the road to the Coulin Pass

**BEINN EIGHE;** *file hill*
**Ruadh-stac Mor;** 1010m; (OS Sheets 19 and 25; NG951611); M120; *big red peak*
**Spidean Coire nan Clach;** 993m; (OS Sheets 19 and 25; NG966597); M150;
  *peak of the corrie of stones*

Beinn Eighe is the easternmost of the threesome of Torridonian giants, but unlike its neighbours it is characterised by the pale quartzite screes and rock of the long ridge which links its several peaks on the north side of Glen Torridon. The great corries of Beinn Eighe face north into desolate country seldom penetrated by hillwalkers, while the long scree flanks above Glen Torridon give the mountain an air of impregnability.

Ruadh-stac Mor, the highest of Beinn Eighe's peaks, is on a spur to the north of the main ridge. It cannot be seen from Glen Torridon, but there is a good view of it from Bridge of Grudie on the Loch Maree road. Spidean Coire nan Clach is on the main ridge near the centre of the massif where the short spur of Stuc Coire an Laoigh juts out above Glen Torridon. The finest feature of the mountain is Coire Mhic Fhearchair, with its dark loch mirroring the Triple Buttress that forms the headwall of the corrie. This is one of the finest corries in Scotland.

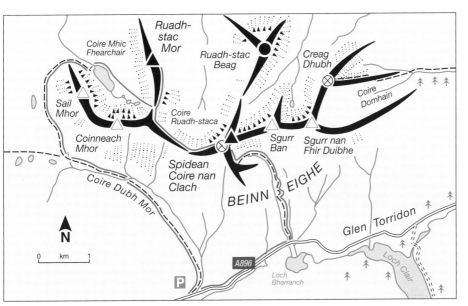

The Triple Buttress of Coire Mhic Fhearchair

218

Looking east from Liathach to Beinn Eighe and distant Fionn Bheinn

Looking west from Sgurr nan Fhir Duibhe to Sgurr Ban and Spidean Coire nan Clach. Ruadh-stac Mor is far to the right

Both mountains can be climbed separately but the most rewarding route is the one which climbs them both. Start in Glen Torridon from the car park at NG958569 and ascend the well constructed path uphill into Coire Dubh Mhor between Liathach and Beinn Eighe to reach the watershed. Above a small lochan take the right fork and traverse around the flanks of Sail Mhor into the magnificent glacial splendour of Coire Mhic Fhearchair with its idyllic lochan and mighty Triple Buttress. Go round the east side of the lochan and continue on a path beside the burn passing some small pools to ascend through, or alongside the scree, then up a stony gully to gain the obvious col. Climb north out of the col and continue on easier ground for 1km to the summit of Ruadh-stac Mor. (9.5km; 924m; 3h 30min).

Return to the col and climb the path up the other side then continue past a cairn to the east end of the level mossy summit of Coinneach Mhor where a splendid ridge leads down south-east to a low point at 822m, then upwards to reach the trig point at 972m on Spidean Coire nan Clach; the 993m summit lies 200m to the north-east. (12.5km; 1218m; 4h 50min).

Return to the trig point and descend the spur southwards towards Stuc Coire an Laoigh before dropping east down the headwall into Coire an Laoigh to follow a good path all the way back to the road beside the burn. Parking at the start of the path for an ascent of Spidean Coire nan Clach via this route is restricted and the main car park 2km away should be used.

The complete traverse of Beinn Eighe including its Munros and Munro Tops is one of the finest outings in Scotland. From the north end of a layby NH025610 at Cromasaig just outside Kinlochewe, gain a track then a good path leading pleasantly above the Allt a' Chuirn, crossing its right branch to climb an increasingly rocky spur onto Creag Dhubh. The jagged ridge and its 'Black Carls' give Grade 1 scrambling to reach Sgurr nan Fhir Duibhe (963m). Next is Sgurr Ban (970m), then Spidean Coire nan Clach (993m). Coinneach Mhor (976m) is easily taken in but the splendid Sail Mhor (980m) involves some logistical decision making as a considerable detour is required here if the intention is to climb both it and Ruadh-stac Mor (1010m). In descent there is a difficult and exposed Grade 2 scramble 'The Ceum Ghrannda' down the side of the Triple Buttress, easier in re-ascent (Highland Scrambles North, SMC). This could be avoided by a detour from the Ruadh-stac Mor col, thence beneath the Triple Buttress and up the slope on the right to Sail Mhor. Either way, return via Coire Mhic Fhearchair and the Coire Dubh path. (23km road to road; 9hrs). A potential 9km walk (1hr 30mins) along the road regains the start.

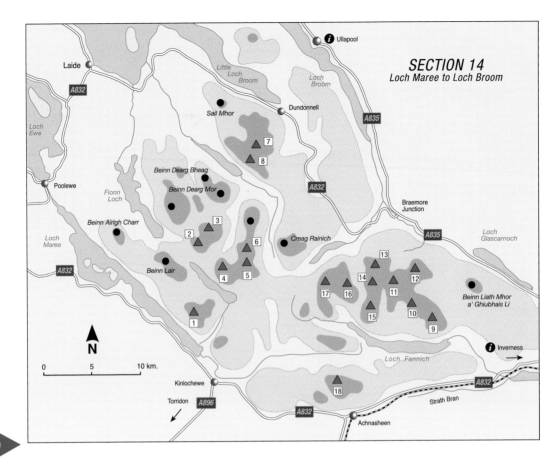

# SECTION 14

## Loch Maree to Loch Broom

**ⓘ VisitScotland Information Centres**
**Inverness**; Castle Wynd, Inverness, IV2 3BJ, (01463 252401), open Jan–Dec
**Ullapool**; Argyle Street, Ullapool, IV26 2UB, (01854 612486), open Easter–Oct

Roger Robb

Slioch from Loch Maree

### Slioch; 981m; (OS Sheet 19; NH004690); M170; *the spear hill*

The head of Loch Maree is dominated by Slioch, a magnificent Torridonian sandstone mountain rising like a huge castle above its foundation of Lewisian gneiss. It is one of the great sights of the Northern Highlands, well seen across the loch, and its summit commands fine views of the surrounding mountains, some of them in the wildest part of Scotland. Around three-quarters of its perimeter Slioch is defended by towering sandstone buttresses, steep crags and scree. Only on its south-east side, in Coire na Sleaghaich above Gleann Bianasdail, are there any easy routes to the summit.

From the large car park at Incheril 1km east of Kinlochewe, follow the footpath north-west alongside fields, then along the wooded bank on the north-east side of the Kinlochewe River. The path reaches the shore of Loch Maree, and 1km further crosses the Abhainn an Fhasaigh by a footbridge. Once across the bridge, turn north-east up the path which leads through Gleann Bianasdail to Lochan Fada.

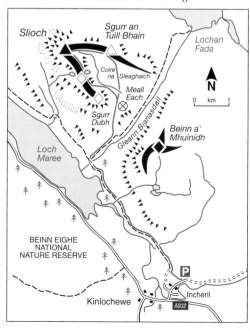

In about 750m bear due north, following a less distinct path up to the col between the rocky point of Sgurr Dubh and the lower knoll of Meall Each. Beyond the col continue north-west then west below the north face of Sgurr Dubh for 750m and climb a short steep slope to reach a col on the south-east ridge of Slioch. Climb this ridge, passing over a knoll and descend past two lochans on its crest, and continue more steeply over a false summit, across a wide col and past the trig point to reach the true summit. (10km; 940m; 3h 50min). It is a fine view-point, being perched at the top of the great north-west buttresses of the mountain.

To make a traverse of the mountain, go east along a narrowing ridge to Sgurr an Tuill Bhain (934m). From there a bearing due south leads down across Coire na Sleaghaich to the col between Sgurr Dubh and Meall Each where the uphill route is rejoined.

# The Letterewe and Fisherfield Hills

North of Slioch and Loch Maree, the Letterewe and Fisherfield forests are a wild and uninhabited tract of mountainous country with no road access. The five Munros and one Corbett in this area, the 'Fisherfield Six', are collectively the remotest in Scotland, their inaccessibility only rivaled perhaps, by Seana Bhraigh and Lurg Mhor. The routes to these six mountains from points on the perimeter of this great wilderness are very long, and hillwalkers have to be fit to walk or bike in, climb their peaks and come out in a single day. The four points of access are Kinlochewe in the south-east, Loch a' Bhraoin in the east, Poolewe in the west and Corrie Hallie near Dundonnell in the north.

The alternative approach to these mountains involves either wild camping or bivouacing in the interior of the area, or staying in bothies, of which there are two. Shenavall in Strath na Sealga is a good cottage from which all five Munros are accessible, and can in fact be climbed in a single day by those who are fit. However, it is very popular and often uncomfortably crowded. The barn at Carnmore at the east end of Fionn Loch has been restored, and there is a sign saying "walkers and climbers are welcome to use the barn". Another option is the Lochivraon Bothy at the west end of Loch a' Bhraoin, reached by a rough track that can be biked.

There is a good network of well-engineered stalkers' paths throughout the area, but also an absence of footbridges at some crucial river crossings, so during and after heavy rain some of these crossings may be impossible. The two most obvious examples of this problem are the Abhainn Srath na Sealga and the Abhainn Gleann na Muice, both near Shenavall.

**A' Mhaighdean;** 967m; (OS Sheet 19; NH008749); M187; *the maiden*
**Ruadh Stac Mor;** 919m; (OS Sheet 19; NH018756); M273; *big red stack*

**A'MHAIGHDEAN**

**222**

**RUADH STAC MOR**

A' Mhaighdean and Ruadh Stac Mor stand in the centre of the Letterewe wilderness, the former a cliff-girt bastion which is one of the most spectacular viewpoints in Britain. These two are among the most highly prized Munros for hillwalkers by virtue of their remoteness and the beauty of their setting. It is worth saving them for a fine day. The very long approach from Poolewe is described, together with an approach from Kinlochewe.

The Poolewe approach starts from a car park on the left immediately after turning-off south on the east side of the bridge across the River Ewe. Walk or bike along what soon becomes a private road by the river. When the road ends take the track on the left and continue past Inveran to reach Kernsary. In a further 500m take a track on the right and go through a gate into the forest where the track deteriorates; bikes are best left here unless very dry. Times given are on foot from Poolewe; (6km; 80m; 1h 20min). Continue almost to the end of the track

The view north-west from A' Mhaighdean towards Dubh Loch and Fionn Loch

*Greg Strange*

A' Mhaighdean and Dubh Loch from the north-west

then go along a path to exit the forest by a gate and stile at NG910789. Older maps do not show the higher line of this stalkers' path which is well above the burn.

Follow the path past Loch an Doire Crionaich and take the short-cut path across the entrance to Srathan Buidhe, the glen separating Beinn Airigh Charr and Meall Mhèinnidh, there is a bridge 400m upstream if required. Continue past a small lochan then make a gradual descent to gain the south-east end of the Fionn Loch where A' Mhaighdean soars up beyond the adjoining Dubh Loch.

Cross the causeway between the lochs and go along the path towards Carnmore (17km; 320m; 4h 10min), then take the path which climbs east into the glen of the Allt Bruthach an Easain. The easiest route is to follow this path north-east to Lochan Fèith Mhic'-illean then take the branch which ascends south-east above Fuar Loch Mòr to gain the col between A' Mhaighdean and Ruadh Stac Mòr then climb each mountain from there. However, a better

A'MHAIGHDEAN

RUADH STAC MOR

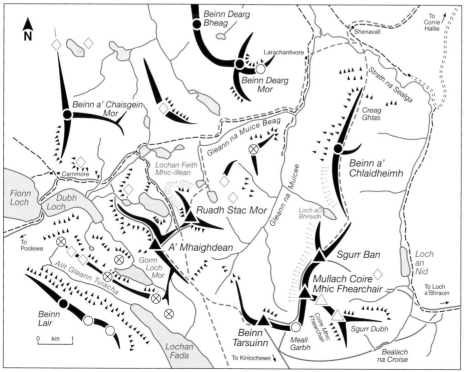

Ruadh Stac Mor

route is to cross the Allt Bruthach an Easain and traverse south-east to the burn flowing out of Fuar Loch Beag and climb the long stepped crest of A' Mhaighdean's north-west ridge. This has many crags but most difficulty can be avoided and the scenery is impressive. Where the ridge narrows in the upper section, cross a neck then cut down left and go right through a notch to pass right of a small pinnacle then a larger one to gain broken ground leading to the domed plateau at Point 948m. The summit lies some 400m away to the south, perched above cliffs (21km; 1050m; 6h 30m).

Descend north-east from A' Mhaighdean by easy, mainly grassy slopes to the col at about 750m, where there is a bivouac site in a cave under a large boulder. This might be useful for a night's shelter if this expedition is too long for a single day. From there Ruadh Stac Mor seems well defended by a ring of sandstone crags, but there is a path which zigzags up the steep hillside through an obvious break and although fairly straightforward, this is eroded in places and care is required, especially when returning the same way. Easier ground above leads through scree and boulders to gain the trig point. (22.5km; 1210m; 7h 10min).

Return by the route of ascent to the col and take the stalkers' path (not completely shown on the OS map) which starts there and makes a descending traverse between the crags and screes of Ruadh Stac Mor above and the dark waters of Fuar Loch Mor below to reach the outflow of Lochan Feith Mhic'-illean. Go south-west along the path which leads down the Allt Bruthach an Easain to Carnmore and the long return journey to Poolewe. The total distance, without the help of a car, is nearly 45km.

Although not as scenically attractive a route to A' Mhaighdean as that from Poolewe, the approach from the Incheril car park 1km east of Kinlochewe, using a bike to just short of Lochan Fada, then cutting across the slopes of Beinn Tarsuinn, is certainly the shortest. From the car park at Incheril NH038624, also the starting point for Slioch, follow the track north-east alongside the Abhainn Bruachaig to fork left at the Heights of Kinlochewe then climb Gleann na Muice to a fork at NH070667. The continuation up the glen is a wide surfaced path which can be cycled to a fence at NH063681 (8.5km, 1h 15min). On this latter section some dismounts will probably be required to cross drainage channels. From the fence a stalkers' path leads to Lochan Fhada. Walk along the waters edge crossing a burn, then at NH045705, just before the inlet of the next burn, climb the hillside to the right of the burn following an old cairned route leading towards the rocks of Creag Ghlas Mhor. Swing around the head of the burn then take a rising traverse line across the hillside aiming for A' Mhaighdean and passing beneath a small rocky spur. Join the 'baggers' path off Beinn Tarsuinn, avoiding the peat hags at the bealach on their left, and climb to the summit of A' Mhaighdean (9.5km, 3h 30min from the bike). Ruadh Stac Mor is easily taken in (11km, 4h 30min from the bike). On the return, an obvious traverse line leads across the slopes of A' Mhaighdean from just above the bealach between the hills, following the 760 and 770m contours, passing well above the crags of Stac a' Chaoruinn, to regain the upward route, which is descended to the bealach. Including Beinn Tarsuinn is now perhaps an option, otherwise retrace the route of ascent. (Distance on foot 21km, 7h 50min and by bike 17km, 2h 10min).

A'MHAIGHDEAN

RUADH STAC MOR

Sgurr Ban and Mullach Coire Mhic Fhearchair from Beinn Tarsuinn

**Beinn Tarsuinn**; 937m; (OS Sheet 19; NH039727); M238; *transverse hill*
**Mullach Coire Mhic Fhearchair**; 1018m; (OS Sheet 19; NH052735); M115;
   *summit of the corrie of Farquhar's son*
**Sgurr Ban**; 989m; (OS Sheet 19; NH055745); M157; *white peak*

This is another hard to reach group with two possible approaches; from Incheril near Kinlochewe and from the A832 road near the east end of Loch a' Bhraoin. Bikes can be used on both routes to save time and effort, but from the former, Sgurr Ban is still a very long way away. The latter gives a shorter, route if one wants to climb all three peaks in one day, either on foot or using a bike.

From the car park at Incheril NH038624, 1km east of Kinlochewe, follow the track north-east alongside the Abhainn Bruachaig to fork left at the Heights of Kinlochewe then climb Gleann na Muice to a fork at NH070667. The continuation up the glen is a wide surfaced path leading to a fence at NH063681. It is possible to bike to here (8.5km; 1hr 15min). Continue by a path to the south-east end of Lochan Fada. From there the going is rough and boggy at first, but improves as height is gained. Head north until the craggy hillside at about 500m is passed, then bear towards Beinn Tarsuinn along a gently rising ridge and a steeper slope of stepped sandstone leading to the summit. (14km; 920m; 4h 40min). Beinn Tarsuinn has a narrow crest extending north-west in the direction of A'Mhaighdean, and fills the head of Gleann na Muice as a grand bastion.

Descend east to the Bealach Odhar (c730m) below Meall Garbh and follow a well-worn deer path across the north-west face of this little peak to the next bealach (750m) below Mullach Coire Mhic Fhearchair. The final climb to the summit of this mountain goes up a broad ridge of shattered quartzite boulders. (16km; 1200m; 5h 40min).

The continuation of the traverse to Sgurr Ban goes down a steep slope of quartzite boulders and up a less steep ridge to the flat stony summit of Sgurr Ban. (17.5km; 1370m; 6h 10min). The return to Kinlochewe is long and tiring. Go back over Mullach Coire Mhic Fhearchair and along the path on the north-west side of Meall Garbh by the outward route to reach the bealach below Beinn Tarsuinn. Then go south down a shallow corrie to rejoin the ascent route near Lochan Fada.

The Loch a' Bhraoin approach is the best way to Sgurr Ban and makes possible the ascent of nearly 1500 metres of low-angled quartzite slabs on its east face, a delightful feature which is unique in the Scottish hills. Leave the A832 road near Loch a' Bhraoin and follow the track along the north side of the loch to reach Lochivraon cottage and bothy. Although quite rough

Looking up Gleann na Muice to Beinn Tarsuinn

it is possible to cycle to here (6km; 45mins). After about 1km the track becomes a path which crosses the burn at NH101729 and continues past the ruin at Feinasheen to descend into the fine strath of Loch an Nid. Cross the strath and climb west beside the burn which flows down from the Sgurr Ban - Mullach Coire Mhic Fhearchair col, and reach the little flat col just west of Meallan an Laoigh. From there go west-north-west up the extensive sheets of quartzite slabs which are a feature of the east face of Sgurr Ban. By going slightly further north, starting at 280m above Loch an Nid, slabs can be followed to 800m on the hillside, a distance of 1500m. In dry weather the walk up these slabs is perfectly easy, but in wet weather a little more care is needed. The summit dome is covered with sharp boulders which give rough walking. (12.5km; 830m; 4h 10min).

To continue the traverse of these three mountains, reverse the route described previously to reach Mullach Coire Mhic Fhearchair (14km; 1030m; 4h 50min) and Beinn Tarsuinn (16km; 1250m; 5h 40min). Descend from this peak south-east then east across the lower part of Coire Mhic Fhearchair to reach the Bealach na Croise, follow the path north-east down from this pass for about 1.5km and then bear away east-north-east to reach the path leading to Loch a' Bhraoin. The total distance for this circuit is about 32km, most of it rough going although use of a bike to Lochivraon does make this easier despite the biking being quite hard. Map on page 223.

226

BEINN TARSUINN

MULLACH COIRE
MHIC
FHEARCHAIR

SGURR BAN

## The Fisherfield Six

Despite the 2012 demotion of Beinn a' Chlaidheimh from Munro to Corbett status, the complete traverse of the Fisherfield range of five Munros and one Corbett is a magnificent expedition and remains as one of Scotland's great hillwalking challenges. This expedition is quite possible for fit hillwalkers in a single day, particularly if Shenavall is used as the base for the trip. This is a very popular bothy and frequently overcrowded in summer. However, useage may be restricted during the stalking season. There is good camping along the north bank of the Abhainn Srath na Sealga. The earlier remarks about river crossings are very relevant as the Abhainn Srath na Sealga has to be crossed both at the beginning and the end of the day, and it is a sizeable river in normal conditions; in spate it is likely to be quite impassable.

From Shenaval cross this river and climb up the north-west shoulder of Beinn a' Chlaidheimh, a steep and rough ascent with small sandstone crags, most of which can be easily avoided. At the top a fine narrow ridge leads to the summit. Continue south over a knoll, then south-east to the col (c.600m) east of Loch a' Bhrisidh. At that point the quartzite slopes of Sgurr Ban are reached, and a long climb south-west leads to its summit. Continue to Mullach Coire Mhic Fhearchair and Beinn Tarsuinn as already described.

From Beinn Tarsuinn descend the fine narrow ridge west then north-west, and drop down west to the low boggy bealach at about 520m which is the watershed between Gleann na Muice

Peter Hodgkiss

Sgurr Ban, Beinn a' Chlaidheimh and Ruadh Stac Mor from the path to Shenavall

and Lochan Fada. The long ascent to A' Mhaighdean is up a broad grassy ridge, and the route continues to Ruadh Stac Mor as already described. The bivouac cave on the bealach between these two mountains may be very welcome on this long expedition.

The most direct return to Shenavall goes along the north-west ridge of Ruadh Stac Mor for almost 500m, then north-east down quite easy slopes towards Lochan a' Bhraghad. From there go north along the stream flowing from the lochan to reach the stalkers' path at the head of Gleann na Muice Beag. This path leads down to Gleann na Muice 1.5km upstream of Larachantivore. Wade across the Abhainn Gleann na Muice and finally cross the level boggy Strath na Sealga to wade its river opposite Shenavall. Map on page 223.

Mullach Coire Mhic Fhearchair from Bealach Odhar at the foot of Beinn Tarsuinn

Rab Anderson

Bidein a' Ghlas Thuill

**AN TEALLACH;** *the forge*
**Bidein a' Ghlas Thuill;** 1062m; (OS Sheet 19; NH069844); M72;
   *pinnacle of the grey-green hollow*
**Sgurr Fiona;** 1060m; (OS Sheet 19; NH064837); M73; *either white peak or wine peak*

    An Teallach is deservedly regarded as one of the finest of Scottish mountains. Forming a high massif between Little Loch Broom and Loch na Sealga, it is seen to best advantage from the A832 road crossing the divide from Braemore to Dundonnell. This aspect is dominated by three eastward projecting ridges, Glas Mheall Mor, Glas Mheall Liath and Sail Liath, and the two great corries which they enclose, Glas Tholl and Toll an Lochain. The highest summit lies at the head of the central ridge, and the other Munro, Sgurr Fiona, is at the upper end of the pinnacled crest

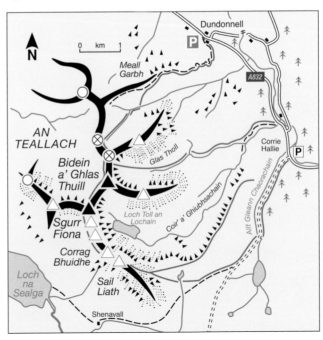

Corrag Bhuidhe (left) and Sgurr Fiona

which curves round the southern corrie to end at Sail Liath. An Teallach is largely composed of dark red Torridonian sandstone, but its dramatic rocky outline is enhanced by the Cambrian quartzites which cap its eastern spurs and form distinctive light grey screes.

Two routes of ascent are widely used. The shorter one starts near Dundonnell Hotel, but it hardly does justice to the mountain; it does, however, avoid all difficulties. Leave the A832 road 500m south-east of the hotel beside a small house and follow a very rough path which zigzags

Corrag Bhuidhe and Sgurr Fiona from Loch Toll an Lochain

Donald Bennet

Sail Liath and Corrag Bhuidhe from Sgurr Fiona

up the steep and in places rocky shoulder of Meall Garbh. Higher up either continue up the broad ridge which becomes smooth and gravelly, or follow a path in the corrie to its south. Both routes lead to a wide stony ridge at a slight knoll at NH067858. Continue south up to a second knoll, Sron a ' Choire, from where a short ascent south-east leads to a top (unnamed on the OS 1:50,000 map) at the edge of Glas Tholl, the big northern corrie. This can be bypassed to the south where an imposing but easy ridge is climbed to reach the summit of Bidein a' Ghlas Thuill. (6km; 1120m; 3h 20min). Sgurr Fiona lies 1km south-west and is reached by descending easily to a col and climbing the steep and in places rocky ridge for 140m. (7km; 1260m; 3h 50min).

A much finer route begins at the Corrie Hallie car park on the A832 road at NH114850. Follow the track south through the birches of Gleann Chaorachain for 3km to the point where the Shenavall path strikes off south-west, then follow this path for a further 1km and bear west to the lochan at the foot of Sail Liath. A good alternative to this route is to leave the track about 500m from Corrie Hallie, cross the Allt Gleann Chaorachain and climb south-west to reach the edge of the long sandstone escarpment above Coir' a Ghiubhsachain. This edge gives a very fine walk along a sandstone pavement to the lochan at the foot of Sail Liath, with splendid views of the mountain above Toll an Lochain.

Climb west from this lochan, at first up grassy slopes, then over quartzite boulders and scree to Sail Liath (954m), the first peak on the ridge. Descend some rocky steps and cross a little knob at the top of the Cadha Gobhlach, *forked pass*, then traverse Stob Cadha Gobhlach (960m) and climb easy rocks to Corrag Bhuidhe Buttress.

From there traverse a narrow horizontal ridge and climb to the base of the first tower of Corrag Bhuidhe. This is the steepest part of the An Teallach traverse; the direct line follows the crest of the ridge and includes a steep and exposed pitch, but it is possible to find easier alternatives on the south-west side of the tower. The narrow crest of Corrag Bhuidhe (1047m) gives excellent but very exposed scrambling over four airy rock towers, followed by the leaning spire of Lord Berkeley's Seat. However, all difficulties can be avoided by going along narrow paths on the south-west side of the ridge below the crest, but much of the character of the traverse is lost by going this way. The spectacular part of the ridge ends with a climb up to the shapely peak of Sgurr Fiona. (7.5km; 1300m; 3h 50min).

The descent north to the col is steep and rocky, but there is no difficulty, and the last 140m pull up to Bidein a' Ghlas Thuill crowns one of the best days to be had in the Highlands. (8.5km; 1440m; 4h 20min).

The return to Dundonnell can be made by the first route described above. To return to Corrie Hallie go down to the col 500m north of Bidein and descend very steeply east into the Glas

On the ridge of Corrag Bhuidhe

Tholl, taking special care if there is any snow. Go down the corrie along the north side of the stream and continue by an intermittent path across the heather-clad slopes and sandstone slabs to the Garbh Allt waterfalls where a better path is joined. This leads down the west bank of the stream to a pine wood and the path disappears into impenetrable thickets of rhododendron where a machete would be very useful. Cross to the other side of the stream and force a way down the overgrown path to the road 750m from the Corrie Hallie car park.

231

AN TEALLACH

The traverse path below the rocky ridge of Corrag Bhuidhe

# The Fannaichs

This range of mountains contains nine Munros which lie between Loch Fannich and the A835 road from Garve to Ullapool. Seven of these Munros form a fairly continuous chain, with short side ridges, whilst two are western outliers, separated from the others by a low bealach at a height of about 550m. One Munro lies south of Loch Fannich, between it and the A832.

The northern side of the Fannaichs, between the A835 road and the main mountain massif, has a lot of very rough ground - vast expanses of tussocky heather, rough grass, peat and boulders, which make for tiring walking if paths are not followed. By contrast, the upper parts of the mountains are much less rough, and most of them give good easy going along broad smooth ridges of moss and short grass.

On the south side of the main ridge the approaches from Loch Fannich can only be reached along a private road. This is not accessible to cars, but it is possible to bike the 12km from the A832 road at Grudie Bridge Power Station to Fannich Lodge.

**An Coileachan;** 923m; (OS Sheet 20; NH241680); M266; *the little cock*
**Meal Gorm;** 949m; (OS Sheet 20; NH221696); M215; *blue hill*

AN COILEACHAN

MEALL GORM

These two hills are at the south-eastern end of the main ridge of the Fannaichs, a few kilometres north of Loch Fannich. An Coileachan has an imposing appearance when seen from the road leading to Loch Fannich, and its east-facing Garbh Choire Mor looks impressive, particularly in winter. From there the main Fannaich ridge extends north-west for several kilometres to the highest peak, Sgurr Mor. Meall Gorm is a rounded hill about halfway along this ridge. It has some fine northern corries which hold lonely lochans at the sources of the Abhainn an Torrain Duibh.

The shortest way to these two hills is from the Torrandhu Bridge parking area by the A835 at the north-west end of Loch Glascarnoch beside the weather station. Walk up the west bank of the Abhainn an Torrain Duibh, which becomes the Abhainn a' Ghiubhais Li and after 4km cross the burn by a bridge at NH252712 and head south up a broad ridge to Meallan Buidhe. Beyond this small hill descend to a col and climb the north ridge of An Coileachan. (8km; 650m; 3h). Descend north then north-west along the main ridge, down to the Bealach Ban then up to the South-east Top of Meall Gorm (922m) and along a broad level ridge to Meall Gorm, passing a small stone-built stalkers' shelter on the way. (11km; 850m; 4h).

Return to the Bealach Ban and descend north-east to the col below Meallan Buidhe to retrace the ascent route back to Loch Glascarnoch. Alternatively, continue the traverse north-west along the broad ridge over Meall nam Peithirean (974m) to Sgurr Mor and join the route described next from where Beinn Liath Mhor can be gained; the reverse of the route on p234 and 235.

232

Meall Gorm from Sgurr Mor

*Donald Bennet*

Sgurr nan Clach Geala (left) and Sgurr Mor from Meall Gorm

In wet conditions a lot of water is funnelled off these hills down the main drainage lines into the Abhainn an Torrain Duibh then Loch Glascarnoch. In such times the burn crossings may be dangerous. Use of the unmarked track through the Altan Wood forestry plantation to the east of the Abhainn an Torrain Duibh and the unmarked bridges at NH264721 and NH252712 can allow these hills to be accessed with only a little added effort. These bridges can also provide access to Beinn Liath Mhor Fannaich and Sgurr Mor, as well as the extended outing described on p234 and 235.

THE FANNAICHS

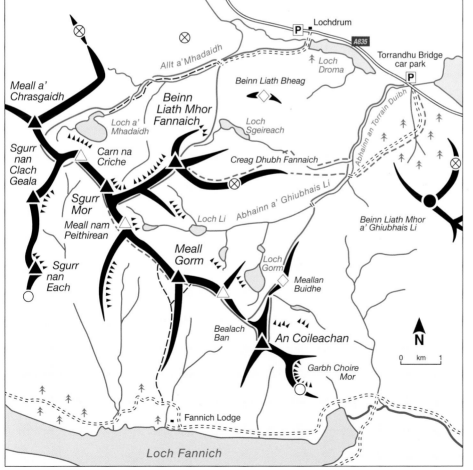

Beinn Liath Mhor Fannaich (left), Sgurr Mor and Carn na Criche from the road to Ullapool

**Sgurr Mor;** 1110m; (OS Sheet 20; NH203718); M43; *big peak*
**Beinn Liath Mhor Fannaich;** 954m; (OS Sheet 20; NH219724); M209; *big grey hill of Fannaich*

234

SGURR MOR

BEINN LIATH
MHOR FANNAICH

Sgurr Mor is the central and highest mountain in the Fannaichs, standing near the middle of the long ridge which extends from An Coileachan to Meall a' Chrasgaidh. Its upper part is a steep cone, and the mountain is prominent from many viewpoints, especially from the head of Loch Broom to the north. The north-east face drops very steeply to the corrie of Loch a' Mhadaidh. The ridge going north-east from Sgurr Mor leads to Beinn Liath Mhor Fannaich, a prominent hill in views from the Ullapool road to the north for it stands out in front of its neighbours.

The traverse of these two mountains can most conveniently be made from the dam at the west end of Loch Droma. From there follow the track beside the pipe which carries water from the Allt a' Mhadaidh to Loch Droma. Cross the Allt a' Mhadaidh at a small dam and continue beside this stream up the path which leads eventually to Loch a' Mhadaidh. Go round the west side of the loch and climb steeply to the col between Meall a' Chrasgaidh and Carn na Criche. It is a very short distance from the col north-west to Meall a' Chrasgaidh, which can be easily included in this walk. From the col go south-east up a broad ridge then east to Carn na Criche (961m) and after another short drop climb the summit cone of Sgurr Mor. (10km; 900m; 4h). The final ridge is quite narrow and steep enough on both sides to give a sense of exposure, and particularly in winter it should be treated with respect.

Descend south-east at first for a short distance, then turn north-east down the ridge leading to Beinn Liath Mhor Fannaich. There is a stalkers' path just below the crest of this ridge on its south-east side and a stone shelter near the knoll on the ridge. From the lowest point at about 850m a short steep climb leads to Beinn Liath Mhor Fannaich. (12km; 1020m; 4h 30min). Go north-east down an open corrie towards Loch Sgeireach and round the west end of the loch to descend north to the end of the track at the Allt a' Mhadaidh. Sgurr nan Clach Geala could also be included, as could Sgurr nan Each, however an arduous re-ascent of the steep south ridge of Sgurr nan Clach Geala and the extra distance might make this more difficult a day than most would desire. Map on page 233.

Starting from the Torrandhu Bridge car park by the weather station at the west end of Loch Glascarnoch, Meall Gorm and An Coilleachan can easily be linked with Beinn Liath Mhor Fannaich and Sgurr Mor to provide a very fine walk (8h). Climb Beinn Liath Mhor Fannaich first via Creag Dhubh Fannaich with the crossing of the Allt an Loch Sgeirich generally being made at least 1km upstream; a potential problem in spate though 2km upstream an island at NH247726 usually provides a crossing place. This point can also be reached utilising the track through the Altan Wood forestry plantation on the other side of the glen, as suggested by the land owners signpost at the car park, and by crossing the Abhainn a' Ghiuthais Li via a bridge at NH264721. This is perhaps a better route if the burns are in spate, however, in the forest there

Bill Brooker

Sgurr Mor from Beinn Liath Mhor Fannaich

is no bridge for the crossing of the Alltan Odhar Mor at NH276734, which although narrow could present a minor problem at the start of the day if dry feet are required; normally it can be jumped just above or below where the track fords it.

Return from An Coilleachan via Meallan Bhuidhe and the bridge over the burn at NH252712. The normal route continues down the left bank to cross the Allt an Loch Sgeirich (no bridge, although only a problem in spate) and join the route of ascent. Before this however, the bridge at NH264721 allows the track through the Altan Wood forestry plantation to be gained after a short ascent. This leads back to the road and although the crossing of the burn at NH276734 has no bridge this is less of a problem at the end of the day.

THE FANNAICHS

Looking north-west from Sgurr Mor beyond Meall a' Chrasgaidh to An Teallach

Alan O'Brien

Sgurr nan Clach Geala from Carn na Criche

**Meall a' Chrasgaidh;** 934m; (OS Sheet 20; NH184733); M243; *hill of the crossing*
**Sgurr nan Clach Geala;** 1093m; (OS Sheet 20; NH184715); M53; *peak of the white stones*
**Sgurr nan Each;** 923m; (OS Sheet 20; NH184697); M267; *peak of the horses*

MEALL A'
CHRASGAIDH

SGURR NAN
CLACH GEALA

SGURR NAN EACH

These three peaks of the Fannaichs lie just east of the path which crosses the bealach from Loch a' Bhraoin to the head of Loch Fannich. They are on a ridge extending from Sgurr nan Each in the south, over Sgurr nan Clach Geala to Meall a' Chrasgaidh which also lies at the north-west end of the main Fannaich ridge. Sgurr nan Clach Geala may well be considered to be the finest of the Fannaichs, its tapering buttresses, soaring ridges and high hanging corrie combining in classic mountain architecture.

Two starting points are possible for the traverse of these peaks: either the west end of Loch Droma and following the ascent route described for Sgurr Mor, or the road near Loch a' Bhraoin at the north-west corner of the Fannaichs. The latter gives the shorter approach and is described.

Start from the A832, 6km south-west of Braemore Junction and walk along the track to Loch a' Bhraoin, then along a path to cross its outlet by a footbridge. Continue south-east on the path to cross the Allt Breabaig by another footbridge at NH163746, then follow the path on the east side of the stream for 500m as it climbs the hillside, before striking east uphill, easily selecting a way through steep mossy grass, heather and boulders. Higher up trend right towards the north-west ridge of Meall a' Chrasgaidh until the slope lessens and leads to the top over patches of grass and weathered rock. (5.5km; 690m; 2h 30min).

From the summit descend a smooth slope south-east then south round the wide corrie whose lush grass in summer provides feeding for the deer, hence the name Am Biachdaich, *the place of fattening*. A lochan lies on the col at the head of this corrie at the start of the ridge which rises above the great east-facing cliffs of Sgurr nan Clach Geala. The upper part of this ridge is quite narrow and gives an easy and enjoyable walk along the brink of the crags which plunge into the corrie below. The summit is an excellent viewpoint from which to appreciate the layout and character of the Fannaichs, all but one of which can be seen from there in clear conditions. (7.5km; 960m; 3h 20min).

There is an easy descent south by grass slopes to the 807m col of the Cadha na Guite. The ridge crest beyond rises gradually to the summit of Sgurr nan Each in an elegant curve with steep crags falling into Coire Mhoir on the east. (9.5km; 1080m; 4h).

Sgurr nan Each from Sgurr nan Clach Geala

Return north along the ridge to the Cadha na Guite and descend west down grassy slopes to the bealach at the head of the Allt Breabaig. From there follow the path north to the east end of Loch a' Bhraoin to rejoin the track leading back to the day's starting point.

237

MEALL A'
    CHRASGAIDH

SGURR NAN
    CLACH GEALA

SGURR NAN EACH

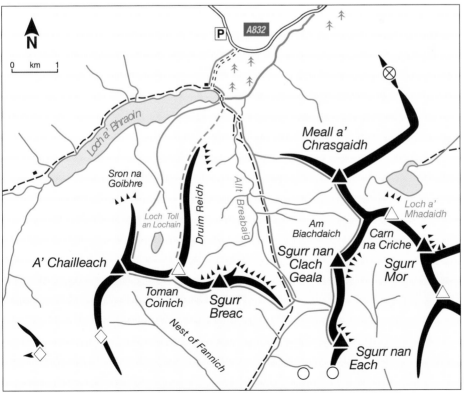

Sgurr Breac from Toman Coinich

**Sgurr Breac;** 999m; (OS Sheet 20; NH158711); M138; *speckled peak*
**A' Chailleach;** 997m; (OS Sheet 19; NH136714); M144; *the old woman*

SGURR BREAC

A' CHAILLEACH

These two hills are the most westerly of the Fannaichs, and lie south of the A832 road from Braemore Junction to Dundonnell. They are connected to the main group by the bealach at the head of the Allt Breabaig at a height of 550m, from where a ridge extends west over Sgurr Breac and Toman Coinich to A' Chailleach. Northward from this ridge the two spurs of Sron na Goibhre and Druim Reidh enclose the corrie of Toll an Lochain.

From the A832, 6km south-west of Braemore Junction, walk along the track to Loch a' Bhraoin then follow a path to cross its outlet by a footbridge. Go south-east to cross the Allt Breabaig by another footbridge and continue south on the path on the east side of the stream. This path continues up the east side of the glen until it reaches the bealach leading over to Loch Fannich. From there climb the east ridge of Sgurr Breac, quite steeply through little rock outcrops at first, then up an easy-angled ridge. (8km; 750m; 3h 10min).

Continue by traversing Toman Coinich (935m), or skirting its summit on the south side, and descending to the bealach at 810m. Ascend the ridge along the rim of the Toll an Lochain to its junction with the Sron na Goibhre spur, then bear south-west along the gently rising crest to the summit of A' Chailleach. (10km; 1020m; 4h).

Return north-east to the junction of ridges above the Toll an Lochain and descend the spur of Sron na Goibhre, which is steep at first and well marked by fence posts. Avoid the rock outcrops at the north end of this ridge by descending north-east down steep and boulder-strewn grassy slopes towards the stream in the Toll an Lochain. Follow this stream downhill for some distance, then go diagonally down the steep grassy hillside north-east towards Loch a' Bhraoin to regain the track leading back to the day's starting point.

An alternative route to these two hills, which is shorter than the traverse described above, is by the Druim Reidh. After crossing the bridge at the outflow of Loch a' Bhraoin, go south and climb a steep grassy slope between the crags below the north end of the Druim Reidh to reach a flat area at its north end. Follow a very obviously eroded path up this ridge to Toman Coinich, from where the two Munros can be climbed along the connecting ridge. Map on page 237.

On the summit ridge of Fionn Bheinn

**Fionn Bheinn;** 933m; (OS Sheets 20 and 25; NH147621); M246; *white hill*

The only Munro of the Fannaichs to lie south of Loch Fannich, Fionn Bheinn rises directly on the north side of the A832 road at Achnasheen. With its smooth grassy slopes and subdued contours, it presents an undistinguished appearance to the south and keeps its more interesting north side concealed from most visitors.

The easiest approach is directly from Achnasheen, by following the Allt Achadh na Sine, keeping on its north-east side and gaining the nose of Creagan nan Laogh. From there ascend north-west by gradual slopes of mossy grass to reach the summit in just over 1km. (5km; 780m; 2h 30min).

A different route for the descent, longer but more interesting than the ascent route described above, allows the mountain to be traversed. It goes east, skirting the edge of the steep slabby face which plunges into the Toll Mor, and follows the ridge east then south-east down a steeper slope close to the rim of another slabby corrie, the Toll Beag. Where the slope levels out at Sail an Tuim Bhain a prominent stone wall leads east and can be followed, with a few gaps, until it intersects an old grassy path crossing the hill from north to south. Turn right along this path which leads downhill towards a small plantation, now partially felled. Continue through the wood by a narrow fire-break and down the east bank of the stream to the A832 road 1km east of Achnasheen.

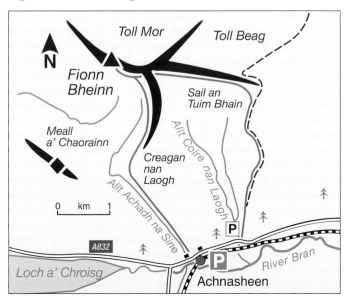

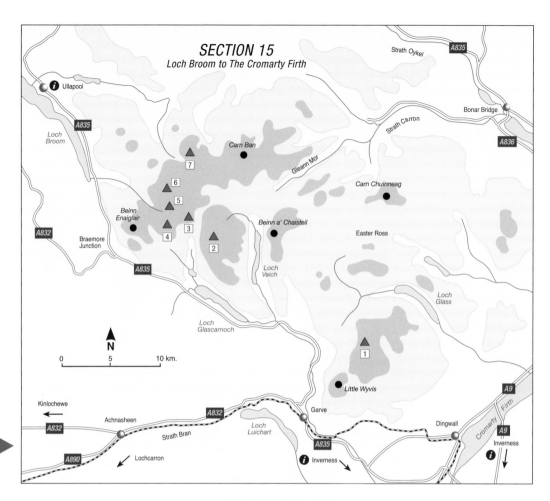

## SECTION 15

### Loch Broom to the Cromarty Firth

**ⓘ** VisitScotland Information Centres
**Inverness**; Castle Wynd, Inverness, IV2 3BJ, (01463 252401), Jan–Dec
**Ullapool**; Argyle Street, Ullapool, IV26 2UB, (01854 612486), Easter–Oct

*Hamish Brown*

Ben Wyvis from the Glascarnoch River

**BEN WYVIS;** *possibly from the Gaelic fuathas, meaning terror*
**Glas Leathad Mor;** 1046m; (OS Sheet 20; NH463684); M85; *big greenish-grey slope*

Ben Wyvis is a solitary mountain, far to the east of other northern hills, whose isolated position makes it a good viewpoint. The highest summit, Glas Leathad Mor, is a high level ridge with two impressive corries on its eastern face, and long uniform grass slopes sweeping up from the dark forests, now being clear felled, on the west. These steep grass slopes can be an avalanche hazard in winter when there is snow on the mountain. The approach from the west is the one most used, as any other route is much longer.

Park in the walkers' car park on the east side of the A835 road from Garve to Ullapool 750m south of Garbat and follow the footpath on the north bank of the Allt a' Bhealaich Mhoir up the forested hillside. Above the forest ascend steeply up the ridge to reach An Cabar (*the antler*) (946m), the end prow of the Wyvis ridge. The summit of Glas Leathad Mor lies 2km north-east along a mossy ridge which gives delightful walking. (6.5km; 920m; 3h).

As an alternative to returning by the route of ascent, traverse the mountain by continuing down the north ridge and climbing Tom a' Choinnich (953m). Descend its grassy south-west ridge to the Allt a' Gharbh Bhaid and follow this stream downhill to the Garbat Forest. Continue through the forest along a narrow path on the north bank of the stream to reach a wide forest road. Go south along it to rejoin the path up the Allt a' Bhealaich Mhoir and follow this downhill.

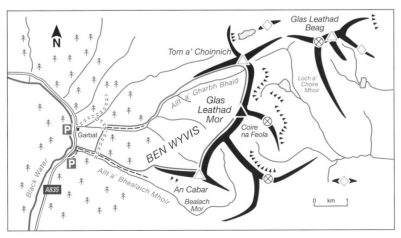

Am Faochagach from Cona' Mheall

### Am Faochagach; 953m; (OS Sheet 20; NH303794); M210; *the heathery place*

The great range of rounded hills which forms the heart of the Strathvaich Forest between Loch Glascarnoch and Strath Vaich culminates in Am Faochagach. Like its lower outliers, it is a massive rounded hill, well seen from the north-west end of Loch Glascarnoch, from which it lies 6km to the north.

**AM FAOCHAGACH**

**CONA' MHEALL**

**BEINN DEARG**

The shortest approach to the hill is from the A835 road at the north-west end of Loch Glascarnoch, starting at the bridge over the Abhainn an Torrain Duibh. The first 1.5km across the level strath is over rough boggy ground, normally very wet underfoot, and includes the crossing of the Abhainn a' Gharbhrain. In normal conditions this crossing will entail wet feet; in wet conditions (which some might regard as normal) the crossing may well be impossible, a diversion up river to try a higher crossing may be no more successful and the only option may be a long walk round the north side of Loch a' Gharbhrain. Am Faochagach is, therefore, a mountain for reasonably dry conditions, or a hard winter's day when frost grips the ground.

Apart from these obstacles, the ascent is straightforward and a faint path can be followed for most of the way. Go roughly north from the road across the bog to the river crossing, then bear north-east up the Allt na h-Uidhe. The going becomes easier as bog and tussocky heather give way higher up to smooth grassy slopes, and the main spine of the range is reached 2km south of Am Faochagach. From there the going is very easy along the level grassy ridge and past a few cairns. Finally, a short steeper slope, where the effects of solifluction are evident, leads to the flat summit of Am Faochagach crowned by two cairns a few metres apart. (7km; 690m; 2h 50min).

If this is your only hill for the day, return by the same route. However, it is quite possible to make this the start of a longer traverse by going north-west over Meallan Ban, then down to the outflow of Loch Prille and up the east ridge of Cona' Mheall to join the route described next.

### Cona' Mheall; 978m; (OS Sheet 20; NH275816); M176; *adjoining hill*
### Beinn Dearg; 1084m; (OS Sheet 20; NH259812); M57; *red hill*

Beinn Dearg is the highest mountain north of the road from Inverness to Ullapool, and with its surrounding peaks it forms a fine group between Loch Glascarnoch and the head of Loch Broom. It is a mountain with some very fine crags and corries, in particular Coire Ghranda on its south-east side which has some huge cliffs on the flank of Beinn Dearg and a dark lochan in its depths. The north-west ridge of Beinn Dearg goes for 6km on the south side of Gleann na

The cliffs of Beinn Dearg above Loch a' Choire Ghranda

Sguaib, and for almost half this length it is lined with a succession of buttresses and gullies. On the opposite side of Coire Ghranda is Cona' Mheall, a smaller peak but one with fine character. Its best feature is the narrow south ridge which rises steeply above the foot of Coire Ghranda and has a narrow crest from which cliffs and boulder slopes drop steeply on both sides.

The approach from the south has very much the same character as the mountains, rough and wild. Leave the A835 road near the south-east end of Loch Droma, where there is parking space in a small quarry. Head north up the rough hillside to meet an old path which continues north-east over the low ridge ahead and drops to a grassy meadow, the site of a long-since abandoned shieling at the north-west end of Loch a' Gharbhrain. Cross the Allt a' Gharbhrain, notoriously difficult or even impossible in spate, and continue north over trackless peat and heather towards Loch Coire Lair. Halfway along the loch start climbing towards the lip of Coire Ghranda where the stream comes down over bare slabs; a very faint path helps in places, but the climb is steep, traversing grass ledges across and up the slabby hillside.

Coire Ghranda is in a superb setting with the cliffs of Beinn Dearg across the loch. Climb directly towards the end of the south ridge of Cona' Mheall, scrambling steeply up grass and easy rocks to reach the more level crest. This is narrow, but quite easy with two short descents and a little scrambling, and the ridge becomes broader as it leads up to the bouldery summit. (7.5km; 750m; 3h).

Descend west down easy slopes of stones and grass to the wide bealach at the head of Coire Ghranda. On the west side of this bealach a stone wall will be found, which can be followed south-west uphill towards Beinn Dearg. At the point where the wall turns right, bear south up the

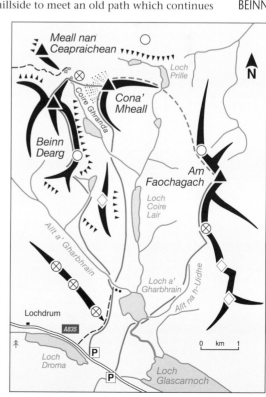

Beinn Dearg from the south ridge of Cona' Mheall

*Alan O'Brien*

**CONA' MHEALL**

stony plateau to the cairn of Beinn Dearg. (9.5km; 1000m; 3h 50min).

244

A few metres east of the cairn descend a steep ridge towards Coire Ghranda, south-east at first then south along the edge of the very steep cliffs above Loch a' Choire Ghranda. Beyond a flat col go over a rounded stony top and south-west for a further 500m, then descend an open grassy gully south-east to the south end of Loch nan Eilean, a wonderfully wild and lonely place. Continue down the left bank of the burn from the loch and along the Allt a' Gharbhrain

**BEINN DEARG**

Cona' Mheall from Loch nan Eilean

*Alan O'Brien*

Donald Bennet

Coire Ghranda

**Meall nan Ceapraichean;** 977m; (OS Sheet 20; NH257826); M177; *hill of the stubby hillocks*
**Eididh nan Clach Geala;** 927m; (OS Sheet 20; NH258842); M257; *web of the white stones*

  These two mountains form the northern half of the Beinn Dearg group, but they do not have the character of either Beinn Dearg or Cona' Mheall. Meall nan Ceapraichean rises to the north-west of the wide bealach which is in the centre of these three mountains. To the west and north it is steep and craggy, but to the east it drops in gradual slopes to the headwaters of the River Carron. Eididh nan Clach Geala is 1.5km north of Meall nan Ceapraichean across the corrie in

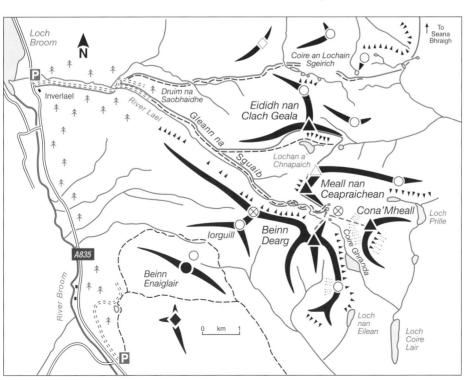

Eididh nan Clach Geala from Ceann Garbh

which lies Lochan na Chnapaich, but it has no very distinctive features except a line of broken crags overlooking this lonely lochan.

The best approach is from the A835 at the head of Loch Broom at the start of a forestry road, where there is a car park beside the telephone box next to the white cottage. Walk or bike up the forestry road for 3km through the Lael Forest into the lower part of Gleann na Sguaib. Beyond the forest follow a stalkers' path up this glen on the north-east side of the River Lael past some fine falls and a beautiful little lochan nestling below the cliffs of Beinn Dearg to reach the wide bealach at the head of the glen. There, two more lochans lie in a desolate stony landscape, and Beinn Dearg is less than 1km away to the south-west. It can be included in the traverse of Meall nan Ceapraichean and Eididh nan Clach Geala without much extra effort, as can Cona' Mheall 1km to the east.

MEALL NAN
CEAPRAICHEAN

EIDIDH NAN
CLACH GEALA

SEANA BHRAIGH

From the bealach climb north-west up the easy-angled ridge of Meall nan Ceapraichean. (10km; 970m; 3h 40min). Continue north then north-east along a broad stony ridge to Ceann Garbh (968m). Descend north-east, easily at first, but lower down small crags and rock bands have to be circumvented and a bealach is reached at NH265838. From there an easy grass slope leads to Eididh nan Clach Geala where there are two cairns, the north-west one being the summit. (12.5km; 1150m; 4h 40min). Just below the cairn, on the north-west side, are the white quartzite boulders which may well give the mountain its name.

Descend west down a broad grassy ridge for 500m, then turn south-west into the corrie to the west of Lochan na Chnapaich where a good stalkers' path is joined and followed downhill to the main path in Gleann na Sguaib.

## Seana Bhraigh; 926m; (OS Sheet 20; NH281879); M262; *old height*

Seana Bhraigh, which occupies a remote situation in true wilderness country in the heart of Ross-shire, competes with A' Mhaighdean and Lurg Mhor for the title of the most distant Munro. It is the eastern outlier of the Beinn Dearg group, a high plateau bounded on its north by the deep dark hollow of Luchd Choire

No matter which way one goes to reach Seana Bhraigh, the approach from the nearest public road is long. The two most practicable routes are from Inverlael at the head of Loch Broom, and up Strath Mulzie from Oykel Bridge in Strath Oykel. The latter route involves a long approach up an estate road and it is possible to drive up this unsurfaced road to a walkers' car park at NH326953, some 200m before Corriemulzie Lodge. From here it is possible to bike further up this strath, almost to the foot of the mountain. The Strath Mulzie route has the advantage of showing the finest side of the mountain: the great corries at the head of the strath and

*Donald Bennet*

The north face of Seana Bhraigh above Loch Luchd Choire

The approach to Seana Bhraigh up the Corriemulzie River

**SEANA BHRAIGH**

the fine ridge which rises from Loch a' Choire Mhoir to Creag an Duine, the eastern promontory of the Seana Bhraigh plateau.

The approach from the west starts from the car park just off the A835 to Ullapool at Inverlael and the first few kilometres are the same as for Meall nan Ceapraichean. Walk or bike through the Lael Forest as far as Glensguaib, then take the stalkers' path out of the forest onto the Druim na Saobhaidhe, crossing the wide upper corrie of Gleann a' Mhadaidh and rounding a spur of the hill above to continue up Coire an Lochain Sgeirich which has a succession of lochans in it.

The path vanishes in a wilderness at about 750m and in poor visibility very careful navigation is required for the continuation to Seana Bhraigh. One way is to find the lochan at NH271856 near the end of the path, go east along a little stream to Loch a' Chadha Dheirg then the tiny feeder lochan 500m east of it, from where a course due north leads up easy slopes to the 906m dome 1km south-east of Seana Bhraigh. Follow the cliff-edge of Luchd Choire north-west to the highest point, where the cairn stands right on the edge of the corrie. (13.5km; 1100m; 4h 50min). Return by the same way.

From the north-east and the car park at Corriemulzie Lodge, follow the track up the strath to the outflow of Loch a' Choire Mhoir. The crossing of the river 1.5km lower down may be a problem and it might be best to stay on the west side of the river. The Coirmor Bothy <www.mountainbothies.co.uk> and Magoos

### Map labels

Knockdamph

Corriemulzie Lodge

P

N

Loch an Daimh

Strath Mulzie

To Glen Achall and Ullapool

Corriemulzie River

0  km  1

Loch a' Choire Mhoir

Luchd Choire

Creag an Duine

Coire Mor

Seana Bhraigh

Loch a' Chadha Dheirg

To Inverlael

At the top of the Creag an Duine ridge of Seana Bhraigh

Bothy are at NH305888 along the side of the loch. From the loch climb steeply south-west beside the stream flowing from the Luchd Choire to reach more level ground. From there the easiest route is up the ridge on the west side of the corrie. It leads past a tiny lochan direct to the summit. (From Duag Bridge: 13km; 830m; 4h 20min).

A much finer route is up the An Sgurr or Creag an Duine ridge on the east side of the corrie. It is steep and narrow, and involves some scrambling, but leads splendidly to the little pointed peak of An Sgurr (905m) from where a short scramble down and up again leads to the edge of the plateau at Creag an Duine. From there a lofty walk over the dome of the South Top (905m) ends at the summit of Seana Bhraigh. The ridge on the west side of the corrie gives the best descent, past the tiny lochan and over Pt.760m.

An Sgurr from Creag an Duine

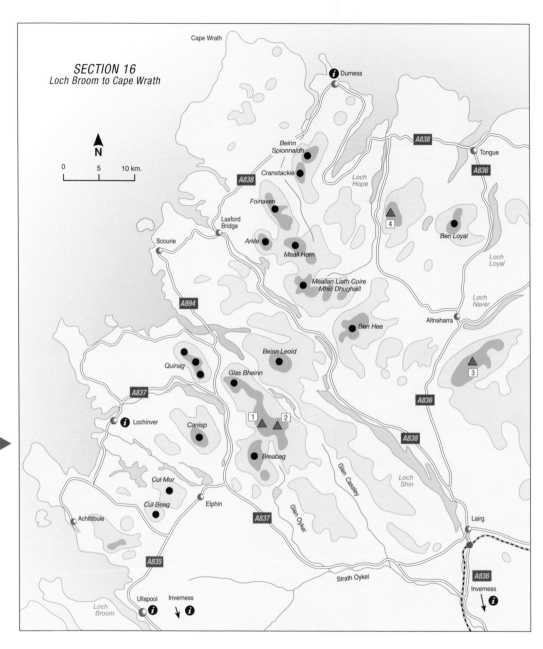

SECTION 16 
Loch Broom to Cape Wrath

Cape Wrath

Durness

A838

Tongue

A836

Beinn
Spionnaidh

Cranstackie

Loch
Hope

Foinaven

Laxford
Bridge

4

Ben Loyal

Scourie

Arkle

Meall Horn

Loch
Loyal

Meallan Liath Coire
Mhic Dhughaill

Loch
Naver

A894

Ben Hee

Altnaharra

Quinag

Beinn Leoid

Glas Bheinn

3

Lochinver

Canisp

1    2

A837

A836

Breabag

A838

Cul Mor

Glen Cassley

Loch
Shin

Cul Beag

Elphin

Lairg

Achiltibuie

A837

Glen Oykel

A835

Strath Oykel

A836

Ullapool

Inverness

Inverness

Loch
Broom

# SECTION 16

## Loch Broom to Cape Wrath

*i* VisitScotland Information Centres
**Inverness**; Castle Wynd, Inverness, IV2 3BJ, (01463 252401), open Jan–Dec
**Ullapool**; Argyle Street, Ullapool, IV26 2UB, (01854 612486), open Easter–Oct
**Lochinver;** Kirk Lane, Lochinver, IV27 4LT, (01571 844373), open Apr–Oct
**Durness;** Durine, Durness, IV27 4PN, (01971 511368), open Apr–Oct

Donald Bennet

Ben More Assynt from Conival

**Conival;** 987m; (OS Sheet 15; NC303199); M158; *adjoining hill*
**Ben More Assynt;** 998m; (OS Sheet 15; NC318201); M141; *big hill of Assynt*
   *(from Norse: ass, a ridge and endi, an end)*

Ben More Assynt and Conival are the highest peaks in Assynt, but they have a hidden secretive character compared to their lower but bolder neighbours like Suilven and Quinag. The traverse of the two mountains is almost invariably done from Inchnadamph on the A837 road between Ullapool and Lochinver. They are rough, rocky peaks, their upper slopes covered with angular quartzite stones and scree which give rough walking, and a feature of interest near the mountains is the Traligill caves which are passed *en route* to them.

From the parking area beside the Inchnadamph Hotel, walk up the main road for 100m then follow the private road on the north bank of the River Traligill. Beyond Glenbain cottage continue along a path below a little plantation to the point where the route to the caves goes down to a footbridge. The route to Conival continues by a good path on the north side of the river in Gleann Dubh to reach a high grassy alp below the Na Tuadhan/Beinn an Fhurain - Conival bealach at 750m. From there the final ascent of Conival is up a rough path over quartzite scree, followed by a fairly level ridge to the large summit cairn. (7km; 920m; 3h).

Ben More Assynt lies 1.5km east along a dipping crest of the same rough, demanding terrain, a mixture of scree and crag, narrow in places. In poor visibility it may be difficult to decide which of two shattered bumps is the summit of the mountain; it is the northern one, with the large cairn and shelter. (8.5km; 1050m; 3h 45min). The simplest return is by the same route.

A more interesting continuation is to go out along the south-east ridge for 1km to the South Top of Ben More Assynt (960m). This traverse involves a narrow, rocky section of ridge sometimes optimistically compared with the Aonach Eagach. However, its 'bad steps' are no more than exposed slabs and there are no difficulties of any consequence, certainly not comparable with the celebrated Glen Coe ridge.

The descent from the South Top, however, is much more likely to cause problems as the south-west face of this peak above the Dubh Loch Mor is steep and craggy, and unless one returns along the ridges one has to descend to this loch. One possibility is to return a short distance north-west along the ridge and descend towards the north end of Dubh Loch Mor. Another possibility is to go south down the ridge towards Carn nan Conbhairean and descend towards the south end of the loch. If in doubt, continue southwards until the slope on the west

Conival from Ben More Assynt

side of the ridge becomes easy. This may well be the best course if visibility is bad or the craggy hillside is wet. A direct descent from the South Top to the loch is not advised.

From the north end of Dubh Loch Mor go west, climbing a little to reach the deeply cut pass between Conival and Breabag Tarsuinn. Once through this pass continue along the dry bed of the Allt a' Bhealaich on a path which leads to the caves near the Traligill River. These are worth a visit, provided you have torches, before continuing down Gleann Dubh to Inchnadamph.

If at the start of the day you intend to do the complete traverse of these two mountains, it is probably better to go in the reverse direction, going first across the Conival – Breabag Tarsuinn pass to Dubh Loch Mor and climbing to the south-east ridge, which is easier than making the descent described above. Then return over Ben More Assynt and Conival.

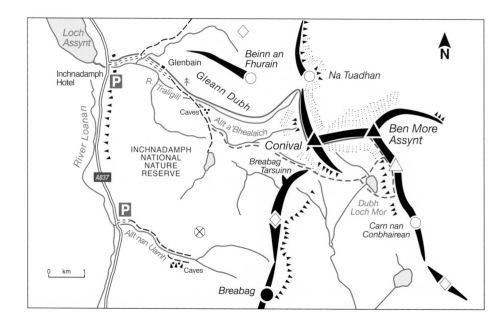

*Hamish Brown*

Ben Klibreck from Strath Vagastie

**BEN KLIBRECK;** *hill of the speckled cliff*
**Meall nan Con;** 962m; (OS Sheet 16; NC585299); M194; *hill of the dogs*

This isolated mountain rises above the desolate moorland of central Sutherland. The vast and featureless character of the landscape in this part of Scotland gives to Ben Klibreck an equal impression of remoteness, although in fact it is only 4km from the A836 road between Lairg and Tongue.

The spine of the mountain is a long curving ridge between Loch Naver and Loch Coire, and the summit, Meall nan Con, is the highest of several tops along this ridge. The north-west side of the mountain facing Altnaharra is quite steep, and on the west side, some distance below the summit, there is a prow of broken crags. By contrast, the south-east slopes are carved into wide grassy corries above Loch a' Bhealaich and Loch Choire.

The inns at Crask and Altnaharra are possible starting points for the ascent, but the shortest and easiest route begins from the A836 road through Strath Vagastie near NC545303, where there is a roadside parking place. Cross the river and go east across the moor to the south end of Loch na Glas-choille, and from there follow the line of a fence to the outflow of Loch nan Uan. In bad weather, if the river in Strath Vagastie is in spate, start at a footbridge at NC537289 near Vagastie, where there is verge parking for a number of cars, and cross the moor directly, initially on a path, past Loch Bad an Loch towards the south end of Loch nan Uan.

The face of Ben Klibreck immediately above Loch nan Uan is very steep, with crags to the north-east under Meall nan Con. The easiest ascent goes east from the loch up steep grassy slopes to the main ridge 1km south-west of the summit where a traverse path is met at the col between Creag an Lochain and A' Chioch. This leads along the mossy ridge to a shallow col to the side of A'Cioch then veers east to climb a steep bouldery slope to gain the summit enclosure and trig point. (5km; 790m 2h 30min).

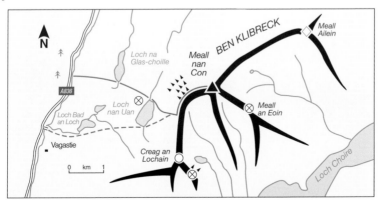

254

Ben Hope from the north-west across Loch Eriboll

Scott Johnstone

Ben Loyal (left) and Ben Hope from Loch Eriboll

## Ben Hope; 927m; (OS Sheet 9; NC477502); M256; *hill of the bay*

Ben Hope, with its Viking name (*hóp*, meaning bay) and splendid isolation, is a worthy peak for the most northerly Munro. Its long west flank above Strath More and Loch Hope is double-tiered and has plenty of crags, but the ascent up this side is not unduly difficult. The easy southern and eastern slopes can only be reached by long approaches, so are seldom used. It would not be difficult to climb both Ben Hope and Ben Klibreck in a single day, with a short drive by car between them.

To reach the mountain, branch west at the cross-roads north of the hamlet of Altnaharra on the A836 road from Lairg to Tongue and follow the narrow road westwards over the moors to descend into Strath More. After several kilometres the interesting broch of Dun Dornaigil is reached, then the farm of Alltnacaillich. About 2km north of Alltnacaillich park near the stream which flows down from the Dubh-loch na Beinne terrace on the west flank of Ben Hope.

Climb up a path beside the stream for 750m north-east and continue up the east tributary which comes down from the vast bowl of the mountain's southern slopes. This leads through a break in the line of cliffs which is clearly seen on the OS map. The path then leads up the broad grassy ridge, not far from the western cliffs, to the little summit plateau, where the trig point is near the north-east edge. The setting is spacious and majestic. The best viewpoint is slightly to the north, but this does not lead to a descent route. (3.5km; 920m; 2h 20min).

Return by the route of ascent, or by the Alltnacaillich variation. This slightly longer alternative starts at Alltnacaillich farm and takes the path up the south bank of the Allt na Caillich (*the old woman's burn*). After crossing the stream above a fine waterfall, the ridge of Leitir Mhuiseil is followed north along the edge of its western escarpment to join the route described above.

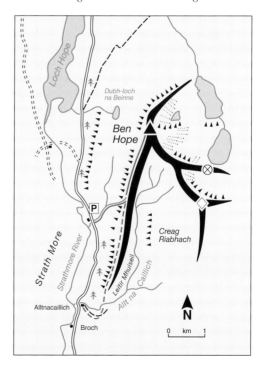

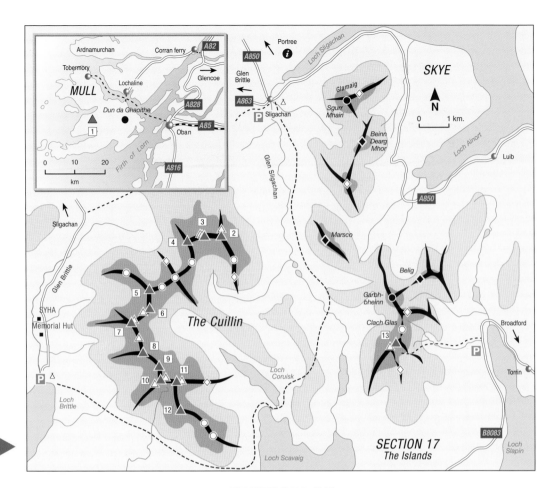

# SECTION 17

## The Islands

---

ℹ️ **VisitScotland Information Centre**

**Skye – Portree**; Bayfield House, Portree, Isle of Skye, IV51 9EL, (01478 612992), open Jan–Dec

Ben More from A' Chioch

**Ben More;** 966m; (OS Sheet 48; NM526331); M189; *big hill*

The only island Munro outside Skye, Ben More dominates the western group of hills on Mull and gives them their impressive form, especially when seen from the south. Splendid views of the Ben More group are also obtained from the B8035 road along which one comes from Salen to reach Loch na Keal and the foot of the mountain. Ben More itself is a fine isolated peak, its summit at the apex of three ridges. Of these the finest is the north-east ridge which leads to A' Chioch, a sharp subsidiary top, and the traverse of this ridge is the best route to Ben More.

Start from the shore of Loch na Keal at the foot of the Abhainn na h-Uamha where there is ample off road parking. Follow paths and sheep tracks along the south-west side of this stream past many attractive pools and waterfalls up the grassy Gleann na Beinne Fada to reach the bealach (c520m) between Beinn Fhada and A' Chioch. Turn south and climb towards A' Chioch; as height is gained the ridge becomes steeper and rockier, and gives a delightful easy scramble up a rocky staircase.

The continuation to Ben More maintains the interest, and the crest of the connecting ridge is remarkably narrow in places. The final ascent from the col is reminiscent of the Aonach Eagach or Liathach, but there are no comparable difficulties, just the same exhilaration and unforgettable views from the summit if the day is clear. (6km; 1060m; 3h 10min).

The quickest descent route is by the broad north-west ridge, following a path in the screes marked by many little cairns. This path continues down the grassy slope on the south-west side of the Abhainn Dhiseig then joins the track to the house at Dhiseig and descends to the road and the large parking area from where the standard up and down route to this hill starts. From here it is a pleasant 1.5km walk along the road back to the start.

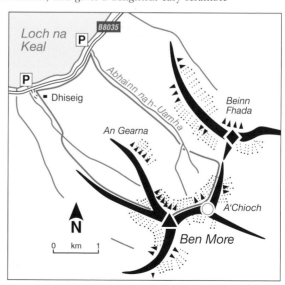

Loch Coruisk

## The Cuillin

The Cuillin are the most challenging mountains in Scotland, almost entirely rocky, with narrow crests and steep sides, and with only a few walking routes to their tops. Climbing these mountains is very different from the perfectly simple hillwalking which is involved in the ascent of all but five or six of the mainland Munros. Most of the Cuillin peaks require some scrambling to reach their summits, and one – The Inaccessible Pinnacle – calls for rock-climbing. Much of the scrambling is fairly easy, but there are places where, for a few metres, the difficulties are more akin to easy rock climbing. There are also many places where the narrowness of the ridges and their exposure are such that a slip might have serious results. In such situations surefootedness and a good head for heights are essential.

The SMC Scramblers' Guide, *Skye Scrambles*, describes all the walking routes to the Cuillin peaks, together with detailed descriptions where scrambling is required, in particular to attain the summit of Sgurr nan Gillean. This guide also contains a description of the full traverse of the Main Ridge, useful for anyone wishing to extend the outings described here and link more peaks.

In spite of the fact that the Cuillin are composed of gabbro, one of the finest and roughest of climbing rocks, there is a great deal of loose rock, and care should be taken at all times. There have been many accidents over the years due to loose rock.

There are some places on the Main Ridge and close to it where the compass is unreliable due to local magnetic anomalies which do not occur on lower ground. Thus in mist you should always know where you are and careful map reading is essential. The Ordnance Survey 1:50,000 map is not really adequate for navigation except on the lower ground. Their 1:25,000 Explorer map covering the Cuillin is more suitable. The Harvey Maps Superwalker map of the Cuillin is probably the best with its 1:25,000 scale and enlarged map of the Main Ridge at a scale of 1:12,500.

All the routes described, except that for Bla Bheinn, are on the Sligachan and Glen Brittle side of the Main Ridge. These places provide the easiest access to the mountains and also most of the accommodation for climbers in hotels, hut, hostel, camp sites etc. Most of the hillwalkers' routes in the Cuillin start from them. Loch Coruisk, on the other hand, is much more remote, the peaks and corries are steeper and wilder on that side, and the routes less well marked by footpaths. As a result the ways to the summits on that side of the Main Ridge are in general more serious.

SGURR NAN
GILLEAN

> **Sgurr nan Gillean;** 964m; (OS Sheet 32; NG472253); M191; *peak of the young men, or more probably peak of the gullies*

Sgurr nan Gillean is a very fine mountain, its summit at the apex of three narrow rocky ridges. It is probably the most familiar of the Cuillin, seen by every tourist on a clear day from the roadside at Sligachan. It was also the first of the Cuillin to be climbed, in 1836 by Professor James David Forbes the physicist and Alpine pioneer, guided by the local forester Duncan MacIntyre. The view from Sligachan, however, fails to reveal Sgurr nan Gillean completely, for its finest feature, the Pinnacle Ridge, is seen 'end-on' and its true character is not apparent.

The usual route of ascent of Sgurr nan Gillean is the so-called 'Tourist Route' first climbed in

*Donald Bennet*

Sgurr nan Gillean

1836, but because of the featureless nature of the lower ground and the rugged and precipitous terrain higher up, route finding may be difficult in poor visibility. Start from the A863 road 200m south-west of Sligachan Hotel, where a path leads to and then crosses the Allt Dearg Mor. Continue south along the path amongst peat hags until in 1.5km it reaches the Allt Dearg Beag. The path follows the west bank for 500m to a bridge, where it divides. Ignore the branch which continues up the burn, but cross the bridge and follow the path which climbs south to reach Coire Riabhach below the lowest rocks of the Pinnacle Ridge.

South of Coire Riabhach climb more steeply up increasingly rocky and stony ground below the east face of the Pinnacle Ridge, still following the path up boulders and scree to reach the south-east ridge of Sgurr nan Gillean. Turn right and climb this ridge, easily at first but with some Grade 3 scrambling and route finding higher up where it becomes narrower, to finish with an airy traverse to the exposed summit of the peak. (6km; 950m; 3h).

SGURR NAN
GILLEAN

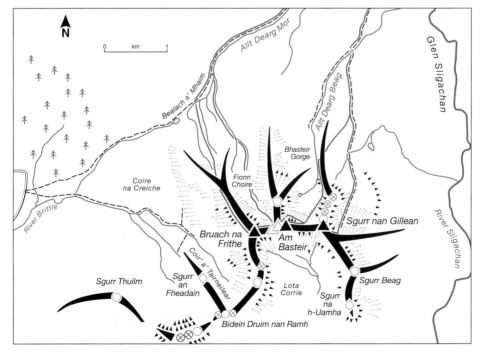

Sgurr nan Gillean from the Basteir Gorge

Am Basteir and Sgurr nan Gillean from Bealach nan Lice

*Hamish Brown*

**Am Basteir;** 934m; (OS Sheet 32; NG466253); M242; *meaning obscure, but probably not, as is commonly supposed, the executioner; maybe the baptiser*

In the view from Sligachan, Am Basteir is the lower peak to the right of Sgurr nan Gillean, with to its right the sharp-pointed Basteir Tooth. It may seem to be a relatively small peak, but on closer acquaintance its true character is evident, a narrow blade of rock, vertical on the north and very steep on the south. Am Basteir can be ascended, with one difficult pitch, by its east ridge, which is the left-hand skyline as seen from Sligachan. However, this ridge is exposed and no place for those without a good head for heights.

From Sligachan follow the 'Tourist Route' to Sgurr nan Gillean as far as a point about 1km beyond the crossing of the Allt Dearg Beag where the path begins to descend slightly towards Coire Riabhach. Branch right on a fairly well-defined and adequately cairned path which climbs south-west onto the broad rocky spur which is due north of Sgurr nan Gillean between Coire Riabhach and Coire a' Bhasteir. From the crest of this spur impressive cliffs on the right drop into the Basteir Gorge, but the path keeps well away from the edge.

Continue up the spur almost to the base of the Pinnacle Ridge where a path leads rightwards on a traverse well below the rocks of Pinnacle Ridge and above the screes of Coire a' Bhasteir. The traverse leads across screes, grass and some easy-angled slabs towards the head of the corrie where a steeper climb up screes and boulders leads towards the foot of the north face of Am Basteir. Keep up to the left to reach the Bealach a' Bhasteir (833m).

From the bealach the route to Am Basteir goes directly up the crest of the east ridge or by sloping ledges just below the crest on the south side. Two-thirds of the way up there is a short vertical drop in the ridge, the difficulty of which has been greatly increased by rockfall. The utmost care should be exercised in its descent and re-ascent. Alternatively, abseil into the gap, leaving the rope for the return. This 'bad step' can be avoided completely by leaving the crest of the ridge early, a short distance above the Bealach a' Bhasteir, where a faint path on the south side leads to an orange-brown slab. Ascend the slab, then cut horizontally leftwards for some distance. Continue round in a slightly exposed position and eventually cross a wall to join a ramp of purple-stained rock. Go up this more easily and soon reach the gap just beyond the 'bad step'. The ridge leads easily to the summit. (5.5km; 930m; 2h 50min).

The summit of Am Basteir is a spectacular place with vertical drops to the north and west. For the scrambler the only sensible route of descent is back down the route of ascent to the Bealach a' Bhasteir. From the bealach, if returning to Sligachan by the ascent route, beware of dropping too low into Coire a' Bhasteir, for there will then be a climb to regain the crest of the spur that leads back to Sligachan. Map on page 259.

Sgurr a' Fionn Choire and Am Basteir from the west ridge of Sgurr nan Gillean

Al Matthewson

*Al Matthewson*

Sgurr a' Fionn Choire (left) and Bruach na Frithe from Am Basteir

## Bruach na Frithe; 958m; (OS Sheet 32; NG461252); M200; *slope of the deer forest*

A fine viewpoint and a peak whose outline would excite attention in any other less imposing environment, Bruach na Frithe is the only one of the Cuillin which is not defended by cliffs. It is not seen in the view from Sligachan, but from a short distance westwards along the road to Dunvegan it appears behind the nearer but lower peak of Sgurr a' Bhasteir.

From a point on the A863 road 600m west of Sligachan take the private road towards Alltdearg House. Pass to the north of the house and follow the path leading south-west along the north-west bank of the Allt Dearg Mor towards the Bealach a' Mhaim, the pass which leads over to Glen Brittle.

At about 300m, still 1km from the pass, the terrain becomes very featureless, especially in bad visibility. To the south of the path the lower part of Fionn Choire is an expanse of grass with patches of stones and no distinguishing landmarks, and several small streams flow down the corrie to unite into the Allt Dearg Mor. In good visibility there is no problem in finding an easy way south onto the crest of the north-west ridge of Bruach na Frithe where it is broad and easy-angled, but if the cloud is low some careful navigation will be required. Continue up the ridge, which becomes narrower and rocky. A well-scratched route goes up ledges on the west flank of the ridge just below the crest, however there is no difficulty in scrambling along the crest all the way to the summit. (7km; 940m; 3h 10min).

An alternative descent route goes down the east ridge of Bruach na Frithe for about 300m to the col on the west of Sgurr a' Fionn Choire. If visibility is bad, a safe descent from there is north into Fionn Choire, which is bouldery for the first few hundred metres down to about 750m. A very easy walk follows over mainly grassy slopes to the path along the Allt Dearg Mor.

If conditions are fair, it is worthwhile traversing Sgurr a' Fionn Choire (935m) from west to east and descending to the Bealach nan Lice. From there the descent north-west into Fionn Choire, passing a spring of clear water a short distance below the bealach, is an easy walk. However, if it is too early to go down, traverse north along the ridge to Sgurr a' Bhasteir (898m), the prominent pointed peak in the view from Sligachan. Descend its north ridge, taking care on loose ground, to reach the col before Meall Odhar and go north-west down to the grassy lower reaches of Fionn Choire. Another option is to descend the north-east ridge and pick a way down to the west of the Basteir Gorge. Map on page 259.

Sgurr a' Ghreadaidh (left) and Sgurr a' Mhadaidh

**Sgurr a' Mhadaidh;** 918m; (OS Sheet 32; NG446235); M277; *peak of the fox*
**Sgurr a' Ghreadaidh;** 973m; (OS Sheet 32; NG445232); M185; *peak of torment, or conflict*

SGURR A'
MHADAIDH

SGURR A'
GHREADAIDH

The central part of the Cuillin Main Ridge is dominated by Sgurr a' Ghreadaidh, a great twin-topped peak. Just to its north Sgurr a' Mhadaidh shows an elegant outline of four peaks, but only the south-west one reaches Munro height. These two mountains are central in the view up Loch Coruisk towards the Cuillin.

On the Glen Brittle side Sgurr a' Ghreadaidh and the highest top of Mhadaidh overlook Coire a' Ghreadaidh, and it is by the northern arm of this corrie, Coire an Dorus, that the ascent of both is most easily made. In the north-east corner of Coire an Dorus an easy scree gully leads up to An Dorus (the door), the col between the two peaks, and it gives the easiest route to both. However, a more interesting though more difficult route which gives a fine traverse of both

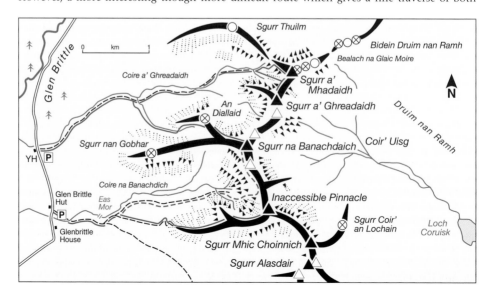

Sgurr a' Mhadaidh, An Dorus and Sgurr a' Ghreadaidh from Coire an Dorus

peaks is described as follows.

From the youth hostel follow the path up Coire a' Ghreadaidh on the south side of the stream for about 2.5km. Cross to the north side and beyond a grassy alp follow the left-hand stream which comes down from the innermost north-east corner of Coire an Dorus. This stream forks at a grassy area below An Dorus, towards which the main right fork heads. Follow the left-hand stream to its end below scree leading to the col on the ridge between Sgurr Thuilm and Sgurr a' Mhadaidh. The easiest route climbs the screes to the right of this col to follow an obvious right slanting break in the slabs before breaking back up left above the slabs to a notch on the ridge above a steep section.

A more difficult route reaches the same point by firstly scrambling to the col. From here it is only a short diversion along the easy ridge to Sgurr Thuilm (879m), a fine viewpoint from which to see Sgurr a' Mhadaidh and its sombre north-west face at the head of Coir' a' Mhadaidh. Returning to the col, traverse a narrow horizontal ridge south-east to the foot of a steep buttress bounded on both sides by dark gullies. The ascent of this buttress is a very fine but in places difficult scramble, with considerable exposure. After about 50m the angle relents and easier scrambling leads to a junction with the route through the slabs. This is difficult to locate in reverse, the route through the slabs being by far the easier option. The way ahead to the summit of Sgurr a' Mhadaidh is by scree covered ledges that lead diagonally up and right. (4km; 900m; 2h 30min).

Descend broken rocks to reach a traverse line leading towards the An Dorus col. The last few metres of the descent are steep and awkward scrambling (Grade 2/3), as are the first few metres of the ascent of Sgurr a' Ghreadaidh on the opposite side of this narrow gap (Grade 3), the right-hand option being the easiest. This is harder on the return descent and memorising the moves is recommended. Continue up the crest of the ridge, soon bearing over to the left side to cross, with hardly any drop, the top of the Eag Dubh (black notch), from which steep gullies fall on both sides. Continue along the crest towards an impressive looking tower which appears to block the ridge. It is something of an imposter, however, as a broad easy scree ledge leads round its west side and a short distance higher the summit of Sgurr a' Ghreadaidh is reached. (5km; 1030m; 3h).

The lower South Peak (970m) is 100m away, but the connecting ridge is narrow and exposed, and the continuation of the Main Ridge southwards gives difficult scrambling with no easy descent for a long way. Unless you want to embark on a long traverse as far as Sgurr na Banachdich, return to An Dorus and descend its screes and boulders to Coire an Dorus where the uphill route is rejoined.

Looking south from the summit of Sgurr na Banachdich to Sgurr Alasdair

**Sgurr na Banachdaich;** 965m; (OS Sheet 32; NG441225); M190; *either peak of smallpox from the pitted appearance of some of its rocks, or peak of the milkmaid*

SGURR NA
BANACHDICH

This fine peak of three summits, of which the northern one is the highest, occupies a central position at the apex of the bend on the Cuillin Ridge and therefore the views from its summit, the easiest of the Cuillin peaks to ascend, are quite spectacular.

Start from the small car park in front of the Youth Hostel (NG 410225) and follow a good path up the side of the Allt a' Choire Ghreadaidh with its lovely gorge and delightful waterfalls. Sgurr nan Gobhar fills the foreground and blocks the view to Sgurr na Banachdaich. After about 1km, opposite a waterslide, a worn trail (mainly used in descent) can be seen coming down the hillside. This cuts the corner but it is perhaps easier to continue on the main path to just in front of the stream that descends Coir' an Eich before breaking off to follow a small path up the side of this. Once in the shallow floor of the corrie, cross the stream and follow a path that zigzags up scree onto the shoulder of An Diallaid. Traces of path lead upwards, beyond the junction with the Sgurr nan Gobhar ridge, over easier-angled slopes of rock and scree to a point where the ground abruptly falls away and one finds oneself in a splendid position atop Sgurr na Banachdaich with dramatic views of the ridge and down Coir'-uisg to Loch Coruisk (4km 950m 2h 15min). The terrain on this final section is featureless and in poor visibility great care should be taken with navigation, especially in descent where the route back into Coir an Eich is not as obvious as one might expect.

An alternative but more complicated route of ascent, or descent, is from near the Glen Brittle Memorial Hut (NG 412216) by a path which crosses the Allt Coire na Banachdaich and goes up the grassy slope on its south side. Level with the Eas Mor waterfall do not take the Coire Lagan path, but follow one on the south side of the stream to enter the wild and rocky inner corrie. Here, great slabs bar direct progress and the route bears right beside the southernmost tributary stream. At the south side of the slabs climb a shallow boulder-filled gully which in wet weather has a little stream flowing down it. Higher up, bear left on a rising traverse above the slabs following traces of a path, then go directly up to the Bealach Coire na Banachdaich (851m).

From the pass climb along the south ridge of Sgurr na Banachdaich over its two subsidiary tops, either along the narrow crest which gives good exposed scrambling, or by traversing easy ledges on the west side just below the crest (4.5km; 950m; 2h 40min). In descent be careful not to go straight down from the Bealach Coire na Banachdaich, but after descending about 100m make a traverse leftwards where traces of a path indicate the way across and down to the boulder-filled gully. Map on page 264.

Gordon Blyth

The Inaccessible Pinnacle (left) and Sgurr na Banachdaich from Sgurr Mhic Choinnich

The Inaccessible Pinnacle and An Stac

*Roger Robb*

## Sgurr Dearg – The Inaccessible Pinnacle; 986m; (OS Sheet 32; NG444215); M164; *red peak*

The most notorious peak in Skye, the Inaccessible Pinnacle is a vertical blade of rock which just overtops nearby Sgurr Dearg. It is the only Munro that calls for rock-climbing ability, and most Munro-baggers have to seek help from their rock-climbing friends or a Mountain Guide to get to the top of this one. The ascent of the Pinnacle should not be attempted without at least one experienced climber in the party, plus a rope and some previous practice in the art of abseiling, and it should probably be avoided on a wet and windy day when the ascent of the Pinnacle's narrow and exposed edge will be distinctly unnerving.

The Inaccessible Pinnacle rises 8m above the top of Sgurr Dearg

*Alan O'Brien*

Climbers on the east ridge of the Inaccessible Pinnacle

The west side of the Inaccessible Pinnacle

Start up the path from the Glen Brittle Memorial Hut on the south side of the Allt Coire na Banachdich. At the point level with the Eas Mor, where the main path to Coire Lagain heads across the moor towards Loch an Fhir-bhallaich, follow another path east up the rising hillside towards the great boulder-strewn west shoulder of Sgurr Dearg. Above the lower grassy slope the path zigzags more steeply up screes and past little crags.

Higher up the ridge narrows and there is some very good and quite exposed scrambling along the crest over some minor bumps to reach the rocky crest of Sgurr Dearg (978m). (3.5km; 970m; 2h 30min).

A short distance to the east is the imposing, possibly even intimidating obelisk of The Inaccessible Pinnacle, showing no easy way up its apparently vertical west ridge. However, the east ridge, which is not seen from the top of Sgurr Dearg, gives a much easier though longer climb which is the normal route up the Pinnacle. Its start is reached by cautiously descending scree and slabs below the south face.

Though only Moderate in standard (in rock-climbing terms), and fairly easy-angled, the east ridge is narrow and remarkably exposed, with vertical drops on both sides and a disconcerting lack of really reassuring handholds. If there is a wind blowing, the situation may seem to be precarious. The ridge is about 50m long and there is a stance and belay about halfway up which should be used.

On the descent it is usual to abseil down the short west side, and it may be desirable to have a spare safety rope for the reassurance of those members of the party who are unfamiliar with this technique or overawed by the exposure on this, the most spectacular of Munros. Map on page 264.

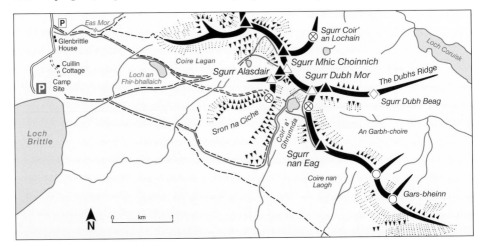

Noel Williams

Sgurr Mhic Choinnich from Coire Lagan

**Sgurr Mhic Choinnich;** 948m; (OS Sheet 32; NG450210); M217; *Mackenzie's peak*

Sgurr Mhic Choinnich, named after the famous Cuillin guide John Mackenzie, is an impressive wedge of rock with steep cliffs falling from its narrow summit ridge into the depths of Coire Lagan. It is one of the more difficult peaks of the Cuillin from the hillwalker's point of view, and the only line of weakness on the Coire Lagan face is the great slope of the An Stac screes to the left of the peak; elsewhere all is steep rock.

Two approaches to Coire Lagan are possible. One starts from the Glen Brittle Memorial Hut and goes up the path on the south side of the Allt Coire na Banachdich to the level of the Eas Mor (*big waterfall*) and then heads south-east past Loch an Fhir-bhallaich to reach Coire Lagan. The other approach starts from the camp site at Loch Brittle and goes straight uphill on a good footpath to Coire Lagan. Continue up the stony path on the north side of the corrie to reach Loch Coire Lagan, set amid huge glaciated slabs.

Bear north-east from the loch to the foot of the An Stac screes which plunge down from the Bealach Coire Lagan, the col between Sgurr Dearg and Sgurr Mhic Choinnich. This slope is ascended with considerable effort, trying to find the most stable stones and boulders up which to make progress; very much a case of two steps up and one step down. Do not aim for the gap

Sgurr Mhic Choinnich (left) and Sgurr Alasdair from the west ridge of Sgurr Dearg

about 120m south-east of the true bealach as it involves rock climbing. Once on the col turn south-east and ascend the north-west ridge of Sgurr Mhic Choinnich, which is airy and exposed and involves some bits of scrambling. (5km; 950m; 2h 50min).

The traverse from Sgurr Mhic Choinnich to Sgurr Alasdair involves Grade 2 and 3 scrambling with an awkward pitch on Sgurr Thearlaich where a rope may be called for. Going in the opposite direction, the traverse to Sgurr Dearg is fairly straightforward provided the steep buttress of An Stac is avoided, so it is quite feasible to combine Sgurr Mhic Choinnich with Sgurr Dearg. However, the easiest descent is back down the route up the An Stac screes.

### Sgurr Alasdair; 992m; (OS Sheet 32; NG449208); M154; *Alexander's peak*

Sgurr Alasdair, named after Alexander Nicolson, the Skye sheriff who made the first recorded ascent in 1873, is the highest peak in the Cuillin. As befits this status, it is a magnificent pointed mountain which rises high above its neighbouring peaks in the south-east corner of Coire Lagan. Its most distinctive feature is the Great Stone Shoot, a 300m-high gully between Sgurr Alasdair and Sgurr Thearlaich, filled with scree and boulders and rising steeply from Coire Lagan to the ridge a few metres below the summits of these two peaks. At one time this was the most famous scree run in the Scottish mountains, but now the passage of hundreds of thousands of climbers has moved most of the scree to the foot of the gully, and the upper half is an unattractive slope of compacted earth and boulders.

Two approaches to Coire Lagan are possible. One starts from the Glen Brittle Memorial Hut and goes up the path on the south side of the Allt Coire na Banachdich to the level of the Eas Mor (big waterfall) and then heads south-east past Loch an Fhir-bhallaich to reach Coire Lagan. The other starts from the camp site at Loch Brittle and goes straight uphill on a good footpath to Coire Lagan. Continue up the stony path on the north side of the corrie to reach Loch Coire Lagan, set amid huge glaciated slabs.

Go a few hundred metres past the loch to the foot of the screes below the Great Stone Shoot and climb the more stable boulders to reach the narrowing of the gully between the cliffs of Sgurr Alasdair and Sgurr Thearlaich. Higher up a zigzag path makes progress fairly easy up the gully to the col between the two peaks, and a short scramble leads to the summit of Sgurr Alasdair. (4.5km; 990m; 2h 40min). It is also possible, but quite difficult and exposed, to climb Sgurr Thearlaich (978m) up a short steep wall on the opposite side of the top of the Stone Shoot.

Return by the same route. The descent of the Great Stone Shoot is slow and tedious.

Sgurr Dubh Mor (left) and Sgurr Dubh an Da Bheinn

**Sgurr Dubh Mor;** 944m; (OS Sheet 32; NG457205); M228; *big black peak*
**Sgurr nan Eag;** 924m; (OS Sheet 32; NG457195); M265; *peak of the notches*

**SGURR DUBH MOR**

**SGURR NAN EAG**

Sgurr Dubh Mor is a fine sharp-topped peak lying to the east of the Main Ridge on a long subsidiary ridge which rises from Loch Coruisk. The lower part of this ridge is formed by a huge expanse of bare gabbro slabs which sweep up to Sgurr Dubh Beag, from where a narrow crest continues to Sgurr Dubh Mor and on to join the Main Ridge at Sgurr Dubh an Da Bheinn (938m). The ascent of this, the Dubhs Ridge, is one of the great Cuillin scrambles and a rope is required for one short abseil. It is the finest route up Sgurr Dubh Mor, however for the walker, the normal approach to this peak is from Glen Brittle by Coir' a' Ghrunnda.

Sgurr nan Eag, the southernmost Munro on the Main Ridge, is not a particularly distinguished peak by Cuillin standards, although it does have some steep crags overlooking An Garbh-choire. It too is most easily climbed from Coir' a' Ghrunnda.

From the Glen Brittle camp site take the path to Coire Lagan for 1km, forking right over a stream and heading east-south-east across the moor to cross the Allt Coire Lagan. Continue ascending gradually along a good path round the base of Sron na Ciche, forking left to reach the foot of Coir' a' Ghrunnda. Climb steeply up the west side of the corrie. The best route stays higher on the hillside, away from the streamway and the slabs. At one point it is difficult to follow as it crosses a boulder-field but is soon picked up again and only comes close to the stream a short distance before the lochan, for the final ascent to it. Go round the lochan's north-west side and climb easy slopes to the col on the Main Ridge 250m north-west of Sgurr Dubh an Da Bheinn, which is then easily climbed. Descend the East Ridge to a col, passing a section at the bottom, either by a gravely path on the left, or by easy scrambling on the right. Sgurr Dubh Mor now rises steeply above and is climbed to the south of the crest by short sections of awkward scrambling separated by ledges. If the going becomes too hard, traverse right and try again. Towards the top, cut across left at a terrace and so gain the knife edged crest, then the summit. (6.5km; 990m; 3h 10min).

Carefully return to Sgurr Dubh an Da Bheinn and descend south along the Main Ridge by very rough rocks. The bealach between Coir' a' Ghrunnda and An Garbh-choire has a prominent gabbro tower astride it, the Caisteal a' Garbh-choire, which can be bypassed along ledges below it on one side or the other. The ridge rises ahead and scrambling close to the crest, or the shallow gully and slopes to the right which are without difficulty, lead to the final fairly level section. The cairn is further back than one might think. at the south-east end. (8km; 1170m; 3h 50min).

Sgurr Dubh an Da Bheinn from Loch Coir' a' Ghrunnda

Return by the route of ascent and before reaching the Bealach a' Garbh-choire descend traces of a path down scree and broken rocks on the west flank of the ridge to the south-east corner of Loch Coir' a' Ghrunnda to rejoin the uphill route.

An alternative return to Glen Brittle, only recommended if the visibility is clear, is to climb north-west from Loch Coir' a' Ghrunnda up a rough bouldery path to Bealach Coir' a' Ghrunnda, the col between Sron na Ciche and Sgurr Sgumain. On its west side descend the Sgumain Stone Shoot, a boulder-filled gully with a well-defined 'path' leading to easy ground at the foot of Sron na Ciche where the path improves and leads across Coire Lagan to join the main route down to Glen Brittle. Map on page 270.

SGURR DUBH
MOR

273

SGURR NAN EAG

Gars-bheinn and Sgurr nan Eag above Loch Coir' a' Ghrunnda

Bla Bheinn and Clach Glas from the crofting land of Torrin

**Bla Bheinn;** 928m; (OS Sheet 32; NG530217); M252; *blue hill from Norse bla, and Gaelic bheinn*

Bla Bheinn is a magnificent isolated mountain. Alexander Nicolson, whose name is immortalised on Sgurr Alasdair, considered it to be the finest mountain in Skye. Girt with precipices and rising directly from sea-level at the head of Loch Slapin, it gives the impression of a hill far higher than it actually is. Though of gabbro rock like the main range of the Cuillin, it stands apart and so offers a superb perspective of the Main Ridge.

Take the road from Broadford to Elgol. As the village of Torrin is approached, the great massif of Bla Bheinn fills the western view on the opposite side of Loch Slapin. Continue round the head of the loch and start the climb at the Allt na Dunaiche, 1km south of there. Follow the path along the north bank of this stream, first past a beautiful wooded gorge and then up the moor toward the foot of Coire Uaigneich.

Cross to the south side of the Allt na Dunaiche and continue along the path to cross the burn tumbling out of Coire Uaigneich and climb more steeply to reach a delightful little grassy alp at 400m. At this point two great slabby buttresses rise to the north-west and between them

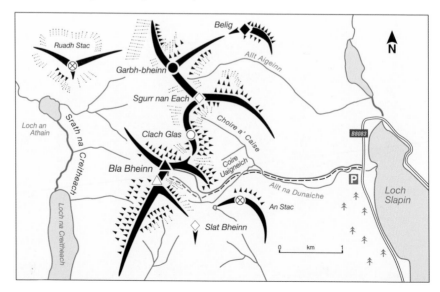

Bla Bheinn from the Cuillin Main Ridge

are steep grass and rocks bounded on the left by a vertically walled gully.

The path bears north, zigzagging up the south flank of the east ridge. At about 600m the grass gives way to scree and rock, and the route continues up the edge of the ridge past the Great Prow, a huge rock tower which projects from the face on the right. A level shoulder is reached and from there the ridge becomes narrower and is followed with a little scrambling to the summit. (4km; 930m; 2h 30min).

The return may be made by the same route. Alternatively, a rapid descent goes south-west from the summit for 150m to the col between the north and south tops. From there plunge down the gully to the south-east to reach the grassy alp of the upward route.

275

BLA BHEINN

Bla Bheinn and Clach Glas across Loch Slapin

# Hillphones

The Hillphones service offers hillwalkers recorded telephone messages detailing stag stalking in various parts of the Highlands from August 1st to October 31st. The messages indicate where stalking is taking place and which walking routes will be unlikely to affect stalking, as well as giving a forecast of stalking activity over the next few days. Recorded messages are generally updated by 8.00 a.m. each day, and calls are charged at normal rates. It usually helps to have a map to hand when calling. There is no stag stalking on Sundays.

The Hillphones service is supported by the Access Forum, and has been organised by the Mountaineering Council of Scotland, Scottish Natural Heritage and the participating estates and aims to improve communications between stalkers and hillwalkers.

Leaflets detailing the precise areas covered by the various Hillphones are updated annually and are available from The Mountaineering Council of Scotland, The Old Granary, West Mill Street, Perth, PH1 5QP, (t) 01738 493942. Further details can also be found on the MCofS's website: <www.mcofs.org.uk> and <www.snh.org.uk/hillphones>.

**1. North Arran**
covering the northern half of the island, (north of the B880) on OS Map 69.
**Tel: Brodick (01770) 302363**

**2. Glen Fyne/Glen Falloch**
including Beinn Bhuidhe, Ben Vane and Beinn Chabhair on OS 50, 51 & 56.
**Tel: Cairndow (01499) 600137**

**3. Balquhidder**
including Beinn a' Chroin and Stob a' Chroin on OS 50 & 51.
**Tel: See postings**

**4. Glen Dochart/Glen Lochay**
including Meall Glas and Sgiath Chuil on OS Map 51.
**Tel: Killin (01567) 820886**

**5. Atholl and Lude**
including Beinn a' Ghlo and Beinn Dearg on OS Map 43.
**Tel: Blair Atholl (01796) 481740**

**6. Fealar**
including Carn an Righ and Beinn Iutharn Mhor on OS 43.
**Tel: Blair Atholl (01796) 481731**

**7. Glen Shee**
including Carn a' Gheoidh and Creag Leacach on OS Map 43.
**Tel: Braemar (013397) 41911**

**8. Callater and Clunie**
including Carn an t-Sagairt Mor and Carn an Tuirc on OS Maps 43 and 44.
**Tel: Braemar (013397) 41997**

**9. Invercauld**
including Ben Avon and Beinn a' Bhuird on OS Maps 36 & 43.
**Tel: Braemar (013397) 41911**

**10. Balmoral/Lochnagar**
including Lochnagar and White Mounth on OS Map 44.
**Tel: Ballater (013397) 55532**

**11. Grey Corries/Mamore**
including Sgurr Eilde Mor and Stob Coire Easain on OS Map 41.
**Tel: Fort William (01397) 732362**

**12. Glen Strathfarrar**
including the Strathfarrar ridge and Sgurr na Lapaich on OS 25 & 26.
**Tel: Inverness (01463) 761360**

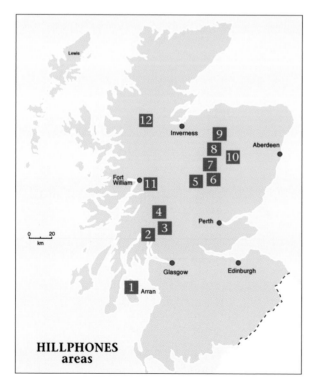

**HILLPHONES areas**

Richard Wood

Looking towards Sgurr an Lochain at the west end of the South Glen Shiel Ridge

# Index

278

# The Munros in Order of Height

| | | | | | |
|---|---|---|---|---|---|
| M1 | Ben Nevis | 1345m | M71 | Cairn of Claise | 1064m |
| M2 | Ben Macdui | 1309m | M72 | Bidein a' Ghlas Thuill – An Teallach | 1062m |
| M3 | Braeriach | 1296m | M73 | Sgurr Fiona – An Teallach | 1060m |
| M4 | Cairn Toul | 1291m | M74 | Na Gruagaichean | 1056m |
| M5 | Sgor an Lochain Uaine | 1258m | M75 | Spidean a' Choire Leith – Liathach | 1055m |
| M6 | Cairn Gorm | 1244m | M76 | Stob Poite Coire Ardair | 1054m |
| M7 | Aonach Beag (Glen Nevis) | 1234m | M77 | Toll Creagach | 1054m |
| M8 | Aonach Mor | 1221m | M78 | Sgurr a'Chaorachain (Monar) | 1053m |
| M9 | Carn Mor Dearg | 1220m | M79 | Beinn a' Chaorainn (Laggan) | 1052m |
| M10 | Ben Lawers | 1214m | M80 | Glas Tulaichean | 1051m |
| M11 | Beinn a' Bhuird – North Top | 1197m | M81 | Geal Charn / | |
| M12 | Carn Eige | 1183m | | Mullach Coire an Iubhair (Laggan) | 1049m |
| M13 | Beinn Mheadhoin | 1182m | M82 | Sgurr Fhuar-thuill | 1049m |
| M14 | Mam Sodhail | 1181m | M83 | Carn an t-Sagairt Mor | 1047m |
| M15 | Stob Choire Claurigh | 1177m | M84 | Creag Mhor | 1047m |
| M16 | Ben More (Crianlarich) | 1174m | M85 | Glas Leathad Mor – Ben Wyvis | 1046m |
| M17 | Leabaidh an Daimh Bhuidhe | | M86 | Chno Dearg | 1046m |
| | – Ben Avon | 1171m | M87 | Cruach Ardrain | 1046m |
| M18 | Stob Binnein | 1165m | M88 | Beinn Iutharn Mhor | 1045m |
| M19 | Beinn Bhrotain | 1157m | M89 | Meall nan Tarmachan | 1044m |
| M20 | Derry Cairngorm | 1155m | M90 | Stob Coir'an Albannaich | 1044m |
| M21 | Cac Carn Beag – Lochnagar | 1155m | M91 | Carn Mairg | 1041m |
| M22 | Sgurr nan Ceathreamhnan | 1151m | M92 | Sgurr na Ciche | 1040m |
| M23 | Bidean nam Bian | 1150m | M93 | Meall Ghaordaidh | 1039m |
| M24 | Sgurr na Lapaich (Glen Cannich) | 1150m | M94 | Beinn Achaladair | 1038m |
| M25 | Ben Alder | 1148m | M95 | Carn a' Mhaim | 1037m |
| M26 | Geal-Charn (Alder) | 1132m | M96 | Sgurr a' Bhealaich Dheirg | 1036m |
| M27 | Binnein Mor | 1130m | M97 | Gleouraich | 1035m |
| M28 | Ben Lui | 1130m | M98 | Carn Dearg (Alder) | 1034m |
| M29 | An Riabhachan | 1129m | M99 | Am Bodach (Mamores) | 1032m |
| M30 | Creag Meagaidh | 1128m | M100 | Beinn Fhada (Kintail) | 1032m |
| M31 | Ben Cruachan | 1126m | M101 | Ben Oss | 1029m |
| M32 | Meall Garbh (Lawers) | 1123m | M102 | Carn an Righ | 1029m |
| M33 | Carn nan Gabhar – Beinn a' Ghlo | 1121m | M103 | Carn Gorm | 1029m |
| M34 | A' Chralaig | 1120m | M104 | Sgurr a' Mhaoraich | 1027m |
| M35 | Sgor Gaoith | 1118m | M105 | Sgurr na Ciste Duibhe | 1027m |
| M36 | An Stuc | 1117m | M106 | Ben Challum | 1025m |
| M37 | Aonach Beag (Alder) | 1116m | M107 | Sgorr Dhearg – Beinn a' Bheithir | 1024m |
| M38 | Stob Coire an Laoigh | 1116m | M108 | Mullach an Rathain – Liathach | 1023m |
| M39 | Stob Coire Easain (Loch Treig) | 1115m | M109 | Aonach air Chrith | 1021m |
| M40 | Monadh Mor | 1113m | M110 | Stob Dearg – Buachaille Etive Mor | 1021m |
| M41 | Tom a' Choinich | 1112m | M111 | Ladhar Bheinn | 1020m |
| M42 | Carn a' Choire Bhoidheach | 1110m | M112 | Beinn Bheoil | 1019m |
| M43 | Sgurr Mor (Fannaichs) | 1110m | M113 | Carn an Tuirc | 1019m |
| M44 | Sgurr nan Conbhairean | 1109m | M114 | Mullach Clach a' Bhlair | 1019m |
| M45 | Meall a' Bhuiridh | 1108m | M115 | Mullach Coire Mhic Fhearchair | 1018m |
| M46 | Stob a' Choire Mheadhoin | 1105m | M116 | Garbh Chioch Mhor | 1013m |
| M47 | Beinn Ghlas | 1103m | M117 | Cairn Bannoch | 1012m |
| M48 | Beinn Eibhinn | 1102m | M118 | Beinn Ime | 1011m |
| M49 | Mullach Fraoch-choire | 1102m | M119 | Beinn Udlamain | 1011m |
| M50 | Creise | 1100m | M120 | Ruadh-stac Mor – Beinn Eighe | 1010m |
| M51 | Sgurr a' Mhaim | 1099m | M121 | The Saddle | 1010m |
| M52 | Sgurr Choinnich Mor | 1094m | M122 | Sgurr an Doire Leathain | 1010m |
| M53 | Sgurr nan Clach Geala | 1093m | M123 | Sgurr Eilde Mor | 1010m |
| M54 | Bynack More | 1090m | M124 | Beinn Dearg (Atholl) | 1008m |
| M55 | Stob Ghabhar | 1090m | M125 | Maoile Lunndaidh | 1007m |
| M56 | Beinn a' Chlachair | 1087m | M126 | An Sgarsoch | 1006m |
| M57 | Beinn Dearg (Ullapool) | 1084m | M127 | Carn Liath (Meagaidh) | 1006m |
| M58 | Beinn a'Chaorainn (Glen Derry) | 1083m | M128 | Beinn Fhionnlaidh (Affric) | 1005m |
| M59 | Schiehallion | 1083m | M129 | Beinn an Dothaidh | 1004m |
| M60 | Sgurr a' Choire Ghlais | 1083m | M130 | The Devil's Point | 1004m |
| M61 | Beinn a' Chreachain | 1081m | M131 | Sgurr an Lochain | 1004m |
| M62 | Beinn Heasgarnich | 1078m | M132 | Sgurr Mor | 1003m |
| M63 | Ben Starav | 1078m | M133 | Sail Chaorainn | 1002m |
| M64 | Beinn Dorain | 1076m | M134 | Sgurr na Carnach | 1002m |
| M65 | Stob Coire Sgreamhach | 1072m | M135 | Aonach Meadhoin | 1001m |
| M66 | Braigh Coire Chruinn-bhalgain | 1070m | M136 | Meall Greigh | 1001m |
| M67 | An Socach (Glen Cannich) | 1069m | M137 | Sgorr Dhonuill – Beinn a' Bheithir | 1001m |
| M68 | Meall Corranaich | 1069m | M138 | Sgurr Breac | 999m |
| M69 | Glas Maol | 1068m | M139 | Sgurr Choinnich | 999m |
| M70 | Sgurr Fhuaran | 1067m | M140 | Stob Ban (Mamores) | 999m |

| M141 | Ben More Assynt | 998m |
| M142 | Broad Cairn | 998m |
| M143 | Stob Diamh | 998m |
| M144 | A' Chailleach (Fannaichs) | 997m |
| M145 | Glas Bheinn Mhor | 997m |
| M146 | Spidean Mialach | 996m |
| M147 | An Caisteal | 995m |
| M148 | Carn an Fhidhleir / Carn Ealar | 994m |
| M149 | Sgor na h-Ulaidh | 994m |
| M150 | Spidean Coire nan Clach – Beinn Eighe | 993m |
| M151 | Sgurr na Ruaidhe | 993m |
| M152 | Carn nan Gobhar (Glen Cannich) | 992m |
| M153 | Carn nan Gobhar (Glen Strathfarrar) | 992m |
| M154 | Sgurr Alasdair | 992m |
| M155 | Sgairneach Mhor | 991m |
| M156 | Beinn Eunaich | 989m |
| M157 | Sgurr Ban (Fisherfield) | 989m |
| M158 | Conival | 987m |
| M159 | Creag Leacach | 987m |
| M160 | Druim Shionnach | 987m |
| M161 | Gulvain | 987m |
| M162 | Sgurr Mhor – Beinn Alligin | 986m |
| M163 | Lurg Mhor | 986m |
| M164 | Sgurr Dearg – Inaccessible Pinnacle | 986m |
| M165 | Ben Vorlich (Loch Earn) | 985m |
| M166 | An Gearanach | 982m |
| M167 | Mullach na Dheiragain | 982m |
| M168 | Maol Chinn-dearg (Glen Shiel) | 981m |
| M169 | Meall nan Aighean | 981m |
| M170 | Slioch | 981m |
| M171 | Stob Coire a' Chairn | 981m |
| M172 | Beinn a' Chochuill | 980m |
| M173 | Ciste Dhubh | 979m |
| M174 | Stob Coire Sgriodain | 979m |
| M175 | Beinn Dubhchraig | 978m |
| M176 | Cona' Mheall | 978m |
| M177 | Meall nan Ceapraichean | 977m |
| M178 | Stob Ban (Grey Corries) | 977m |
| M179 | A' Mharconaich | 975m |
| M180 | Carn a' Gheoidh | 975m |
| M181 | Carn Liath – Beinn a' Ghlo | 975m |
| M182 | Stuc a' Chroin | 975m |
| M183 | Beinn Sgritheall | 974m |
| M184 | Ben Lomond | 974m |
| M185 | Sgurr a' Ghreadaidh | 973m |
| M186 | Meall Garbh (Glen Lyon) | 968m |
| M187 | A' Mhaighdean | 967m |
| M188 | Sgorr nam Fiannaidh – Aonach Eagach | 967m |
| M189 | Ben More (Mull) | 966m |
| M190 | Sgurr na Banachdich | 965m |
| M191 | Sgurr nan Gillean | 964m |
| M192 | Carn a' Chlamain | 963m |
| M193 | Sgurr Thuilm | 963m |
| M194 | Meall nan Con – Ben Klibreck | 962m |
| M195 | Sgorr Ruadh | 962m |
| M197 | Stuchd an Lochain | 960m |
| M196 | Beinn nan Aighenan | 960m |
| M198 | Beinn Fhionnlaidh (Appin) | 959m |
| M199 | Meall Glas | 959m |
| M200 | Bruach na Frithe | 958m |
| M201 | Stob Dubh – Buachaille Etive Beag | 958m |
| M202 | Tolmount | 958m |
| M203 | Carn Ghluasaid | 957m |
| M204 | Tom Buidhe | 957m |
| M205 | Saileag | 956m |
| M206 | Sgurr nan Coireachan (Glen Finnan) | 956m |
| M207 | Stob na Broige | 956m |
| M208 | Sgor Gaibhre | 955m |
| M209 | Beinn Liath Mhor Fannaich | 954m |
| M210 | Am Faochagach | 953m |
| M211 | Beinn Mhanach | 953m |
| M212 | Meall Dearg – Aonach Eagach | 953m |
| M213 | Sgurr nan Coireachan (Glen Dessarry) | 953m |
| M214 | Meall Chuaich | 951m |
| M215 | Meall Gorm | 949m |
| M216 | Beinn Bhuidhe | 948m |
| M217 | Sgurr Mhic Choinnich | 948m |
| M218 | Creag a' Mhaim | 947m |
| M219 | Driesh | 947m |
| M220 | Beinn Tulaichean | 946m |
| M221 | Carn Bhac | 946m |
| M222 | Meall Buidhe (Knoydart) | 946m |
| M223 | Sgurr na Sgine | 946m |
| M224 | Bidein a' Choire Sheasgaich | 945m |
| M225 | Carn Dearg (Monadh Liath) | 945m |
| M226 | Stob a' Choire Odhair | 945m |
| M227 | An Socach (Glen Ey) | 944m |
| M228 | Sgurr Dubh Mor | 944m |
| M229 | Ben Vorlich (Arrochar) | 943m |
| M230 | Binnein Beag | 943m |
| M231 | Beinn a' Chroin | 942m |
| M232 | Carn Dearg (Corrour) | 941m |
| M233 | Carn na Caim | 941m |
| M234 | Luinne Bheinn | 939m |
| M235 | Mount Keen | 939m |
| M236 | Mullach nan Coirean | 939m |
| M237 | Beinn Sgulaird | 937m |
| M238 | Beinn Tarsuinn | 937m |
| M239 | Sron a' Choire Ghairbh | 937m |
| M240 | A' Bhuidheanach Bheag | 936m |
| M241 | Beinn na Lap | 935m |
| M242 | Am Basteir | 934m |
| M243 | Meall a' Chrasgaidh | 934m |
| M244 | Beinn Chabhair | 933m |
| M245 | The Cairnwell | 933m |
| M246 | Fionn Bheinn | 933m |
| M247 | Maol Chean-dearg (Torridon) | 933m |
| M248 | Meall Buidhe (Glen Lyon) | 932m |
| M249 | Beinn Bhreac | 931m |
| M250 | Ben Chonzie | 931m |
| M251 | A' Chailleach (Monadh Liath) | 930m |
| M252 | Bla Bheinn | 928m |
| M253 | Mayar | 928m |
| M254 | Mean nan Eun | 928m |
| M255 | Moruisg | 928m |
| M256 | Ben Hope | 927m |
| M257 | Eididh nan Clach Geala | 927m |
| M258 | Beinn Liath Mhor (Achnashellach) | 926m |
| M259 | Beinn Narnain | 926m |
| M260 | Geal Charn (Monadh Liath) | 926m |
| M261 | Meall a' Choire Leith | 926m |
| M262 | Seana Bhraigh | 926m |
| M263 | Stob Coire Raineach | 925m |
| M264 | Creag Pitridh | 924m |
| M265 | Sgurr nan Eag | 924m |
| M266 | An Coileachan | 923m |
| M267 | Sgurr nan Each | 923m |
| M268 | Tom na Gruagaich – Beinn Alligin | 922m |
| M269 | An Socach (Glen Affric) | 921m |
| M270 | Sgiath Chuil | 921m |
| M271 | Carn Sgulain | 920m |
| M272 | Gairich | 919m |
| M273 | Ruadh Stac Mor | 919m |
| M274 | A' Ghlas-bheinn | 918m |
| M275 | Creag nan Damh | 918m |
| M276 | Meall na Teanga | 918m |
| M277 | Sgurr a' Mhadaidh | 918m |
| M278 | Geal-charn (Drumochter) | 917m |
| M279 | Beinn a' Chleibh | 916m |
| M280 | Ben Vane | 916m |
| M281 | Carn Aosda | 915m |
| M282 | Beinn Teallach | 915m |

# SCOTTISH MOUNTAINEERING CLUB

## SCOTTISH MOUNTAINEERING TRUST

Prices were correct at time of publication, but are subject to change

## HILLWALKERS' GUIDES

| | |
|---|---:|
| The Munros | £23.00 |
| The Corbetts and Other Scottish Hills | £23.00 |
| The Grahams & The Donalds | £25.00 |
| North-West Highlands | £22.00 |
| Islands of Scotland Including Skye | £20.00 |
| The Cairngorms | £18.00 |
| Central Highlands | £18.00 |
| Southern Highlands | £17.00 |

## SCRAMBLERS' GUIDES

| | |
|---|---:|
| Skye Scrambles | £25.00 |
| Highland Scrambles North | £19.00 |
| Highland Scrambles South | £25.00 |

## CLIMBERS' GUIDES

| | |
|---|---:|
| Inner Hebrides & Arran | £25.00 |
| Northern Highlands North | £22.00 |
| Northern Highlands Central | £25.00 |
| Northern Highlands South | £25.00 |
| Skye The Cuillin | £25.00 |
| Skye Sea-cliffs & Outcrops | £25.00 |
| The Cairngorms | £25.00 |
| Ben Nevis | £22.00 |
| Glen Coe | £22.00 |
| Highland Outcrops South | £28.00 |
| North-East Outcrops | £22.00 |
| Lowland Outcrops | £22.00 |
| Scottish Winter Climbs | £25.00 |
| Scottish Rock Climbs | £25.00 |
| Scottish Sport Climbs | £28.00 |

## OTHER PUBLICATIONS

| | |
|---|---:|
| Ben Nevis – Britain's Highest Mountain | £27.50 |
| The Cairngorms – 100 Years of Mountaineering | £27.50 |
| Rising to the Challenge – 100 Years of the LSCC | £24.00 |
| Hostile Habitats – Scotland's Mountain Environment | £17.00 |
| Munro's Tables | £16.00 |
| A Chance in a Million? Avalanches in Scotland | £15.00 |
| The Munroist's Companion | £16.00 |
| Scottish Hill Tracks | £18.00 |
| Scottish Hill Names | £16.00 |
| Mountaineering in Scotland (The Early Years) | £24.00 |
| Ski Mountaineering in Scotland | £18.00 |

**Visit our website for more details and to purchase on line:**
**www.smc.org.uk**

Distributed by:
**Cordee Ltd, 3a De Montfort Street, Leicester LE1 7HD**
**(t) 01455 611185 (w) www.cordee.co.uk**